Irish Gardening
for all Seasons

Phyl and Dick Boyce

BOYCE'S GARDENS

MERCIER PRESS

MERCIER PRESS
Douglas Village, Cork, Ireland
www.mercierpress.ie

Trade enquiries to Columba Mercier Distribution,
55a Spruce Avenue, Stillorgan Industrial Park, Blackrock, Dublin

© Phyl and Dick Boyce, 2006

ISBN 1 85635 495 4

10 9 8 7 6 5 4 3 2 1

 Mercier Press receives financial assistance from
the Arts Council/An Chomhairle Ealaíon

Printed in Ireland by ColourBooks Ltd

I Garden Plants

II Garden Basics

Introduction

Have you ever wondered why two people, or even a thousand people, can follow the same gardening basics and read the same books and newspaper articles about good gardens yet no two gardens will ever come out looking the same? Some will be quite successful, many will be a good first effort that will refine over time and a few will be utter failures.

So perhaps it is time to warn the new gardeners, or those who have dabbled but are starting to get serious about their garden, that a garden is never done. If you look at your garden and say, 'It is done,' then you have ceased to have ideas on how to improve things: you are done, not the garden. Be grateful that your garden will always provide you with an outlet for creativity and exercise.

The first rule in gardening is that even if you do everything right, things will go wrong. If you have your soil tested, dig lots of compost into it, research every plant for the right growing conditions, you will still not always get perfection. Slugs may eat your favourite plant, you may have a very dry summer or a wet and cold winter or you may have bought a mislabelled plant. These failures are not your fault. They are tests to see if you have the character to garden and enjoy it.

The second rule in gardening is to know your soil. Many young gardeners have undreamed-of success with plants that experienced gardeners fail with. Soil varies hugely from one garden to the next and even within a garden there can be a variety of soil types. The soil needs to be free draining with lots of organic matter, like compost or farmyard manure, added.

The third rule is that most of us will not do everything right. It is not for lack of trying. Every passionate gardener soon learns that the more you know about plants, the more you find that you do not know. Every year you will learn from your mistakes and do more and more things right. Gardening is a process of striving towards perfection and learning to deal with the setbacks.

The fourth rule in gardening is that our tastes change as we grow older. As young gardeners we have the energy to try a hundred different new plants – variety is the essence of the young gardener. Older gardeners will depend on plants that need less attention so the garden becomes less demanding but even more satisfying.

This book outlines the success of two novice gardeners who started gardening thirty years ago to produce an award-winning garden. Boyce's Garden at Mountrenchard, Foynes, County Limerick, enjoys mild winters with little frost but is on a site exposed to salt-laden winds. The garden is divided into a number of sheltered rooms, linked by winding paths constructed with stone paving and gravel chips. The shelter is provided by a variety of hedges. These informal rooms provide a microclimate for the many colourful and tender plants that grow here. The garden is designed for year-round colour with bulbs, shrubs, trees and herbaceous beds providing interest from early spring to late autumn. It contains a vegetable garden that has become very popular in recent years, proving that more people now want to grow their own vegetables.

This book details the plants grown in the garden, their size and flowering period, and the construction of rockeries, garden pools, paths, steps and topiary. This knowledge has been accumulated, through trial and error, over a period of thirty years. The novice gardener will find advice on design, sowing a new lawn and planting hedges, shrubs and trees. The experienced gardener should enjoy growing the exotic plants and shrubs listed. The chapter on vegetables and herbs should stimulate more gardeners to grow their own vegetables, whether they have a small or large garden.

The development of a garden is a slow process. It is better to start small than spend lots of money on what may turn out to be a disappointment. There is no recipe for an instant garden: the aim of this book is to create the garden of your dreams over a period of years by planting good shrubs and trees and constructing garden features that will add character to your garden. Hopefully you will enjoy the time you spend creating and looking after your garden.

Happy Gardening!

Note: superscript numbers in the text correspond to photographs in the colour section.

Garden Plants

Herbaceous plants

Herbaceous plants have soft green stems that produce little wood growth. The term is used to distinguish such plants from woody plants. All herbaceous plants die down in winter and produce new shoots in spring from dormant roots. The idea in a herbaceous border is to create blocks of colour with different plants jumbled together to mature into intriguing collages of colour and texture. Perennials provide the border with continuity year after year, giving grand performances that peak at different times. The secret to a colourful border is to pick plants that flower from early summer to late autumn. Annuals can be mixed into the herbaceous border to provide quick colour fixes where required. Summer-flowering bulbs such as lilies, canna, dahlias and gladioli can be used to produce splashes of colour at critical times during the summer. These bulbs can be planted directly into the ground or left in pots and placed strategically in the border to create dramatic impact and to jazz up established perennial plantings.

Herbaceous borders did not become popular until the twentieth century, when Gertrude Jekyll brought them into the gardening limelight. In the nineteenth century gardens were large and, with teams of gardeners to care for them, it was possible to have an iris garden, peony beds, dahlia borders, rose beds and autumn gardens to provide seasonal colour. Now gardens are much smaller and there is no team of gardeners so a herbaceous border will contain plants to produce colour from early spring to autumn.[1]

Shape
If the garden is laid out formally, choose a rectangular, oval or circular shape for your border. For the informal garden choose a border with free-flowing curved lines. A one-sided border backed by a wall or hedge is not the best for display or easy maintenance. Access to the rear of the bed is difficult and the backing wall or fence often restricts light and water, leading to tall weak stems. In this border the tallest plants should be planted at the back with smaller plants placed in front. The ideal shape of a border is an island bed that is accessible from all sides and where the plants can be viewed from all sides. This type of bed is easy to fit into most parts of the garden away from the boundary. An open position is the most suitable for the island bed and, since most herbaceous plants prefer sun, a wide choice of plants will be available to plant in it. The size of the bed will depend upon the amount of available space.

Selecting plants
As a general rule, the tallest plants are planted at the rear of a one-sided bed but in the centre of an island bed. In an island bed the maximum height of the plants in the middle should be approximately half the width of the bed. If your bed is 10 feet wide, do not select plants that grow more than 5 feet tall.

To produce continuous display of colour, choose plants that flower in spring, as well as those that flower in summer and autumn. Grouping at least three plants of the same kind together is more effective than the plum pudding model of having single plants dotted about everywhere.

Soil preparation
There is a hard and an easy way to prepare a bed for planting. The hard way is to dig the ground, remove all weeds and add in compost or well-rotted manure. The easy way is to spray the ground with weedkiller, such as Roundup, which will kill the grass and the more

persistent weeds like couch grass, ground elder, thistle and bindweed. Weedkillers work best when plants are in active growth. Weedkillers need a dry period of twenty-four hours after spraying. Read and follow the spraying instructions closely and wear suitable protective clothing and a mask. Another easy way to prepare the ground is to cover it with a layer of weed-block and then cover the weed-block with a layer of bark. Cut holes in the weed block to place plants in the ground.

Herbaceous borders in winter[2]
In winter many gardeners are tempted to savagely cut back plants that have finished flowering. Do not bother. Let the dead stalks stand over the winter and enjoy the architectural forms of the dead stems on a frosty morning. Most herbaceous plants do not need to be cut back until the new shoots emerge in the spring. In fact, the old stems protect the crown and emerging shoots from cold and moisture. The old stalks provide a friendly habitat for beneficial insects, such as ladybirds, to survive the winter.

Herbaceous borders in spring[3]
Remove all weeds and cut the dead stalks – a shredder is ideal to chop up the dead stalks and spread them around the bed. Spread a layer of well-rotted farmyard manure or compost over the bed. Spring or autumn is the ideal time to plant a herbaceous border. Take a trip to your local nursery or garden centre and explore the range of plants available. Choose plants that will provide a long season of interest and a succession of flowers. If possible, buy at least three pots of each plant to allow for the creation of bold drifts of colour through your border. The following are just some plants that you can choose for your herbaceous border.

Acanthus spinosus (bear's breeches)
Height: 3 feet (90 centimetres).
Flowering period: May–July.[4]

This is an architectural plant with handsome dark green leaves whose shapes have been used on Corinthian columns and cornices and in woodcarving. This plant will bring a strong hint of classical elegance to the garden. It produces tall flower spikes, which resemble foxgloves from a distance, with two-tone flowers in shades of purple and white. Once established it is virtually impossible to move so make sure it is planted in the correct position. This is a dramatic plant for growing at the back or in the middle of a large border. *Acanthus* 'Lady Moore' is a smaller plant with a yellowish leaf.

Aconitum (monkshood)
Height: 2–6 feet (60 centimetres–1.8 metres), depending on variety.
Flowering period: most varieties, late summer–autumn.[5]

Aconitum will provide height and colour very similar to their relatives the delphiniums. Aconites grow from tubers, which tend to become congested after two or three years, so they will need dividing and replanting. This is best done in autumn after flowering, replanting only the most vigorous and largest tubers. Tall varieties will require staking. There are many varieties to choose from, some of them flowering early in the year. *Aconitum cammarum* 'Bicolour' produces blue and white flowers on arching branches in July and August. *Aconitum* 'Spark's Variety' produces indigo-blue flowers in August. *Aconitum* 'Ivorine' is a bushy plant, producing yellow flowers in late spring and early summer. They are good for cutting but contact with the foliage can irritate the skin; all parts are toxic if ingested.

Alstroemeria (Peruvian lily)
Height: 3 feet (90 centimetres); dwarf varieties, 8 inches (20 centimetres).
Flowering period: summer.[6–7]

This plant produces erect stems with funnel-shaped flowers in summer. They are often sold in flower shops as a cut flower and they have a vase life of two weeks. They produce an array of vibrant flower colours and bicolours, including red, pink, purple, white, yellow and orange. Many blooms are attractively decorated with spots and flecks. Once established in a warm site they will flower year after year without attention. In exposed sites they will need staking to prevent them falling over when in full bloom. Plant the tubers in late summer or early autumn in fertile soil in full sun. In recent years dwarf varieties have been developed that do not require staking. These are ideal for rock gardens, containers or the front of the herbaceous border. *Alstroemeria* 'Little Miss Isabel' is a dwarf variety that grows about 6 inches (15 centimetres) in height.

The attractive foliage and shapely flowers of aquilegias makes them a beautiful plant for the garden. The common name comes from the Latin name *columba*, which means dove or pigeon. The flower heads resemble the heads of doves and have flared petals that look like the wings of a bird. Aquilegias have been a popular cottage-garden plant for years. They produce flowers in an array of colours that contain most of the visible spectrum. They also produce a range of bicolours, such as blue and yellow, salmon and white or pink and lemon. There are dwarf varieties that grow less than 4 inches (10 centimetres) in height. They are among the hardiest of perennials and easy to grow from seed. They self-seed very easily, which can be a problem if you want to keep your varieties pure because they cross-pollinate with other varieties in the garden. To keep your varieties pure, dead-head to remove old flower heads before they produce seeds.

Aquilegia (columbine)
Height: 2–3 feet (60–90 centimetres). Flowering period: early summer.[8]

Asters are the stars of the autumn border, providing an array of cool, sophisticated drifts right through from September to Christmas. The word *aster* comes from the Greek word for star. Asters are also known as Michaelmas daisies. They produce large daisy-like flowers in various colours but have a tendency to attacks of mildew unless sprayed with a fungicide. New England asters are a variety less likely to suffer from mildew. There are asters for almost all garden situations, including borders and rock gardens. Mulch all asters annually after cutting back in late autumn. Stake taller varieties from early spring. To maintain vigour and flower quality, divide clumps every three years.

Aster (Michaelmas daisies)
Height: 2–5 feet (60–150 centimetres). Flowering period: September– Christmas.[9]

Astilbes are grown for their striking plume-like flowers, which can be up to 14 inches (35 centimetres) long, in a range of colours such as red, pink, purple and white and for their ferny foliage. The dry flower heads fade to decorative shades of brown in the autumn, providing continued interest throughout the winter. Astilbes like a fertile, moist, humus-rich soil; they will not thrive in soils that dry out in summer. Divide and replant every three or four years to maintain vigour and flower quality. *Astilbe* 'Fanal' produces a red flower; *Astilbe* 'Rhineland' has a pink flower; *Astilbe* 'Irrlicht' has a white flower.

Astilbe
Height: 1.5–4 feet (45–130 centimetres). Flowering period: June– August.[10]

Campanula
Height: 6
inches–6
feet (15–180
centimetres).
Flowering
period:
midsummer–
early autumn.[11]

Few flowers can ring in the true glory of summer like the delicate, bell-shaped flowers of the Campanulaceae family. Commonly known as bellflowers, these elegant plants are perennial, easy to grow and work well in any part of the garden.

Extremely versatile, there is a campanula to suit most positions, including deepest shade or the cracks in old masonry. Campanulas vary greatly in size and habit. They may be low clump-forming dwarf, which are ideal for a rock garden, or tall and erect, which suit the herbaceous border. The flowers vary in shape from bell to tubular to star shaped and may also be cup or saucer shaped. Their colours are mostly blue, with a scattering of white and the occasional pink. Borders are the main planting ground for campanulas. The large bells of both blue and white forms of *Campanula persicifolia* are displayed on stems 3 feet (90 centimetres) tall. *Campanula pulla* is an alpine variety that has deep purple-blue flowers. *Campanula garganica* 'Dickson's Gold' is another alpine bellflower with beautiful golden foliage that perfectly complements its blue flowers. There are a number of varieties that will grow in the tiny cracks between paving stones or on walls. *Campanula lactiflora* 'Loddon Anna' produces soft lilac-pink flowers. *Campanula carpatica* 'Bessingham White' has large pure-white flowers.

They are reliable perennials that require no special care. It is worthwhile splitting up the clumps every few years and replanting the strong pieces in soil enriched with compost.

Cerinthe major
Height: 12
inches (30
centimetres).
Flowering
period: late
spring–
autumn.[12]

Cerinthe major is a plant that looks its best in the middle of summer. Commonly called the wax flower, it has been around for hundreds of years but only recently became popular in gardening magazines, so it is quite new to Irish gardens. After it has been baked by the sun, the plant's leaves turn from grey to a luminous blue. The foliage effect is so stunning that it does not really need to flower. But it does, producing purple-blue bracts from which tubular dark-purple flowers appear. The plant produces little black seeds, which are clearly visible as the flower petals fade.

The plant is usually grown as a hardy annual in most gardens; it can be perennial in warmer sheltered gardens. It drops many seeds towards the end of summer, which rapidly germinate where they fall. The subsequent seedlings will not survive the wet and cold of winter

unless they are protected with a cloche. In cold areas it is best to collect seeds and sow them the following spring.

Cerinthe major is a stunning border plant that makes a dense mound 2 feet (60 centimetres) across and 12 inches (30 centimetres) high. It looks fantastic with blue-leaf plants such as eryngiums. Cerinthe major is a plant that thrives in poor, hungry soil; no feeding is required.

Chrysanthemums provide an array of shapes and sizes to fill the autumn border and a varied spectrum of colours such as reds, yellows and whites. Many people call them 'chrysanths' and the Americans call them 'mums'. Chrysanthemums will often survive in full bloom outdoors until the end of November.

**Chrysanthe-
mum**
Height:
3–7 feet (1–2.2
metres).
Flowering
period:
summer–late
autumn.[13]

Chrysanthemums are available as bushy annuals or herbaceous perennials with woody bases. The annual species come from the Mediterranean region, where they grow in dry fields and wasteland. The herbaceous perennials come from China and Japan, where they have been grown for 2,500 years. They were introduced into Europe about 200 years ago.

Chrysanthemums are grown for their showy flower heads in a variety of colours, such as yellow, white, pink, purple and red. They are grown in a multiplicity of forms. For ease of reference, chrysanthemums have been divided into a number of different groups. Florist's chrysanthemums are grown for exhibition and cut flowers. The flower heads come in a variety of shapes, such as single, pompon and spider. It requires considerable skill to grow exhibition-quality blooms. Disbudded chrysanthemums have all the flower buds on each stem removed except for the terminal bud, which increases the size of the remaining flower. In non-disbudded chrysanthemums the buds are allowed to develop freely to produce a spray of flowers on each stem.

Chrysanthemums thrive in rich soil and a reasonable amount of moisture. Do not over-feed them because this will produce lush growth, which invites disease and results in lanky plants that are more likely to flop over. Most chrysanthemums need support but they can be cut back in June to make more compact, sturdier plants. Lift and divide plants every three years to retain vigour and produce stocky stems that are easier to support. Cuttings of young shoots taken in spring will root in a mixture of potting compost and sand. Cuttings taken in March will produce healthy plants for planting outdoors in May.

Cimicifuga (bugbane)

Height: 3–4 feet (1–1.2 metres). Flowering period: late summer–early autumn.[14]

This plant gets its common name, bugbane, because it was once used as an insect repellent to ward off fleas. The plant has been renamed Actaea. It is a native of China, Russia and Japan.

Cimicifuga likes a moist, fertile soil, enriched with lots of compost, in partial shade. The plant is very hardy and will survive several degrees of frost. *Cimicifuga simplex* 'Brunette' has very dark foliage and purple stems. The plant is sure to turn heads when it produces stems covered in slightly purple-tinted white flowers. The flowers really stand out against the dark foliage.

Cirsium rivulare

Height: 4 feet (1.2 metres). Flowering period: early summer.[15]

This plant produces dark-green prickly leaves and tall, erect stems covered with purple pincushion-like flowers. It can be invasive, spreading by means of rhizomes or self-seeding.

Cosmos

Height: 2 feet (60 centimetres). Flowering period: midsummer–autumn.[16]

Most species of cosmos are annuals that are grown from seed, sown each year. *Cosmos atrosanguineus* is a tender perennial that produces a graceful cup-shaped flower with a dark centre and maroon petals. The plant has a fragrance of chocolate and so is often called the 'chocolate plant'. The plant is not fully hardy: it will not survive frost. It grows from a tuber so it can be lifted and stored in a frost-free area for the winter, like dahlias. The plant is slow to start growth in spring – new shoots may not emerge until late spring.

Crocosmia (montbretia)

Height: 2–3 feet, (60–100 centimetres). Flowering period: July–October.[17–18]

Crocosmia is a vigorous bulbous plant that has become naturalised in many parts of Ireland, where it can be seen growing on banks, hedgerows and along the sides of the road. It is a native of South Africa. The plant produces funnel-shaped flowers on stems up to 2 feet (60 centimetres) tall. Over a century of breeding has produced hundreds of crocosmia cultivars so no late-summer garden should be without their warmth of colour in shades of yellow, orange and red. The tufts of sword-like leaves give form to planting schemes

and remain fresh from spring to autumn. One great performer is the hardy, vigorous *Crocosmia* 'Emily McKenzie', which has large burnt-orange trumpets streaked with mahogany, grows over 2 feet (60 centimetres) tall and is one of the best-known bicolour flowers. Alan Bloom has produced many new varieties in recent years; his greatest triumph is *Crocosmia* 'Lucifer', which produces intense flame-red flowers in early July. If you are looking for a yellow crocosmia, try 'Solfatare': it has bronze leaves to complement the yellow flowers. *Crocosmia* 'Star of the East' produces star-shaped apricot-orange large flowers. This is one of the last to flower and often flowers until October. Crocosmias grow from corms that renew themselves each year by making new corms directly below the old ones. The new corms produce next year's shoots and flowers. If planted in a sunny position in free-draining soil they will increase rapidly, making a dense clump that may be divided in the autumn.

Dahlias were once very popular, were almost forgotten for a number of years but are now making a big come back. Dahlias have been called the 'man's plant' because many men seem to enjoy the intricacies of growing a dahlia to exhibition size. Dahlias come from Mexico so they like a warm climate. Dahlias are available in many different sizes and types of flower head, such as decorative, cacti and pompon. They grow from a tuber, which is a thickened root containing buds. Dahlia tubers should be potted up in spring and planted out when the new season's growth is visible and the risk of frost is over. Protect the young shoots from slugs and snails. The plant will spend spring and summer growing and flower profusely in late summer and autumn, when its splash of colour is really appreciated. If your soil is wet and soggy you should lift the dahlia tubers in the autumn when the flowers and foliage have died down and store them in a dry, frost-free place.

Dahlia
Height: 2–4 feet (60–120 centimetres). Flowering period: late summer.[19–21]

The dahlia that appears to have renewed interest in growing these flowers is a cultivar called 'Bishop of Llandaff'. This stunning plant has purple-black leaves and grows 2 feet (60 centimetres) high. The flowers are a vivid red with discreet yellow stamens. Plant dahlias in soil enriched with plenty of well-rotted manure or compost. Plant the tubers so there is a shallow depression around each plant to collect rain – dahlias require lots of water when flowering.

Delphinium
Height:
2–6 feet (60
centimetres–
1.8 metres).
Flowering
period: early–
midsummer.[22]

Delphiniums are the crown jewels of the herbaceous border. They produce tall spikes in a range of colours that cover all three primary colours; although when we think of delphiniums we tend to think of blue. The plant will grow in any fertile, well-drained soil in full sun, with shelter from strong winds. The trouble with most delphiniums is that they grow tall and so need staking. Water plants freely and apply a balanced liquid fertiliser every two to three weeks. An exciting development in delphiniums is the production of dwarf compact varieties, such as 'Fantasia' mix delphiniums. These grow only 2 feet (60 centimetres) tall, require no staking and are just as showy as their taller cousins. If the flowers are removed before they set seed and the plant is given a good feed of fertiliser, the plant may produce more flowers later in the year.

Dicentra
Height: 1–3
feet (30–90
centimetres).
Flowering
period: late
spring–early
summer.[23]

Dicentra spectabilis (bleeding heart) is a graceful plant in the herbaceous border. The plant produces fern-like leaves on stems up to 2 feet (60 centimetres) tall. Heart-shaped flowers hang from the stems in early summer. Dicentra spectabilis produces rose-pink flowers tipped with white; the variety 'Alba' has pure white flowers. The plant is a native of China and likes a well-drained, moist soil in sun or partial shade. After flowering the delicate foliage begins to fade and can leave a hole in the herbaceous border, where pots of summer-flowering bulbs can be plunged in to fill the gap. Dicentras do not like disturbance of their fragile roots so digging around dicentras can kill them. The best way to propagate dicentras is to take root cuttings in early spring when the plant is dormant and grow them on in sandy compost. The new cuttings can be planted out a year later.

Dierama
Height:
3–6 feet (1–1.8
metres).
Flowering
period: late
summer.[24]

Dierama (angel's fishing rod or wand flower) is a plant to admire from all parts of the garden. The common name, angel's fishing rod, comes from the plant's slender, graceful curving stems. The plant is evergreen, producing clumps of long, narrow grass-like leaves up to 3 feet (90 centimetres) tall. In late summer the plant produces elegant arching, wiry stems up to 6 feet (1.8 metres) tall, bearing funnel-shaped pinkish-purple flowers. The tall stems move like fishing rods in the wind. The plants are hardy in all but the coldest

regions and look wonderful when grown in gaps in the paving around a garden pool, where their elegance is reflected in the water. Dierama should be planted among low-growing plants to accentuate the plant's arching stems.

Plant the bulbs 3–4 inches (7–10 centimetres) deep in the autumn or spring in a humus-rich, well-drained soil in a sheltered position in full sun. Dieramas do not like been disturbed: divisions and young plants are slow to establish and may take three or four years to flower, but once they are established they are trouble free and well worth the patience needed to see them flower. Propagate by division in spring or by seed, sowing in a cold frame as soon as they are ripe. Most of the dieramas come from South Africa and produce flowers that are red, pink, purple or white.

Digitalis (foxglove) is a plant that brings grace and architecture to the summer garden. One of the great beauties of this plant is that it is equally at home growing in a herbaceous border or between shrubs or planted among pale old roses at the back of a border. The Latin name *digitalis* refers to the flower shape, looking like fingers or digits. The common foxglove, *Digitalis purpurea*, can grow to 6 feet (1.8 metres) tall, has soft green leaves and a strong stem that can carry hundreds of tubular rosy-purple flowers. There are many varieties of digitalis now available in a range of colours like white, yellow and pink, many of the flowers are richly spotted and blotched inside. *Digitalis* 'Excelsior Hybrids' produce flowers in a range of pastel shades. *Digitalis grandiflora* has deep-cream flowers with distinctive rusty markings on the inside. Although all digitalis are herbaceous, a tree from China called *Paulownia tomentosa* (foxglove tree) has large pale-green leaves and produces pinkish-lilac foxglove-like flowers.

Digitalis
Height: 3–6 feet (1–1.8 metres). Flowering period: early summer.[25]

The outstanding feature of eryngiums is the unusual metallic-looking flowers they produce. *Eryngium giganteum* or 'Miss Willmott's Ghost' is a short-lived herbaceous plant. This plant gets its common name from Miss Willmott's habit of distributing seeds in friends' gardens and the plant's silvery-grey bracts, which have a ghostly quality when they appear. Miss Willmott's Ghost

Eryngium **(sea holly)**
Height: 1–5 feet (30 centimetres– 1.5 metres).[26]

Flowering period: mid–late summer. will die once it has flowered; however it will seed itself around the garden and the resulting seedlings will flower in their second year if there is not too much competition from other plants. *Eryngium X oliverianum* produces heads of large deep-blue flowers from July to September on stems that grow up to 2 feet (60 centimetres) tall. Each flower contains a central cone surrounded by narrow silver prickly bracts. Even in the autumn, when the flowers are brown and dry, the eryngium remains interesting. *Eryngium bourgatii* grows 18 inches (45 centimetres) tall, produces blue branching stems with blue cone-shaped flowers with silver bracts. Most eryngiums are native to the dry, rocky coastal areas of Europe and North Africa where they produce large tap roots. Most eryngiums need sunny, free-draining soil; they are ideal for stony soil or gravel beds. Plant between autumn and spring; cut flower stems down to ground level in late winter.

Euphorbia (milkweed) Height: 3 feet (90 centimetres). Flowering period: spring–early summer.[27] Euphorbias make up one of the most diverse plant families in the world. They are called spurges because they were once used in medicine for their purgative qualities. Euphorbias are grown for their subtle qualities of structure and foliage colours, which can outshine the brightest of flowers and blend in with their surroundings. The majority of the flowers are small and yellowish-green in colour, although some are burnt orange.

Euphorbia characias is one of the most popular. A native of the Mediterranean, it loves the sun. This shrubby species is handsome in appearance and remains evergreen in the winter. It produces a huge cylindrical head of yellow-green flowers in late spring and summer.

Euphorbia griffithii 'Fireglow' has dark-green foliage and produces bright-red flowers that last for weeks. The flowers are bracts, which are petal-like leaves on the top of each stem. The only problem with this plant is that it can be invasive, as the rhizomes tend to spread out and grow through other plants. In the spring cut out any shoots that are growing into other shrubs.

All euphorbias prefer a sunny position but will grow perfectly well in semi-shade. They do best in well-drained soil but will survive almost anywhere, provided the soil does not remain waterlogged. A word of warning on euphorbias: they produce a white sap when cut that is highly poisonous and can irritate the eyes and skin. Always wear gloves when handling these plants.

Euphorbia mellifera is an evergreen shrub from Madeira. It needs a sheltered position and protection in winter, except in the mildest parts of the country. It has apple-green foliage and golden-tan flowers in late spring. The flowers are followed by warty fruit that burst open in late summer, like a furze bush, propelling its seeds over a great distance. The bursting of the pods can be clearly heard on a warm day. *Euphorbia pulcherrima* (poinsettia) is a native of Mexico and is widely sold as a pot plant for Christmas.

Filipendula Height: 3–8 feet (1–2.4 metres). Flowering period: late spring–late summer.[28]

This is a hardy clump-forming perennial with large palmate leaves that grows 3 to 8 feet (1 to 2.4 metres) tall. Plumes of tiny, fluffy, red, pink or white flowers are produced from late spring to late summer on single or branched stems well above the foliage. The plant likes a moist humus-rich soil. *Filipendula palmata* is great for a wet, boggy part of the garden.

Francoa (bridal wreath) Height: 2–3 feet (60–90 centimetres). Flowering period: midsummer.[29]

This is a tender perennial from Chile. In midsummer the plant produces flower stems, 2 to 3 feet (60 to 90 centimetres) high, covered with small cup-shaped flowers that are pink with red markings. Francoa likes a well-drained soil and a sunny, warm position with shelter from wind. It can be grown as an edging for a border.

Galega (goat's rue) Height: 5 feet (1.5 metres). Flowering period: midsummer.[30]

This is a bushy, vigorous perennial with soft green or blue-green leaves that produces long clusters of numerous pea-like flowers that can be coloured white, blue, mauve or bicolour. The flowers are produced in midsummer and the plant can grow up to 5 feet (1.5 metres) tall. The plant likes a moist soil in full sun and needs staking.

Gaura Height: 3–4 feet

Gaura lindheimeri is a slender clump-forming perennial from Texas. The flowers are produced above the foliage on erect spires up to 2 feet (60 centimetres) tall. These spires continue to grow throughout

(1–1.2 metres). the flowering period, which can extend from late spring to early
Flowering autumn. The individual flowers have four petals and are white when
period: late they open in the morning, fading to rose-pink in the evening. Only a
spring–early few flowers are open at any one time and each flower drops off after
autumn.[31] blooming to leave a neat, clean stalk. The plant likes a moist, well-
drained soil but can tolerate drought and shade because it has a long
tap root. *Gaura* 'Crimson Butterflies' is a new cultivar from Australia
that has bronze foliage with crimson flowers.

Gazania Gazanias are a tender perennial, most of which come from South
Height: 8 Africa. They love full sun and produce a great splash of colour in
inches (20 hot, dry positions. They produce grey-green foliage that sprawls in
centimetres). clumps across the ground and large daisy-like flowers in a range of
Flowering yellow and orange shades. The flowers remain closed on dull days and
period: will open when the sun comes out. Gazanias are not hardy: plants
summer.[32] can be lifted in the autumn and stored in a frost-free glasshouse or
you can take cuttings in the autumn. The plant can be raised from
seed, sown in spring with gentle heat and planted out after the last
frost.

Geranium If you are looking for a plant that is easy to grow and will flower
(cranesbill) for weeks on end, then the hardy geraniums are your plant. Their
Height: 1–2 sheer versatility sets them apart from other herbaceous plants and
feet (30–60 there is at least one variety for every garden, whether large or small,
centimetres). dry, damp or shady. Hardy geraniums should not be confused with
Flowering their cousins the pelargoniums, which are grown as pot plants in the
period: mid- greenhouse. The name geranium comes from *geranos*, the Greek for
summer–mid- crane. This refers to their beak-like seed capsule, hence their common
autumn.[33–34] name: cranesbills.

The colour range of geraniums is not comprehensive: the most
common colours are blue, pink, maroon and white. Plant geraniums
in bold groups or drifts for dramatic effect. Although most are long
flowering, the variety 'Johnson's Blue' produces seemingly endless
displays of flowers. This variety produces no seeds so all the energy
of the plant is used to produce flowers. Another useful quality of
geraniums is their ability to form attractive ground cover, even in the
deepest shade. Geraniums will grow in most soils except an extremely

waterlogged one. *Geranium* 'Ann Folkard' produces a mass of yellow-green leaves in spring. In midsummer it produces saucer-shaped, silky magenta flowers with black veins that lead down to a black eye at the centre. This exceptional display continues from midsummer to mid-autumn. Old flowering stems can be cut back to the central crown throughout the summer to keep the foliage looking fresh. *Geranium maderense* is evergreen in a mild winter and produces flat pinkish-magenta flowers with a magenta centre. This plant is a native of Madeira and can grow 4 to 5 feet (1.2 to 1.5 metres) tall. The plant is short lived but if conditions are right it will self-seed.

Geum (Avens)
Height: 1–2 feet (30–60 centimetres). Flowering period: spring–summer.[35]

Geums are spring- and summer-flowering perennials that grow with a base of leaves and produce tall, thin flower stems up to 18 inches (45 centimetres). They are great plants to bring bright colour to the garden in spring before the main flowering season gets under way. They have saucer-shaped five-petalled flowers in shades of cream, yellow, orange, pink or red. There are small geums suitable for the rock garden; the larger ones can be grown at the front of a border. They like humus-rich, well-drained soil in full sun; avoid soil that is waterlogged in winter. Cut back the old flower stems to give more flowers later in the year. *Geum* 'Blazing Sunset' is a striking plant, flowering in spring to produce double scarlet flowers that last a long time. *Geum* 'Lady Stratheden' produces clusters of semi-double yellow flowers.

Helleborus
Height: 12–18 inches (30–45 centimetres). Flowering period: late winter–mid-spring.[36–37]

Hellebores are marvellous plants for shady gardens. Most of them do not require a lot of shade but they tolerate it. The best-known species are *Helleborus orientalis* (lenten rose) and *Helleborus niger* (Christmas rose) but they are by no means the only hellebores worthy of space in any garden.

The flowers of the lenten rose are open, cup-shaped with a nodding head. They come in mute colours of green, white, pale pink and primrose yellow through to the most exquisite plum-purple. All these colours may be enhanced by varying degrees of dark-red spots and the flower outline can be round or slightly star shaped. Growing to about 12 inches (30 centimetres) tall, they make an excellent ground cover under trees.

Helleborus niger, also known as the black hellebore because of its black roots, is the best known species of the Christmas rose family. It produces nodding flowers that open as early as January and continue on until April. *Helleborus niger* has been crossed with other species to produce some interesting hybrids such as 'Potter's Wheel', which has bowl-shaped white flowers with a green centre. Breeding new varieties of hellebores has reached almost cult status in recent years. Breeders have produced double flowers with colourful nectars. Hellebores that bloom well will produce seeds that will germinate to produce seedlings. These seedlings must be removed to prevent competition with the parent plant. The seedlings can be potted up and grown on to produce plants that will flower after about three years; however, the flower may not be the same colour as the parent plant. Named cultivars of hellebores do not come true from seed and this is the reason why choice plants are so expensive: these cultivars are propagated by division.

Most hellebores grow well in shade, in soil with plenty of organic matter added to it. All hellebores prefer a sheltered position, away from the effects of strong icy winds in winter that can damage the emerging blooms and leaves. To expose the flowers to their maximum potential, cut off the dead and decaying leaves. Hellebores, like roses, can suffer from a type of black spot that at best is unsightly and at worse can kill the plant. Spraying with a systemic fungicide, drenching the whole plant, will help prevent the disease. A badly affected plant should have the worst-affected leaves removed and burned.

***Hemerocallis* (daylily)**
Height: 2 feet (60 centimetres). Flowering period: late spring–late summer.[38]

Hemerocallis are herbaceous perennials with thousands of named cultivars to choose from. They are clump forming with dark-green leaves and grow up to 2 feet tall (60 centimetres). The flowers come in a variety of shapes, such as circular, star-shaped and trumpet, which remains a popular choice. The flowers range in colour from almost white through yellow and orange to dark purple and deep red. Most flowers last for only one day but new flowers are produced each day. Hemerocallis like fertile, moist but well-drained soil and full sun. Dig lots of compost into the soil before planting. Give the new plant much care in its first season and it will reward you with lots of blooms in later years. Feeding is essential: a sprinkling of a high-potash fertiliser in spring followed by a mulch of compost will

encourage strong growth and plenty of flowering stems. Water freely from spring until the buds develop; dry conditions and excessive shade will reduce flowering. It takes a few years for hemerocallis to become fully established but once established they can tolerate drought. Divide every two to three years to maintain vigour.

Heucheras are a group of perennials that come from North America. They grow as tufts of foliage from which spires of small flowers are produced from spring to summer. There are two basic types of foliage colouration. The first is bronze-purple, which lasts throughout the year. The second is green leaves with white or silver patches between the veins. Grow in well-drained, neutral soil in sun or partial shade. The woody rootstock tends to push up out of the soil so place a mulch around the plant each autumn; replant after a few years with the crown just above soil level. Heucheras are useful plants for ground cover. One of their strengths is that they can be evergreen and their foliage remains attractive throughout the winter.

Heuchera
(coral flower)
Height: 1–2 feet (30–60 centimetres). Flowering period: early summer.[39]

Hostas have fabulous foliage with delicate architectural shapes that blend in very well with so many other plants in garden design. They may be used as ground cover or as an edge to paths and lawns. There are dwarf varieties that reach only a few inches tall to giants that grow a few feet tall. Hostas are available in a wide variety of colours and textures; the shapes and sizes of the leaves vary greatly. The leaves can be anything from lance shaped to almost circular and can be more than 14 inches (35 centimetres) long. The leaf is often deeply textured with permanent veins and can be either matt or gloss. Leaf colours range from the coolest of silver blues to deep greens and yellows. Many varieties are variegated with white, cream or gold, often with a distinct margin around the edge or streaked as if a paintbrush were dragged lengthways down the leaf. Although hostas are grown for foliage they also produce flowers. The flowers are trumpet or bell shaped, appearing above the leaves on long stems, and come in shades of purple, mauve and white. All hostas like a moist soil and generally improve in leaf colour with age. They tend to grow best in dapple to full shade. It is important to prepare the soil well before planting, as hostas are long lived and can be quite happy

Hosta
(plantain lily)
Height of foliage: 1–2 feet (30–60 centimetres). Flowering period: midsummer; foliage, spring–autumn.[40]

in the same spot for over thirty years. Add well-rotted manure or compost to feed the plant and retain moisture. The only real problem with hostas is that slugs and snails like them so take measures to control them.

Japanese anemone
Height: 4–5 feet (1.2–1.5 metres). Flowering period: late summer–mid-autumn.[41]

The saucer-shaped blooms of these flowers will add grace and colour to the garden in late summer and autumn. The flowers are produced on tall, slender stems that do not need staking. The centre of each flower is covered with a circle of stamens that are often golden in colour. They can be slow to establish themselves in heavy clay soils. Once established, they are mainly trouble free. They like a fertile, neutral soil in light shade but will also do well in an open border. Japanese anemones can be slightly invasive in a light soil so keep them under control by digging up the extremities of the clump. *Anemone hybrida* is the most widely grown variety, producing a pink flower. It is easily grown from divisions or bits of the suckering roots. *Anemone* 'Hadspen Abundance' has deep-red-coloured flowers; the edges of the petals have a pinkish white colour that highlights the red. *Anemone* 'Honorine Jobert' is an old variety that produces clear-white flowers. Most species are best planted in the autumn. Japanese anemones should not be confused with the St Brigid or De Caen group of anemones: these are tubers that flower in spring.

Kitaibela vitifolia
Height: 8 feet (2.4 metres). Flowering period: midsummer–early autumn.[42]

This is a tall herbaceous perennial that comes from Slovenia and Macedonia. The leaves are vine-like, hence the name 'vitifolia'. The plant grows up to 8 feet (2.4 metres) tall and produces cup-shaped, mallow-like white flowers with five petals from midsummer to early autumn. The plant likes a deep, fertile soil in full sun.

Kniphofia **(red hot poker or torch lily)**

Kniphofias have been out of fashion in gardens for some time but recently have become a popular plant in garden design. They produce spires of colour from knee height to head height above a clump of arching, strap-shaped green leaves. The flowers are red, orange, yellow, white or greenish white. Numerous cultivars have

been produced that range in size from dwarf plants of 20 inches (60 centimetres) high to tall plants up to 5 feet (1.5 metres) tall. Kniphofias come from South Africa, where they grow in wet, marshy soil, so they like similar conditions in the garden and lots of sun. These plants may die from cold and wet in the winter so add grit or gravel to the soil when planting to improve drainage. They like lots of moisture in spring when the new growth emerges. *Kniphofia* 'Little Maid' is a popular plant in small gardens: it forms a small clump of leaves and produces flower spires 2 feet (60 centimetres) tall, coloured creamy white.

Height: 20 inches–5 feet (60 centimetres–1.5 metres). Flowering period: late summer–early autumn.[43]

These are large perennials that come mostly from China. Some of them can grow to 6 feet (1.8 metres) tall. These plants are grown for their large leaves and tall spires of yellow daisy-like flowers. Ligularia grow best in moist, well-drained soil that contains lots of organic matter. The plants do not like prolonged periods of dryness. They prefer partial shade rather than full sun. The leaves are large, can grow to a width of 20 inches (50 centimetres) and are often attacked by slugs and snails. The plants form clumps rather quickly and these can be left for several years without needing division. *Ligularia dentata* 'Desdemona' has large round, brown leaves that are deep purple underneath and produces orange flowers, which butterflies love.

Ligularia
Height: 3–6 feet (1–1.8 metres). Flowering period: Midsummer–early autumn.[44]

To most gardeners the name lobelia conjures up the pretty and delicate plant bought at the garden centre for your hanging basket or for edging a flower border. These annuals are easy to grow and can be raised from seed. There are perennial varieties that can be grown beside water or in a mixed herbaceous border. There are aquatic species for a pond. Lobelias like a fertile, moist soil in full sun or partial shade. To improve the flowering performance of annuals give them a liquid fertiliser every two weeks in spring and early summer and a fertiliser, low in nitrogen, every two weeks after that. Grow aquatics in baskets of acid soil at the margin of a pool.

Lobelia cardinalis is a short-lived moisture-loving plant with green leaves and a display of bright-red flowers from July to August. Many other colourful forms have been bred from this plant. *Lobelia*

Lobelia
Height: 6 inches–6 feet (15 centimetres–1.8 metres). Flowering period: summer–mid-autumn.[45]

cardinalis 'Queen Victoria', with its dark, almost black, foliage and red flowers, is one of the true stars. *Lobelia erinus* cultivars are low-growing bushy or trailing annuals with small leaves that produce flowers from summer to autumn in a range of colours such as blue, white, pink, red and purple. *Lobelia dortmanna* (water lobelia) produces pale-blue to pale-violet flowers in summer.

Lobelia tupa is a giant of a plant, very tropical in appearance, growing to a height of between 4 and 6 feet (1.2 to 1.8 metres) with a spread of 3 feet (90 centimetres). This lovely plant has pale-green leaves and scarlet-red flowers. The flowers are produced on spires up to 18 inches (45 centimetres) long from midsummer to mid-autumn. The plant is a native of Chile and will not tolerate temperatures below -10°C. It likes a moist soil enriched with well-rotted manure or compost. The plant can be propagated from seeds sown from February to March; do not cover the seeds – they need light to germinate.

Lupinus (lupin)
Height: 3–5 feet (1–1.5 metres).
Flowering period: early–midsummer.[46]

Lupins are one of the traditional flowers of the early summer border. They are upright perennials grown for their spires of large pea-like flowers, which appear above the attractive foliage. Lupins produce flowers in every colour of the spectrum, including bicolours. Flowering continues for six to eight weeks and if the plants are dead-headed they will often produce a few late flowers in early autumn. Although they will grow in neutral to acid soil, lupins like a slightly acid, well-drained soil. Lupins are fairly short-lived, especially if grown in limy soil.

Lychnis (campion)
Height: 2–4 feet (60 centimetres–1.2 metres).
Flowering period: early–midsummer.[47]

These are perennials with erect, branched stems that produce five-petal star-shaped flowers in early summer. The larger species are grown in a herbaceous border; there are alpine species suitable for the rock garden. They like a moderately fertile, well-drained soil in full sun. *Lychnis alpina* is a dwarf plant that grows to 6 inches (15 centimetres) tall and produces purple-pink flowers, ideal for rock gardens. *Lychnis chalcedonica* (Maltese cross) grows 3 to 4 feet (1 to 1.2 metres) tall and produces scarlet flowers from early to midsummer. This plant needs staking.

The larger species of this plant are suitable for a moist herbaceous border. The plant produces saucer- or cup-shaped flowers with five petals that are usually white or yellow in mid- to late summer. *Lysimachia punctata* produces yellow flowers and can be invasive. *Lysimachia punctata* 'Alexander' has grey-green foliage edged with creamy-white colour and produces attractive spires of brassy-yellow flowers in midsummer. It contributes foliage interest all season long and is not invasive. The plant likes a moist, well-drained soil that does not dry out in summer and full sun.

Lysimachia **(loosestrife)** Height: 2–3 feet (60–90 centimetres) Flowering period: Mid–late summer.[48]

Meconopsis is one of the most exquisitely beautiful of all the flowering plants that you can grow in the garden. They are not the easiest of plants to grow but are well worth trying. Meconopsis come from Tibet and China. They are deciduous perennial plants, which can be short lived. In summer they produce pendant to horizontal, saucer-shaped, bright-blue flowers with yellow stamens. The flowers are produced at the top of the stems, which can be 4 feet tall.

Meconopsis Height: 18 inches–4 feet (45 centimetres–1.2 metres). Flowering period: summer.[49]

Meconopsis likes a humus-rich, neutral to slightly acid soil, moist but well drained. It likes a cool, shady position in the shadow of a north-facing wall. The plant will rot in the winter if the soil becomes too wet. It thrives in partial shade with shelter from cold, drying winds.

Meconopsis betonicifolia (Himalayan poppy) produces blue flowers with gold stamens: the petals are like silk and the gold stamens stand out against the blue petals. The plant flowers in June and July and is one of the easier ones to grow.

Meconopsis x sheldonii 'Slieve Donard' is another beautiful blue flower, which was produced in the 1960s at Slieve Donard Nursery in County Down. This plant is a hybrid that does not produce viable seed; the plant is propagated vegetatively by division after flowering or in early September.

Meconopsis cambria (Welsh poppy) produces cup-shaped yellow flowers from spring to autumn. This plant has a long tap root, is very hardy and will thrive almost anywhere in the garden. The plant grows 18 inches (45 centimetres) tall.

Monarda (bergamot)
Height: 3–5 feet (90 centimetres–1.5 metres).
Flowering period: August–September.[50]

Monardas produce flowers in a range of colours from scarlet to white, which attract plenty of bees. The plant flowers from early August into September, adding a splash of colour to the late-summer border. The seed heads will give continued interest well into the winter. The plant grows 3 to 5 feet (90 centimetres to 1.5 metres) tall.

Monarda 'Cambridge Scarlet' produces a good bright-red flower. *Monarda* 'Beauty of Cobham' has pale-pink flowers and purple-green foliage. *Monarda* 'Croftway Pink' is a clump-forming plant with pink flowers. There are numerous new varieties, mostly bred in Holland; many of them are named after Native American tribes and signs of the zodiac. *Monarda* 'Aquarius' has pale-violet flowers and 'Scorpion' has violet flowers. *Monarda* 'Cherokee' has pink flowers while 'Sioux' has white flowers.

Monardas like sun or very little shade and thrive in most soils, except very dry or clay. Keep them well watered over summer. They are best planted behind smaller plants that will hide the lower parts of their stems. They are mobile plants and gradually move outwards from the original planting site so after a few years they may need digging up and replanting. Divide the plants in spring when they start to grow.

Myosotidium (Chatham Island forget-me-not)
Height: 2 feet (60 centimetres).
Flowering period: May.[51]

Myosotidium hortensia is a perennial that grows wild on Chatham Island off New Zealand. The flowers resemble the forget-me-not (myosotis) plant. This beautiful plant is not commonly grown because it only survives in mild climates where the summers are not too hot. It produces thick, fleshy stems and large bright-green succulent leaves up to 12 inches (30 centimetres) long, which are kidney- to heart-shaped and deeply ribbed. It produces small blue flowers in dense rounded heads in May. The plant grows up to 2 feet (60 centimetres) tall with a spread of 2 feet (60 centimetres).

Mysostidium needs to be grown in well-drained, humus-rich soil. It needs a sheltered position with partial shade from the sun: a north-facing position is ideal. The plant thrives in coastal gardens where the soil is moist but well drained. It likes a mulch of seaweed or seaweed-based fertiliser once a month. Cover the plant in winter because it will not survive temperatures much below freezing point.

The plant can be propagated by collecting seeds after the flowers

decay and sowing the seeds in potting compost when fresh. The plant is almost extinct in the wild due to grazing and trampling by animals.

Herbaceous peonies will provide a reliable display of colour each year without too much trouble. The flowers are every bit as beautiful as roses; most are strongly scented and make excellent cut flowers. The Chinese peony (*Paeonia lactiflora*) was introduced into Europe at the end of the eighteenth century and became a favourite in borders. Since then thousands of varieties have been bred and were planted in many cottage gardens. Flowers vary in size from singles to doubles, with most flowers having a red or pink colour. There are a few varieties with yellow and white flowers.

Paeonia (peony) Height: 2–3 feet (60–90 centimetres). Flowering period: early summer.[52]

Peonies grow best in a fertile soil but will tolerate a sandy soil if given a regular mulch of compost. They do not like a water-logged soil, especially in winter. They prefer neutral or alkaline soil and do not like acid soil with a pH of less than six. They are very hardy so they are ideal for gardens in colder areas. They flower best in full sun but will tolerate partial shade. Peonies flower in early summer. After flowering the foliage becomes tatty so it is best to plant them behind low-growing plants to conceal the decaying foliage.

Plant peonies in autumn to allow the roots time to get established. Since they grow for years if undisturbed, prepare the ground well, adding lots of compost. Peonies take time to settle down and may not flower in the first or second year. Most peonies are self-supporting but large flowering varieties can droop under the weight of the flowers. Place a plant support around the clump as the flowers emerge so the stems can grow through it. *Paeonie* 'Sarah Bernhardt' produces large rose-pink flowers with ruffled inner petals. *Paeonie officinalis* 'Ruba Plena' has vivid crimson flowers.

Few hardy perennials have such magnificent flowers as the oriental poppy. Clumps of big, bold red flowers are a sign of the arrival of summer sunshine. Scarlet was the only colour available until the 1940s when new varieties were introduced in a range of shapes and colour shades, including bright pinks, pale pinks and pure whites. Further developments in the 1980s saw lilacs and blue tones introduced. The

Papaver (poppy) Height: Oriental, 2–4 feet (0.6–1.2 metres);

Iceland, 12 inches (30 centimetres) Flowering period: Oriental, late spring–midsummer; Iceland, summer.[53]

oriental poppies (*Papaver orientale*) bloom in June, growing 2 to 4 feet (60 centimetres to 1.2 metres) in height. Their sturdy stems, topped with fat buds, rise from a lush carpet of evergreen foliage. The buds open to reveal crumpled petals that delicately unfurl into a luxuriously cup-shaped flower. The flowers often measure 9 to 10 inches (22 to 25 centimetres) in width. Some of them have a black blotch in the centre of the petals and all have a large number of purplish-black stamens in the centre of the flower.

The Iceland poppies (*Papaver nudicaule*) are smaller plants, growing about 12 inches (30 centimetres) in height. They are also favourites in the garden for their petals of white, lemon, yellow and orange, which are beautifully crinkled and have a delicious fragrance. They bloom all through the summer if the flowers are cut every day. *Papaver orientale* 'Cedric Morris' produces very large pink flowers with frilled petals. *Papaver rhoeas* (Flanders poppy) produces bowl-shaped red flowers. *Papaver alpinum* (Alpine poppy) is a low-growing poppy, 6 to 8 inches (15 to 20 centimetres) high, suitable for the rock garden, which produces flowers in shades of white, yellow and red.

Penstemon
Height: 1–2 feet (30–60 centimetres). Flowering period: mid-summer – mid-autumn.[54–56]

Penstemons can be deciduous, semi-evergreen or evergreen perennials, depending on how mild the garden is. The plant produces foxglove-like flowers in a range of colours from pink to purple; there are also some varieties with yellow and blue flowers.

The flowering power of penstemons is increased by continuous dead-heading throughout the summer. All penstemons hate having their roots cold and wet in the winter. They thrive in well-drained, fertile soil with full sun and ample water during dry spells. Add plenty of compost and grit to the soil before planting.

Do not prune the plant in the autumn: the summer growth will protect the crown of the plant over the winter. Wait until April or May, when the new growth starts to emerge, to cut back any new growth above the ground to about 15 inches (40 centimetres). Severe frost or old age will eventually kill your penstemons so take cuttings in late summer or early autumn to produce new stock for the following year.

A wide variety of penstemons are available to choose from: *Penstemon* 'Apple Blossom' produces bell-shaped pale-pink flowers with a white edge from midsummer to mid-autumn; *Penstemon* 'Sour

Grapes' has greyish-blue flowers with a purple tinge on the outside; *Penstemon* 'Rubicon' has bright-red flowers with a white throat.

The persicaria species contains annuals and perennials that may be evergreen, semi-evergreen or deciduous. They grow in any moist soil in full sun or partial shade. *Persicaria polymorpha* is a large herbaceous plant that can grow to 6 feet (1.8 metres) tall, making it an ideal plant for the back of a border. The plant has large, pointed green leaves and produces masses of soft-white flowers that fade to a pink-bronze colour in late summer. *Persicaria affinis* (*Polygonum affine*) is a matt-forming evergreen perennial with lance-shaped, dark-green leaves that turn a bronze-red colour in the autumn. The plant produces short spires covered in red flowers from midsummer to late autumn; these flowers fade to a pale pink and eventually brown to provide colour during the winter. *Persicaria virginiana* 'Painter's Palette' has variegated leaves with V-shaped brown marks, yellow patches, deep pinkish-red tinges and red midribs – the colour mix is like a painter's palette. It produces slender spires up to 12 inches (30 centimetres) long with cup-shaped green flowers that change to red in the autumn.

Persicaria
Height: 12 inches–6 feet (30 centimetres–1.8 metres). Flowering period: early summer–mid-autumn.[57–58]

Phlox is a plant that will fill the herbaceous bed with colour in late summer. Varieties of *Phlox paniculata* come in many shades, ranging from white through pink to mauve and magenta. They are greedy plants, needing lots of well-rotted manure or compost when planted. Grow phlox in well-drained soil in full sun. If some of the growing tips of the new shoots are pinched out when they are about 12 inches (30 centimetres) tall, the plants will grow bushier and produce more flowers over a longer period. A common problem with phlox is powdery mildew, often caused by the roots becoming too dry. The problem can be reduced by planting phlox in an open, airy place, so there is good air circulation around the plant, and keeping the roots cool with a mulch. Most phlox grow to 3 to 4 feet (1–1.2 metres) tall, while some varieties, like *Phlox drummondi*, only grow 18 inches (45 centimetres) in height. The stems of phlox are quite strong so they do not need staking. At the top of each stem, the five-petal flowers lie almost flat, providing a comfortable landing for

Phlox
Height: 3–4 feet (1–1.2 metres). Flowering period: summer–early autumn.[59]

bees. The flowers are usually fragrant. Propagate all phlox in autumn or spring by dividing the clump and discarding the dead part at its centre. *Phlox paniculata* 'Balmoral' has pink flowers; *Phlox paniculata* 'Hampton Court' has mauve-blue flowers, *Phlox paniculata* 'Mother of Pearl' has white flowers with a pink tinge.

Polygonatum (Solomon's seal)

Height: 2–3 feet (60–90 centimetres). Flowering period: late spring–midsummer.[60]

Polygonatum is a popular herbaceous plant in gardens, as it is very graceful and beautiful. It has a creeping rhizome or underground stem that produces stems in spring that grow up to 2 feet (60 centimetres) or more in height. The lower half of the stem is straight and bare; the top half has large oval-shaped leaves on one side of the stem, pointing in the same direction and bending over gracefully. You have to look closely to see the flowers, which grow from the base of the leaves and hang down beneath them to form drooping clusters. The bell-shaped flowers are a creamy-white colour, topped with a yellowish-green rim.

The plant likes a well-drained soil and a shady position since it is a native of woodlands. If the plant is given space it will thrive and multiply very rapidly. *Polygonatum multiflorum* 'Striatum' has creamy-white stripes on the leaves. *Polygonatum stewartianum* produces a straight, erect stem, 3 feet (90 centimetres) tall, with purple-pink tubular flowers. The flowers are followed by red berries in the autumn.

Pulmonaria (lungwort)

Height: 10 inches (25 centimetres). Flowering period: spring.[61]

Pulmonaria or lungwort are a group of evergreen, low-growing perennials with slowly spreading rhizomes. The name is derived from the Latin word *pulmo*, meaning lung, probably because the spotted leaves resemble the lungs. Practically evergreen, pulmonarias generally have colourful flowers and striking foliage. They are grown for their early flowers, often among the first perennial flowers in late winter or spring, and for their elliptic or oblong hairy leaves, which are often attractively spotted white or silver. The funnel-shaped flowers are produced in a variety of colours from dazzling white through to pinks and reds and a full range of blues. After flowering, new summer leaves develop, showing off the markings at their best. Pulmonarias are good ground-cover plants for a shady position.

There are a number of varieties to choose from, such as *Pulmonaria*

officinalis 'Sissinghurst White', which has spotted green leaves and white flowers. *Pulmonaria* 'Mawson's Blue' produces dark-blue flowers. *Pulmonaria saccharata* 'Argentea' has leaves that are almost completely silver and flowers that open red.

Pulmonarias can be planted in most locations and are as useful in a summer display as in a spring one. Plant between autumn and spring, 10 inches (25 centimetres) apart, in moist humus soil that is not waterlogged. Mature plants should be lifted every three to four years, divided into small chunks and replanted. The big advantage of pulmonarias is that slugs do not attack the leaves and this is one of the reasons many gardeners are now growing pulmonarias instead of hostas. They have attractive foliage and more attractive flowers than hostas.

Pulsatilla is grown for its fern-like leaves and silky bell- or cup-shaped flowers that are produced in spring and early summer. The flowers are followed by spherical seed heads, silvery white in colour, on stems above the leaves. Pulsatillas will thrive in most soils as long as they are well drained, get plenty of moisture in spring and have full sun. Since they only grow 8 to 10 inches (20 to 25 centimetres) in height, they are ideal plants for rockeries and scree beds. *Pulsatilla vulgaris* produces bell-shaped flowers in shades of deep to pale purple, while *Pulsatilla vulgaris* 'Alba' produces pure-white flowers. Dead-heading prolongs the flowering period but stop towards the end of the flowering season so that the seed heads remain to be enjoyed. Pulsatillas resent root disturbance and may be difficult to establish so plant when small and leave undisturbed.

Pulsatilla
Height: 8–10 inches (20–25 centimetres). Flowering period: spring.[62]

Rodgersias are very large, coarse-looking perennials, most famous for their ability to stand up to wet soils and shaded positions. They flower in late spring to early summer, producing large flower panicles up to 2 feet (60 centimetres) long, depending on variety. They are easy to grow, producing a stout, creeping rhizome that forms a large clump in time. They like a humus-rich, moist soil with shelter from cold, drying winds. In the sun they take on a bronze tinge. The leaves are shaped like those of the horse chestnut tree and change to a bronze colour in sun and in the autumn. *Rodgersia*

Rodgersia
Height: 3–5 feet (1–1.5 metres). Flowering period: late spring–early summer.[63]

aesculifolia produces white flowers on stems up to 5 feet (1.5 metres) tall. *Rodgersia pinnata* 'Superba' produces pink flowers on red stems.

Rudbeckia (coneflower)
Height: 18 inches–6 feet (45 centimetres–1.8 metres). Flowering period: late summer–mid-autumn.[64]

Rudbeckias are late-flowering herbaceous plants that range in height from 18 inches (45 centimetres) to 6 feet (1.8 metres). Some varieties can become invasive and spread through the herbaceous border. They produce large yellow or orange daisy-like flowers with dark centres; the flowers can be 5 inches (12 centimetres) wide. The plant flowers from late summer to mid-autumn. The plant will grow in any moderately fertile soil that does not dry out. *Rudbeckia fulgida* grows 3 feet (90 centimetres) tall, producing an orange-yellow flower. *Rudbeckia hirta* 'Becky Mixed' is a dwarf plant that grows 10 inches (25 centimetres) tall and produces flowers in shades of yellow, orange and red.

Salvia (sage)
Height: 18–24 inches (45–60 centimetres). Flowering period: summer–late autumn.[65]

The salvia or sage family is very diverse, containing annuals, herbaceous and evergreen perennials and shrubs. The common sage, *Salvia officinalis*, has been grown for centuries for use in cooking. Most *Salvia* types are native to Mexico so they can be tender plants. *Salvia patens* produces intense royal-blue flowers from summer to late autumn and grows to a height of 18 to 24 inches (45 to 60 centimetres). The plant likes a fertile, moist soil in full sun. The plant is not reliably hardy and will need the protection of a cloche in winter in mild gardens. In cold gardens it is recommended to lift and store the plant in a frost-free greenhouse.

Scabiosa (pincushion flower)
Height: 16 inches–3 feet (40–90 centimetres). Flowering period: summer.[66]

These are hardy perennials and herbaceous plants that are used for cut flowers as well as garden decoration. The name *scabiosa* is derived from 'scabies' because the plant is supposed to irritate the skin. The plant grows up to 3 feet (90 centimetres) tall and produces fragrant flowers from summer to early autumn. The stamens stand above the petals like pins stuck in a pincushion. The plant does best in deep, rich soil. If the soil is heavy the plant is likely to die during the winter. *Scabiosa columbaria* 'Butterfly Blue' was discovered in an Irish garden over forty years ago by David Tristram, who brought international attention to it. It grows 16 inches (40 centimetres) tall

and produces flowers from late spring to late summer. The flowers can be 2 inches (5 centimetres) in diameter with an outer ring of frilly, lavender-blue petals and a paler domed centre with protruding stamens. The flowers are produced singly on stiff stems. This plant is propagated from cuttings or plant division: it does not reproduce from seed.

𝒮edums have the advantage of looking good almost all the year round. The stonecrop or ice plant, as sedums are commonly called, belong to a family of succulent-leafed, sun-loving plants with fleshy leaves that act as a sort of moisture store for the plant. They are happy almost anywhere, excellent for dry areas of the garden with poor soil and almost thrive on neglect. *Sedum spectabile* (ice plant) produces new grey succulent foliage in spring. The stems slowly become fatter as spring and summer progress and the foliage takes on the frosty bloom that gives the plant its common name. The grey flower heads that form in summer are very similar to heads of broccoli. In late August, after the foliage is fully developed to a height of 2 feet (60 centimetres), each stem is topped with flat heads of starry flowers, deep pink at first, deepening to a bronze-red colour in October, which continues until the first frost arrives. The old flower heads can be left on the plant to protect the crown throughout the winter. Cutting these heads in spring reveals the new growth and the cycle starts all over again. *Sedum maximum* 'Atropurpureum' has leaves that are deep purple. Sedums can be planted in the herbaceous bed with late-flowering plants.

There are many small varieties of sedums that are suitable for an alpine bed or on the edge of a trough. There are tender species that will only survive in a greenhouse – *Sedum morganianum* is one such species. This is a pendant evergreen perennial with greenish blue leaves that produces small pale-pink flowers in summer.

Sedum
Height: 1–2 feet (30–60 centimetres). Flowering period: autumn.[67]

𝒮olidago provides late colour in the herbaceous border. Some varieties may start to flower in July but most varieties will not flower until late August and will continue until the end of September. In the past solidago had a poor reputation for its invasive tendencies. Some of the older hybrids gave the plant a bad name and they can

Solidago
(golden rod)
Height: 2–5 feet (0.6–1.5 metres).

Flowering period: late summer to autumn.[68]

often be found in neglected herbaceous borders. New varieties are now available, which have contributed to new interest in solidago. The more elegant solidagos are those with mimosa-like yellow flowers. *Solidago* 'Golden Shower' grows to 2 feet (60 centimetres) tall. There are dwarf varieties that fit better into planting schemes. *Solidago* 'Goldkind' has soft-yellow flowers and grows to about 20 inches (50 centimetres).

Thalictrum (meadow rue)
Height: 3–5 feet (90 centimetres– 1.5 metres). Flowering period: summer.[69]

This species is grown for its attractive foliage and feathery flowers; the taller species are excellent backdrop plants for a border. The plant thrives in moist, humus-rich soil in partial shade. *Thalictrum delavayi* has slender stems and produces fluffy yellowish-white flowers in clusters. The plant grows 4 feet (1.2 metres) tall and flowers from midsummer to early autumn. *Thalictrum delavayi* 'Hewitt's Double' has mauve pompon-like flowers. This plant needs to be divided and replanted every two to three years to maintain vigour.

Tradescantia
Height: 16–24 inches (40–60 centimetres). Flowering period: early summer to autumn.[70]

There are many varieties of tradescantia, some of them with purple-flush or variegated leaves that are tender and only suitable for greenhouses. The hardy tradescantias can be grown in moist, fertile soil in full sun. The *Andersoniana* group of tradescantias have narrow lance-shaped leaves and produce saucer-shaped flowers in a range of colours, from blue, purple, pink to red and white. The plant grows 16 to 24 inches (40 to 60 centimetres) tall and will flower from early summer to autumn. After flowering, cut back the flower stems to prevent seeding and to encourage more flowers.

Verbascum
Height: 3–6 feet (90 centimetres– 1.8 metres). Flowering period: early to late summer.[71]

Verbascum has been grown in gardens since the middle ages. Untouched by changes in gardening fashions, the popularity of verbascum remains and with the introduction of new cultivars it will maintain its place in the list of good garden plants.

Most of the 360 species of verbascum come from Turkey and the western part of Asia, where they enjoy the very-well-drained soil and baking sun. The majority will find it difficult to survive our cold, wet gardens.

The species that is most familiar to gardeners is *Verbascum*

olympicum. It grows up to 6 feet (1.8 metres) tall, with a candelabra of branches covered with golden-yellow flowers. The plant has a long tap root, which makes it difficult to transplant. Most of the biennial verbascums produce masses of seed and will spread through the garden if left unchecked.

The most common perennial verbascum grown in gardens is *Verbascum chaixii*. This plant is only half the height of the large biennials and, branching from the bottom, gives a more delicate look to the garden. Cutting down the flower spikes after they have flowered will produce a second and sometimes a third flowering.

This plant has been used by nurserymen to produce new cultivars such as the Cotswold group of verbascum cultivars. This group includes *Verbascum* 'Gainsborough' and *Verbascum* 'Cotswold Queen', which produce flowers in a colour range from white through pink to apricot and white. They have violet anthers that give the flowers their distinctive dark eye. Some of the new introductions, such as *Verbascum* 'Helen Johnson', produced twenty years ago in Kew Gardens, have renewed interest in verbascums. This plant has large buff copper-pink flowers, a colour seldom seen, grows 3 feet (90 centimetres) tall and flowers over summer. Unfortunately the plant is difficult to grow and even under ideal conditions will rarely live more than two years, often dying during the first winter.

Take root cuttings each year to produce new plants for the following year. Cut a piece of the root, about the thickness of a pencil, into 2 inch (5 centimetre) sections. Place them in a seed tray and cover with a layer of compost and horticultural grit, water well and do not allow the compost to dry out. New shoots will appear long before the cuttings produce any real roots of their own so do not pot up your new plants until you are sure they rooted. Wait until you see roots appearing through the drainage holes at the bottom of the tray. Pot them up in small pots and plant out in the spring. Root cuttings can be taken at any time but early autumn is the traditional time.

If you cannot live without verbascums treat them like bedding plants and buy new ones each year.

Verbena
Height: 5 feet (1.5 metres).

This genus of plants contains annuals, which are grown in hanging baskets, and perennials, some of which are suitable for the herbaceous border. *Verbena bonariensis* is a very popular perennial

Flowering
period:
midsummer to
early autumn.[72]

plant in herbaceous borders. Whether the plant is grown as a single specimen or in large groups, it is eye catching. The plant produces a dense cluster of tiny pale-purple flowers at the top of a stem that can grow to 5 feet (1.5 metres) tall. The plant takes up very little growing space and has very little leaves so it is possible to plant it anywhere in the herbaceous border because it will not obscure any planting around it. The plant was first introduced from South America and flowers from midsummer to early autumn. The plant is not reliably hardy so planting in a well-drained soil with added grit will increase its chances of survival in winter. If growing conditions are right the plant will self-seed.

Trees and Shrubs

Trees

Whatever the size of your garden, make sure that you include at least one tree, preferably more. A tree will reduce the amount of carbon dioxide in the atmosphere and reverse the greenhouse effect. Trees and shrubs create an essential backdrop for perennials and annuals. They provide structure, height and screening as well as giving shelter and shade, even in the depths of winter. Chosen carefully, a tree can have something good to offer for more than one season – flowers in spring or summer followed by colourful bark and autumn foliage. Avoid greedy brutes such as sycamores, willows and poplars that can wreck drains and foundations. You could treat a tree like a temporary resident, allowing it to grow for ten or twenty years and then removing it before it gets too big. Consider planting a tree to mark a special occasion such as the birth of a child or an anniversary. There is not enough space in a small garden to plant a large tree: it will plunge the house and garden into darkness and your neighbours may suffer also. Pick a small tree or choose one that can be pruned regularly to control its size. Many trees respond amazingly well to pruning. A tree can be used to divide one section of a garden from another or conceal part of the garden from the house or screen certain rooms in the house from the general view. Buy a tree with a good strong leading shoot. A tree with a broken or twisted leading shoot or more than one leader should be ignored as it will not grow to form a good trunk and head.

Before you plant your favourite tree erect a piece of wood or cane (the length of the wood should be the estimated height of the tree after twenty years) where you are planning to plant the tree. Look at the piece of wood from different positions in the garden and from the house and move it around until you are satisfied with its location. Consider the shade the tree will cast with the sun or the view it will block. Small trees will establish themselves in the garden more easily than large ones and will require less staking. Do not simply shoe horn your expensive tree into a hole and expect it will survive. Give your tree a good start in life by digging a wide hole, two to three times as wide as the diameter of the pot it is growing in. Mix well-rotted manure or garden compost into the soil. The depth of the hole should be such that when the tree is planted the soil level at its base is the same as it was in the pot. Use a cane to check the hole's depth – many tree deaths can be attributed to planting too deeply. The subsoil at the base of the hole should be broken up and some good topsoil or compost worked in. If drainage is poor add a layer of coarse grit or sand. Place a small stake in the planting hole, remove the tree from the pot and tease out any compacted roots. Damaged roots should be cut off. Fill in and firm around the roots, tie the tree to the stake and water well. In its first few years keep the tree well watered and weed free around its base. Do not apply a fertiliser, as it will only burn the roots at this stage – applying a mulch of well-rotted compost is much better. The following are some trees to consider for a very small garden: Japanese maple, ilex (holly), magnolia, *Cornus kousa*, *Pyrus salicifolia* 'Pendula' (weeping pear) and robinia.

Shrubs
Shrubs, like trees, are woody-stemmed plants that can be deciduous or evergreen. Trees are much larger than shrubs – trees can vary in height from 3 feet (90 centimetres) to 300 feet (90 metres) while most shrubs will not grow taller than 20 feet (6 metres). A tree usually has a single stem, whereas a shrub will have several stems rising from ground level. In recent years many shrubs have been trained into standards that look like a small tree: these are ideal for the small garden or patio where they can be grown in a large pot.

Shrubs provide a permanent structure and add seasonal interest to the garden by flowering at different times of the year. They can be used to define areas of the garden and to disguise eyesores such

as bins and compost heaps as well as neighbouring gardens. Shrubs are very versatile and there is one to suit every design and location, whether your garden is big or small. They range from dwarf plants, suitable for the front of a border, to large specimens that can grow up to 15 feet (4.5 metres) tall and wide. To create an exciting shrub border, pick plants that perform well at different times of the year. Pick shrubs that flower in spring and summer and ones that produce interesting foliage, bark colour and berries in the autumn. Pick a mixture of deciduous and evergreen shrubs and include a few variegated ones to provide colour in winter. While herbaceous plants will give a good show of colour in their first year, shrubs are slower to establish themselves. If you are planning a new shrub border you have two options. Plant the shrubs more densely than recommended and thin them out a few years later by replanting some of them. Plant them so they have enough space to mature and plant annuals between the shrubs in the first few years to provide instant colour. The second option is the cheaper one and easier in the long run. If you have a mature garden with established trees and shrubs take a critical look at what you have. Look at each plant and decide whether you like it enough to keep it. If a shrub has become too large and overgrown, prune it hard or remove altogether. If you decide to keep some shrubs and replace others prune the ones that are retained so that the new plants will integrate with the old ones. Before you buy a shrub check that it likes the conditions in your garden – some plants like an acid soil while others like shade or full sun.

Most shrubs are best planted between autumn and spring when the ground is not too wet or frozen. Shrubs planted in the autumn have their roots settled into the ground for growth in spring. Tender and evergreen shrubs are best planted in spring if the garden is cold and exposed. Most shrubs are sold as pot grown plants, so they can be planted any time of the year but will need to be watered frequently. Dig the planting hole as deep and twice as wide as the rootball of the shrub. Mix in some well-rotted manure or garden compost and after planting apply a layer of mulch around the stems. Cut out any dead or diseased stems and stems that are growing towards the centre of the plant. The best way to select shrubs for your garden is to visit gardens open to the public where you will see a variety of shrubs growing and make a note of the ones that you like. The following are some of the trees and shrubs that you could choose for your garden.

Abutilion
Height:
6–15 feet (1.8–
4.5 metres).
Flowering
period:
summer–
autumn.[73–75]

Abutilion is an evergreen or deciduous shrub from the tropical regions of Africa, Australia and America. It is grown for its showy, mostly bell-shaped flowers with highly colourful stamens. The flowers are solitary and hang like a pendulum along the stem and are often produced from late spring to autumn. Some varieties, such as 'Thompsonii', have attractive variegated foliage. Some abutilions are tender and will not survive severe frost: these should be grown in a greenhouse or conservatory. Abutilions like a well-drained soil in full sun.

After three or four years abutilions tend to become woody and produce less flowers so replace old plants with new plants raised from cuttings. They grow easily from cuttings taken in late summer. Some varieties worth growing are *Abutilion* 'Kentish Bells', which produces flowers with apricot petals and purple stamens on slender arching stems. *Abutilion pictum* 'Thompsonii' has a large maple-like variegated leaf with salmon-pink flowers and can grow 15 feet (4.5 metres) tall. *Abutilion* 'Ashford Red' has large red flowers. *Abutilion megapotamicum* has slender, arching stems with yellow petals protruding from red sepals.

Acacia (wattle)
Height: 12–30
feet (3.6–9
metres).
Flowering
period: winter–
spring.[76]

Acacias, or wattles as they are called in Australia, are half-hardy trees and shrubs from the southern hemisphere. These plants, also called mimosas, produce yellow flowers in late winter or early spring and are often scented. The flower heads are small and form in clusters along the stem – they may be so densely crowded that they hide the stem and leaves. The leaves are pinnate in shape, which gives a feathery appearance to the plant.

Acacias need a lime-free soil that is well drained and shelter against wind. They need full sun and a south or west wall to protect against frost – they do well in coastal gardens. The branches of acacias can be pruned after flowering to encourage more compact, bushy growth.

Acacia dealbata is the most commonly grown variety. It is a vigorous evergreen tree whose blue-grey fern-like leaves look silvery from a distance. *Acacia baileyana* 'Purpurea' is a plant worth looking for: the tips of the shoots are purple and it looks great even when it is not in flower.

**Acer
(maple)**
Height:
3–70 feet (90
centimetres–21
metres).
Flowering
period:
attractive
foliage, spring–
autumn.[77–78]

This large group of deciduous and evergreen trees and shrubs contains plants that vary in size from small to very large. They are grown for their foliage, which may be variegated, and produce beautiful autumn colour – some of them have very attractive barks. There is at least one acer to suit every garden, whatever the size.

Acer palmatum is commonly called the Japanese maple. This plant is widely grown in gardens for its attractive foliage. The first things you will notice about Japanese maples in a garden centre are their delicate-shaped foliage and their price. Many varieties are grafted, which is a labour-intensive business and explains their high cost. These varieties vary in height from 3 to 30 feet (90 centimetres to 9 metres), with a wide range of foliage colour and shape. The foliage in spring and early summer is soft and brightly coloured: some have green, others smoky-purple or bright-orange-and-red coloured foliage. Later in the summer the shades darken to green, bronze and purple. In the autumn the spring colours return again to the foliage.

One of the best-known varieties is *Acer palmatum atropurpureum*, which has large bronze leaves that turn a brilliant red in the autumn. The 'Dissectum' group of plants are small and mound shaped with arching branches that will reach a height and spread of about 6 feet (1.8 metres) after ten or more years. The leaves are each deeply and finely cut to give a lacy, almost fern-like effect.

Acer palmatum 'Senkaki' produces orange-yellow leaves that turn yellow in the autumn. Once shed, the falling leaves reveal bright red shoots. Japanese maples like a well-drained soil with shelter from wind, especially in spring when the new foliage is emerging. They prefer a slightly acid soil to give the best colour but will grow well in lime soils also. They can be grown in pots and containers – shelter from cold winds is the one thing they require.

Other acers worth growing are *Acer negundo* 'Variegatum', which has a white margin on the leaves; *Acer griseum* (paper-bark maple), which has a peeling orange-brown bark; *Acer platanoides* 'Crimson King', which has very dark red-purple foliage and can grow up to 40 feet (12 metres) tall; *Acer shirasawanum* 'Aureum', which has bright-yellow leaves that turn red in the autumn and grows 20 feet (6 metres) tall; and *Acer davidii* 'Serpentine', which produces beautiful green-and-white patterns on its bark.

Acradenia
Height: 10 feet (3 metres). Flowering period: early summer.[79]

Acradenia is a genus of two species of evergreen shrubs from Australia. *Acradenia frankliniae* is an erect-growing, small to medium sized shrub. It has pretty, fragrant, glossy dark-green leaves and produces flat clusters of star-shaped white flowers in early summer. The plant is slow growing and will ultimately reach a height of 10 feet (3 metres). It can be grown outdoors in mild climates in a well-drained, fertile soil in partial shade with shelter from cold, drying winds. In frost-prone gardens grow the plant in a glasshouse in lime-free compost. Water freely and apply a liquid fertiliser monthly during the growing season; water sparingly in winter.

Aralia
Height: 30 feet (9 metres). Flowering period: summer.[80]

Aralia spinosa (devil's walking stick) is a deciduous tree or shrub with a thorn-covered stem. It has large dark-green pinnate leaves and produces white flowers in summer. It grows up to 30 feet (9 metres) tall and likes a fertile, humus-rich soil in sun or partial shade with shelter from strong wind.

Arbutus unedo (strawberry tree)
Height: 25 feet (7.5 metres). Flowering period: September–November.[81]

This is a spreading shrubby tree with a shedding brown bark and glossy bright-green leaves. It is attractive in the autumn when the white flowers, often tinged pink, are produced and the fruit from last year are turning red. The tree gets its name from these fruit, which look like strawberries but sadly don't taste like them. Grow the plant in a fertile soil with lots of well-rotted garden compost mixed in and stake well. It likes full sun and shelter from cold winds. The plant requires minimal pruning; remove any broken, diseased or crossing branches in late autumn or winter. An excellent tree for coastal gardens.

Aucuba (laurel)
Height: 10 feet (3 metres). Flowering period: mid-spring.[82]

Aucuba is a plant often found in old gardens; it is not planted very much in new gardens. It is a useful plant for shaded areas, as it can grow, even thrive, under the shade of large trees. *Aucuba japonica* (spotted laurel) is an evergreen shrub that grows 10 feet (3 metres) tall. The plant can be pruned to control its size. The female plants produce bright-red berries in the autumn but to produce berries a male cultivar must also be planted. Variegated cultivars are ideal for brightening up a dull corner by adding hints of bright yellow or gold.

Aucuba crotonifolia is a female plant with leaves liberally splashed and speckled with yellow spots. The variegated plants like partial shade from cold winds that scorch the leaves.

T his group of plants consists of tender evergreen shrubs or small trees that are natives of Argentina and Chile. *Azara microphylla* is a small tree with sprays of small dark-green leaves. It produces tiny yellow, scented flowers on the undersides of the twigs in early spring. This is the hardiest of the azaras: it tolerates full shade and can grow up to 30 feet (9 metres) tall. A variegated form of this plant has pale-green leaves with a white margin. *Azara lancelolata* is a tender shrub that will blacken when exposed to cold winds. It produces bright-yellow flowers in small clusters in mid-spring. Azaras like a fertile, humus-rich soil with shelter from cold winds.

Azara
Height: 15–30 feet (4.5–9 metres)
Flowering period: spring.

B erberis is a useful plant for hedging, screening and ground cover. This is a large genus of evergreen and deciduous shrubs. *Berberis darwinii* is a vigorous upright, evergreen shrub about 8 feet (2.4 metres) tall. The leaves are spine-toothed like a miniature holly. In April and May the plant is covered with brilliant orange-yellow flowers that are followed in the summer by blue-black berries. The plant was introduced into England from Chile by Charles Darwin. It makes an excellent hedge and with its prickly leaves it will keep out all intruders.

Berberis
Height: 5–10 feet (1.5–3 metres).
Flowering period: spring.[83–84]

There are many other berberis to choose from, many of them deciduous. Varieties of *Berberis thunbergii* are the most commonly grown berberis. This deciduous shrub was first found growing wild in Japan. Its neat growth habit, with arching branches, has ensured that it has remained a popular garden plant. *Berberis thunbergii* 'Rose Glow' is a deciduous shrub with red-purple leaves that have a fleck of white in summer. *Berberis thunbergii* 'Aurea' is a small shrub that grows to 5 feet (1.5 metres) tall. It has bright yellow leaves and should be planted in shade – plants with yellow leaves do not like direct sun. *Berberis x stenophylla* is an evergreen shrub with long arching branches that are covered with deep-yellow flowers in late spring.

Berberis are very hardy plants that will grow in almost any well-drained soil in full sun or partial shade. There are dwarf species that are suitable for the rock garden or large shrubs that can be used as a hedge or as a specimen shrub.

Betula (birch)
Height: 5–80 feet (1.5–24 metres). Flowering period: catkins, spring.[85]

The elegant and graceful form of birch has ensured that it has become a popular garden tree. There are about sixty species and most are grown for their unusual bark, colourful autumn foliage and catkins in spring. Many are suitable for a small garden, grown as a single specimen or planted in small groups.

Betula pendula is perhaps the most elegant of the genus and over the years many improved varieties with better weeping characteristics have been introduced. *Betula pendula* 'Tristis' is a narrow, slim tree with slender, pendulous branches and good white bark. *Betula pendula* 'Youngii' is a weeping birch that can grow to 25 feet (7.5) tall. *Betula pendula* 'Purpurea' has dark-purple leaves and purple-tinged bark; it grows 30 feet (9 metres) tall. 'Golden Cloud' has yellow leaves. Birches are very adaptable to their surroundings and will grow in any soil, although they thrive in moist well-drained soils.

Buddleja (butterfly bush)
Height: 12 feet (3.6 metres). Flowering period: midsummer to autumn.[86–87]

Buddleja davidii is a great garden plant because of its fine large flowers in striking colours and its ability to attract butterflies. It will thrive in a wide range of soils, flower prolifically, require minimum maintenance and is easily propagated. It could be argued that it is too vigorous for a small garden – it is now seen growing along hedgerows and waste ground. There are many varieties with less vigorous growth habits and equally appealing flowers.

The flowers are large, long and cone-shaped, made up of thousands of tiny tubular flowers. Buddlejas will flower for a long period, starting in midsummer. *Buddleja davidii* 'Black Knight' produces purple-blue flowers; 'White Profusion' has white flowers with a yellow eye; and 'Harlequin' has green leaves with a cream margin and dark red-purple flowers. *Buddleja globosa* produces fragrant dark-orange and yellow flowers in the shape of a ball.

Buddlejas reach a mature height of about 12 feet (3.6 metres) with a spread up to 15 feet (4.5 metres). The spread of these plants makes them unsuitable for small gardens. It is possible to train buddlejas into standards by removing all the lower branches and only allowing one stem to grow up, cutting the top when it has reached 5 feet (1.5

metres) to form a bushy head. These standardised plants will fit in any garden and there is space underneath the plant to grow bulbs. Prune these plants after flowering.

Callistemon makes an excellent garden plant, as it has so many positive features. It is grown for its fine arching habit and, above all, the beautifully coloured bottlebrush flowers that stand out against the darker background of its narrow leaves. It is evergreen. The plant gets its common name from the bristle-like flowers that look like old-fashioned bottlebrushes. The flower consists of a mass of stamens rather than the colourful petals found in most flowers. The tips of the stamens can be coloured yellow.

It is a native of Australia, where it has a very long flowering season, usually beginning in late spring and continuing throughout the summer. In this country it will flower from July through to August.

Callistemons are adapted to cope with seasonal waterlogging as well as extended periods of drought. They do not like acid soil so do not plant them near your favourite camellias or azaleas. They like full sun. Callistemons are not very hardy and will tolerate temperatures down to about -5°C. They are well worth experimenting with to see what varieties will survive our colder winters.

Most callistemons will grow from 6 to 20 feet (1.8–6 metres) tall and with the lower branches removed will make an attractive shaped tree. Stake young plants when training them into a tree. They should be pruned after flowering to maintain the shape of the plant. Prune the plant just below the old flower head.

Callistemon citrinus is probably the best-known bottlebrush – it produces bright-red flowers in summer and grows about 12 feet tall. *Callistemon brachyandrus* has red flowers with the tips covered in yellow pollen and grows about 9 feet (2.7 metres) tall. *Callistemon pallidus* (lemon bottlebrush) produces pale lemon-coloured flowers in early summer.

Callistemon **(bottlebrush)** Height: 6–20 feet (1.8–6 metres). Flowering period: summer.[88–89]

Camellias are one of the star plants in the garden in early spring. The dark, glossy foliage of the plant always looks well, even after flowering. Camellias originated in China and Japan, where they were cultivated thousands of years ago. They were very popular in

Camellia Height: 6–28 feet (1.8–8.5 metres).

Flowering period: late winter to late spring.[90–91]

Victorian times and after that interest in them waned. In the 1930s the English gardener Williams produced a number of new hybrids that were hardier and more free flowering.

There are many varieties of *Camellia x williamsii* available now. Camellias are easily grown in open ground or in pots. They like a neutral or acid soil – if your soil is limy grow them in containers filled with lime-free compost. Plant camellias in dapple shade to avoid early morning sun, which will burn the flowers in frosty weather. They may be pruned in spring, after flowering, to keep the plant bushy and restrict its size. When planting camellias add a generous supply of humus and peat. Do not plant them too deeply – the top of the root-ball should be slightly higher than the surrounding ground. A good layer of mulch on top of the soil will retain moisture and protect the shallow roots. Water a new plant thoroughly, once a week, during its first year. In summer they produce fat flower buds for the following year and can lose these buds if the plant becomes too dry. Camellias are not heavy feeders so fertilisers should be used sparingly.

Camellia japonica is a large plant that can grow up to 28 feet (8.5 metres) tall; it flowers in early spring, producing flowers in a range of colours, such as red, white and pink, depending upon the variety. *Camellia x williamsii* 'Donation' has large pink flowers from late winter to spring, can grow to 15 feet (4.5 metres) tall and flowers from late winter to spring. 'Golden Spangles' has variegated foliage with pink flowers.

Ceanothus (California lilac)
Height: 3–10 feet (1–3 metres).
Flowering period: summer.[92]

Ceanothus is a dazzling shrub with dark-blue flowers borne on arching branches and glossy dark-green leaves. This dense evergreen shrub is ideal for a sunny mixed border on neutral to acid soil. Coming from California, the plant needs well-drained soil, full sun and shelter from cold winds. It flowers from May to June in different shades of blue – one variety that produces a white flower (*Ceanothus incanus*). The plant can grow up to 10 feet (3 metres) tall. There are low-growing species that are excellent for ground cover or the rock garden, such as *Ceanothus thyrsiflorus var. repens*, which grows 3 feet (1 metre) high.

Chaenomeles are one of the brightest early flowering ornamental shrubs. They produce richly coloured flowers on bare stems in early spring. The flowers come in a range of colours, such as white, pink and dark reds, before the new leaves emerge. They are easy to grow, with some of them producing golden fruits that make delicious preserves. They grow in most soils and conditions – the exception is very limy soil, which causes yellowing of the leaves. To keep them in shape they can be pruned immediately after flowering.

One of the most attractive ways of growing quince in the garden is to train it as a wall climber. The plant can be trained as a fan against a wall by tying its shoots onto horizontal wires; then give it a summer trim to cut back badly placed shoots. To cover the dull foliage of chaenomeles, train a climber such as a late-flowering clematis to grow through it and you will get two displays of flowers from the same area. The largest and most vigorous members of the family can grow up to 10 feet (3 metres) tall.

Chaenomeles japonica produces orange to red flowers and grows 3 feet (1 metre) tall. *Chaenomeles* 'Rowallane', produced in Northern Ireland, grows 3 feet (1 metre) tall and has red flowers.

Chaenomeles (flowering quince)
Height: 3–10 feet (90 centimetre–3 metres).
Flowering period: spring.[93]

This group of plants are evergreen shrubs native to Mexico. *Choisya ternata* (Mexican orange flower) is a round medium-sized shrub that will grow 5 to 10 feet (1.5–3 metres) tall. Even if it never flowered it would be a valuable evergreen shrub. It has glossy dark-green leaves that produce a slight smell of oranges when crushed. It is a plant widely used by flower arrangers for its foliage. The flowers are a bonus – fine heads of white, fragrant flowers are produced in late spring to cover the whole shrub; in mild autumns it can produce a second show of flowers. Choisyas can be planted in spring in any well-drained, fertile soil in sun or light shade. No regular pruning is required – the shrub can be trimmed to shape after flowering. Other varieties worth growing are *Choisya* 'Sundance', whose new leaves are a brilliant yellow colour. Like all yellow-leaf plants, this needs to be planted in shade from the sun. It also produces white flowers but not as plentiful as *Choisya ternata*. *Choisya* 'Aztec Pearl' forms a small shrub with almond-scented white flowers with a tinge of pink.

Choisya (Mexican orange flower)
Height: 5–10 feet (1.5–3 metres).
Flowering period: late spring to early summer.[94-95]

Cordyline (cabbage tree)
Height: 25 feet (8 metres).
Flowering period: summer.[96]

Cordylines are a genus of ornamental shrubs and trees grown primarily for their foliage. They usually have a single trunk with several ascending branches, each topped with a large, thick mass of long sword-like leaves; the colours range from green and purple to yellow shaded with dark pink. Cordylines don't seem to mind the soil they are in as long it is well drained – they grow well in coastal gardens. Once established they need little water and will tolerate dry soils. Plant in full sun or partial shade. Remove the lower leaves as they die to form a trunk. *Cordyline australis* (New Zealand cabbage tree) is a slow-growing evergreen sparsely branched tree that produces white flowers in large open panicles in summer. The plant can grow up to 25 feet (8 metres) tall. *Cordyline australis* 'Purpurea' has purple leaves.

Cotinus (smoke tree)
Height: 15–20 feet (4.5–6 metres).
Flowering period: summer.[97]

Cotinus are deciduous shrubs that are grown for the colour of their foliage. Most shrubs, trees and hedges provide foliage in different shades of green. Cotinus provide different colours of foliage, which can transform the garden into something out of the ordinary. *Cotinus coggygria* (smoke tree) is a bushy tree or shrub with mid-green leaves that turn red in the autumn. The plant produces smoke-like clusters of flowers. Many varieties of cotinus produce purple foliage. *Cotinus* 'Grace' produces purple leaves that turn a brilliant red in late autumn; it grows 20 feet (6 metres) tall. Purple-leaf forms give the best colour in full sun. Cotinus are fully hardy and will thrive in most garden soils. If the plant has space to grow, the only maintenance needed is to tidy up the plant in late winter or early spring. In small gardens the plant can be kept in check by pruning.

Coprosma
Height: 5–15 feet (1.5–4.5 metres).[98]

This group of tender evergreen shrubs or small trees are mostly natives of New Zealand. They are mainly grown for their attractive foliage, which is variegated in many species. The plant likes a neutral to slightly acid soil that is moist but well drained. The plant is not fully frost hardy so it will only survive in mild regions. *Coprosma repens* is a small tree or shrub that can grow up to 15 feet (4.5 metres) tall. They produce brightly coloured berries in the autumn if a male and female plant are both grown. *Coprosma repens* 'Pink Splendour' has brilliant dark-pink tones that are more pronounced in cool weather.

The cornus or dogwood species are mostly deciduous trees or shrubs, grown for their wide range of ornamental effects. Some of them are grown for their flowers in spring (flowering dogwoods); others are grown for the colour of the stems in winter. Dogwoods such as *Cornus alba* are prized for their brilliant autumn foliage and outstanding winter beauty provided by colourful stems, which range in colour from yellow to red and almost-black purple. These dogwoods will grow in wet ground where many other plants would fail. They should be cut back hard in spring to within 12 inches (30 centimetres) of the ground. The new growths will have excellent bark colour. They are often used to decorate the embankments and roundabouts of new roads.

Cornus canadensis (creeping dogwood) is a creeping perennial that produces white flowers in late spring. It likes a humus-rich, well-drained soil.

The flowering dogwoods, such as *Cornus kousa*, are grown for their white flowers in early summer and stunning autumn foliage. *Cornus kousa* produces creamy-white flowers that sit on the branches; the flowers are flushed with pink before they fade. Sometimes the plant produces berries like strawberries that turn red in the autumn. Flowering dogwoods thrive in well-drained neutral to acid soil with shelter from cold north and east winds. They can grow up to 23 feet (7 metres) tall.

Cornus alternifolia 'Argentea' (pagoda dogwood) and *Cornus controversa* 'Variegata' have graceful horizontal tiered branches that look like a wedding cake. The variegated leaves have a wide creamy-white margin and the plant is covered with creamy-white clusters of flowers in early summer. These should be allowed to grow naturally with the minimum of pruning – just remove branches that grow vertically.

Cornus (dogwood) Height: 10–25 feet (3–7.5 metres). Flowering period: early summer.[99–100]

Corokia is a tender evergreen shrub or small tree that comes from New Zealand. It can grow from 8 to 10 feet (2.4 to 3 metres) tall and produce small star-shaped yellow flowers with five petals in late spring. In the autumn the plant produces pretty orange berries. *Corokia cotoneaster* has thin, wiry stems and is often referred to as the 'wire net bush'. The plant thrives in well-drained, humus-enriched soil in full sun with shelter from cold winds – it does very well in

Corokia Height: 8–10 feet (2.4–3 metres). Flowering period: late spring.[101]

coastal gardens. Since the plant is slow growing it does not require regular pruning; to keep the plant in shape, it can be trimmed or lightly cut back after flowering.

Correa (Australian fuchsia)
Height: 3–10 feet (90 centimetres–3 metres).
Flowering period: autumn to spring.[102]

Correa is a small genus of only twenty species of evergreen shrubs or small trees from Australia. We grow the plant as a climber on a north-facing wall that is sheltered form north and east winds. The plant is frost tender so in frost-prone areas it can be grown in a greenhouse. The plant likes a fertile, moist but well-drained neutral to acid soil in full sun. It can grow up to 10 feet (3 metres) tall. *Correa pulchella* produces tubular fuchsia-like flowers in shades of pink and orange right through the winter from autumn to spring. If you have a mild garden and want a plant that flowers for months over the winter then a correa is worth growing.

Corylus (hazel)
Height: 20 feet (6 metres).
Flowering period: catkins, spring.[103]

One of the most bizarre small trees that can be grown in the garden is *Corylus avellana* 'Contorta' (corkscrew hazel). The Americans call it Harry Lauder's walking stick after a vaudeville comedian who used a twisted cane as a walking stick. It is one of the few winter trees that really looks at its best with its leaves removed. It grows what are allegedly flowers, the catkins that hang from it, in early spring. In summer it produces crinkled crêpe-paper-like leaves that look as if they are suffering from some pest attack. Characterised as a large shrub, it can grow up to 20 feet (6 metres) in height and width. Because the plant is grafted it has a tendency to produce suckers that grow straight from the rootstock and these must be removed. Some varieties are grafted 4 feet (1.2 metres) above the ground to produce a standard. The twisted branches are widely used in flower arranging.

Cotoneaster
Height: 6 feet (1.8 metres).
Flowering period: summer.[104]

Most of the 200 species of cotoneasters come from the temperate regions of China and the Himalayas and include evergreen and deciduous shrubs and small trees. They will survive in poor soils provided they are not subjected to waterlogged conditions. They are grown for their autumn and winter displays of red berries – some species produce yellow or black berries. In winter, birds find the

berries irresistible and so the plant is often used to attract wildlife to the garden. In summer the plant produces masses of white flowers that attract bees and the close-growing density of the small branches provides suitable nesting sites for small birds. The most commonly planted species is *Cotoneaster horizontalis*, often grown as a ground-cover shrub or close to a wall, where it grows like a climber. Cotoneasters are prone to attack from the bacterial disease fireblight, which results in the foliage wilting and turning brown. It is best to remove every infected branch from the plant to prevent the disease from spreading.

Crinodendron hookerianum is an evergreen shrub or small tree from Chile. The plant is grown for its dark-green foliage and its bell- or lantern-shaped flowers that are produced in May and June. The plants like a fertile, moist but well-drained, humus-rich acid soil in full sun or partial shade, with the roots kept cool and shaded. Shelter from cold, drying winds. Young growth and flowerbuds can be damaged by hard frost. The plant can be pruned after flowering to remove dead or damaged growth. The lower side branches can be removed to raise the foliage up from the ground and provide space for bulbs or small shrubs. There are only two species of crinodendron: *Crinodendron hookerianum* produces red flowers while *Crinodendron patagua* produces white flowers in late summer and prefers drier conditions.

Crinodendron (lantern tree)
Height: 20–25 feet (6–7.5 metres). Flowering period: summer.[105]

Daphnes are grown for their winter fragrance and profusion of flowers. They are mostly small shrubs that can be deciduous, evergreen or semi-evergreen. They produce fragrant tubular flowers that come in a variety of colours from red-purple to pink, white and lilac. They are suitable for cutting and their fragrance will fill the house with a beautiful scent. Most gardeners think of daphnes as small shrubs but some varieties can grow up to 6 feet (1.8 metres). *Daphne mezereum* can reach 4 feet (1.2 metres) in height, is deciduous and produces pink flowers in late winter and early spring before the leaves appear. *Daphne x burkwoodii* cultivars flower in late spring, producing pink flowers, and can be evergreen in mild winters. *Daphne cneorum* is a hardy, prostrate evergreen shrub that bears fragrant

Daphne
Height: 1–5 feet (30 centimetres– 1.5 metres). Flowering period: late winter–late spring.[106]

clusters of rose-pink flowers in April and May. It can be a difficult plant to establish. It needs cool, moist conditions with soil enriched with compost. It will tolerate a limy soil, unlike most daphnes. This variety is excellent for a shady spot in the rock garden. In general daphnes like a moderately fertile, humus-rich, well-drained but not dry soil. Mulch in the spring to keep the roots cool. Most varieties prefer a slightly acid soil in sun or partial shade. They do not like pruning and resent being moved once established so it is essential to plant them in the right position at the beginning. To gain the maximum pleasure from daphnes, plant them near paths where both the sight and scent of the flowers can be appreciated. If there is one drawback with daphnes it is that all parts of the plant are poisonous, particularly the berries.

Davidia (handkerchief tree)
Height: 50 feet (15 metres). Flowering period: summer.[107–8]

This genus contains one species of deciduous tree that comes from China. When it flowers in late May or early June it appears to be covered with white doves or handkerchiefs fluttering in the breeze. This tree is not frequently planted because it takes years before it flowers. To grow *Davidia involucrata* you need patience – lots of patience. The first time it flowered in Limerick was in Nell Allott's garden in Ballingarry – the tree was 45 years old. The tree has glossy pale-green leaves, resembling those of a lime tree. After the flowers it produces brown golf-ball-sized fruit in the autumn. The plant can be propagated by planting the whole fruit in compost and leaving it outdoors. Germination will normally occur after two winters – it even takes patience to germinate the seeds. The plant likes a fertile, moist, well-drained soil in sun, with shelter from cold winds.

Deutzia
Height: 6 feet (1.8 metres). Flowering period: spring–summer.[109]

Deutzias are prolific-flowering deciduous shrubs that bloom from mid-spring to summer. They can grow up to 6 feet (1.8 metres) tall. They produce pure-white or pinkish flowers with yellow stamens. They are easy to grow and will thrive in any soil that is fairly moist, in a sunny location. Pruning consists of thinning out the shoots that have finished flowering by cutting them back to within a short distance of the old wood.

This is a small group of evergreen trees and shrubs from the southern hemisphere. They are grown for their attractive bark, glossy green leaves and white flowers. The flowers are either male or female – only one type will be found on any one plant so both male and female plants must be planted if seed is required. They like a reasonably well-drained, moist soil with shelter from cold winds. *Drimys winteri* is a small tree that can grow up to 20 feet (6 metres) tall, has large, smooth green leaves and produces clusters of white flowers in summer. *Drimys lanceolata* is a bushy shrub with fragrant mahogany-coloured bark and produces white flowers in late spring.

Drimys
Height: 12–20 feet (3–6m)
Flowering period: late spring–early summer.[110]

This group of mostly evergreen shrubs are grown for their foliage. *Elaeagnus angustifolia* 'Quicksilver' is a fast-growing shrub with silvery leaves. It can tolerate many growing conditions, such as very dry soil and coastal salt winds, which makes it ideal as a hedge in coastal gardens. *Elaeagnus* 'Gilt Edge' has green leaves with a golden yellow margin. *Elaeagnus* 'Maculata' has dark-yellow leaves with a green margin.

Elaeagnus
Height: 12–20 feet (3–6m)
Flowering period: summer.[111]

Embothrium coccineum is a small tree that grows to about 20 feet (6 metres) tall. The tree is evergreen and is covered with orange-red to scarlet tubular flowers in late spring and early summer. The flowering period is brief but spectacular. The plant likes a fertile, deep, humus-rich soil that is neutral to acid.

Embothrium (Chilean fire bush) Height: 20 feet (6 metres). Flowering period: late spring–early summer.[112]

Enkianthus campanulatus is a plant grown for its clusters of delicate bell-shaped creamy-yellow flowers with pinkish-red margins and matt green leaves that turn vivid shades of orange and red in the autumn. It is a deciduous shrub that occurs in the woodlands from the Himalayas to Japan, where it can grow up to 15 feet (4.5 metres) tall. The plant is fully hardy and will grow in moist, humus-rich acid soil that is well drained. It likes full sun in spring and autumn with slight shade in summer. Apply a thick mulch of well-rotted

Enkianthus
Height: 6 feet (1.8 metres). Flowering period: late spring–early summer.[113]

leaf-mould around the base of the plant in spring. It requires little pruning – remove dead and diseased wood and branches that are crossing each other after it has flowered. The plant grows into a small shrub about 6 feet (1.8 metres) high in this country. The plant is trouble free though yellowing of the leaves indicates chlorosis due to the presence of lime in the soil. It is an ideal plant for a shady woodland edge.

Escallonia
Height: 10 feet (3 metres). Flowering period: summer.[114]

Escallonia could be described as one of the mainline shrubs of gardens – there seems to be at least one plant growing in every garden. They are evergreen shrubs and small trees of varying size that come from South America. The have dark-green, glossy leaves and produce flowers in shades of pink and red throughout the summer – if the plant has not been mutilated as a hedge. They are widely used as foundation and specimen shrubs and in hedges. They can take any conditions along the coast but like a reasonably well-drained soil. Slieve Donard Nursery and the Botanic Gardens in Dublin have produced a number of new varieties of escallonia. *Escallonia rubra* 'C. F. Ball' is named after C. F. Ball who worked in Glasnevin and was killed in the First World War. *Escallonia* 'Donard Seedling' produces pink-tinged white flowers. *Escallonia* 'Pride of Donard' has red flowers. *Escallonia laevis* 'Gold Brian' is a relatively new introduction. It has bright-yellow foliage all year round with deep pink flowers in summer.

Eucalyptus
Height: 60–150 feet (18–45 metres). Flowering period: summer.[115]

Eucalyptus is a group of large evergreen trees and shrubs from Australia. They are grown for their aromatic foliage and attractive peeling barks. They are not a tree for the small garden unless they are pruned back hard each spring to control their size. When pruned hard they produce a nice display of young foliage. They make a nice specimen tree but they must be planted in the right spot. They are always dropping leaves and bark so should not be planted near a garden pool. They produce small white or creamy-yellow flowers that have no petals. *Eucalyptus gunnii* (cider gum) has greyish-green leaves and a whitish-green bark.

Euonymus
Height: 3–8 feet (90 centimetres–2.4 metres).[116]

Euonymus is a great plant to make a hedge, edging or ground cover. The evergreen types are valued for their handsome foliage, which is usually multicoloured, and their tolerance to salty winds in coastal gardens. The flowers are insignificant. *Euonymus fortunei* 'Emerald 'n' Gold' is an attractive compact dwarf shrub with dark-green leaves edged with a wide band of brilliant gold and grows about 3 feet (90 centimetres) tall. *Euonymus fortunei* 'Silver Queen' can grow up to 8 feet (2.4 metres) tall and has green leaves with a wide white edge. Euonymus will grow in almost any type of soil. The variegated varieties need sun to produce the best leaf colour.

Euryops
Height: 4 feet (1.2 metres). Flowering period: summer–autumn.

Euryops pectinatus is a vigorous, tender evergreen shrub from South Africa. It has soft grey-green foliage and is covered with yellow daisy-like flowers all through the summer and into the autumn. The plant likes a well-drained soil in full sun. Trim lightly after flowering to control the size of plant. It grows about 4 feet (1.2 metres) and will not survive severe frost.

Fatsia
Height: 5–12 feet (1.5–3.6 metres). Flowering period: autumn.[117]

Fatsia japonica is often grown as a foliage houseplant but will survive outdoors in mild seaside gardens or against a warm wall in colder inland gardens. Hard frost can damage the leaves but the plant will recover if the roots are protected from freezing. The plant has very large palmate leaves, which create a tropical effect. In the autumn the plant produces small whitish flowers followed by clusters of small black berries. Plant in spring to give the plant time to establish itself before the winter sets in. Plant in well-drained soil in full sun with shelter from cold winds.

Forsythia
Height: 10 feet (3 metres). Flowering period: spring.[118]

Forsythia is an early flowering deciduous shrub that can grow up to 10 feet (3 metres) tall. The yellow flowers are produced on thin woody stems in early spring before the leaves appear. Forsythias can be grown as a hedge or planted as individual specimens. The taller varieties are easily trained on a wall as climbers. Although forsythias are not fussy about their growing conditions they perform best in well-drained soil. Forsythias flower on the previous year's growth so pruning should be done immediately after the flowers have faded.

Each year prune back about a quarter of the old stems to within a few inches of the ground. A forsythia that is drastically overgrown from years of neglect may stop flowering. In this case cut the entire plant down to ground level. It may take a few years before it flowers again but the shrub will come back better than ever. *Forsythia x intermedia* 'Lynwood' has large bright-yellow flowers; this cultivar was introduced by Slieve Donard Nursery in 1946.

Fothergilla
Height: 6–10 feet (1.8–3 metres). Flowering period: late spring.[119]

Fothergilla is a deciduous shrub that can grow 6 to 10 feet (1.8–3 metres) tall. The plant produces glossy dark-green leaves. The leaves are noteworthy for turning brilliant reds, oranges and yellows in the autumn. In late spring the plant produces white bottlebrush-like flowers. The bristles on the flower spires are actually stamens – the flowers have no petals. The flowers appear before the leaves and can last for two to three weeks. The plant needs an acid soil – it will not tolerate limy conditions. It does best in a moist, humus-rich soil in partial shade. Fothergilla is a rather slow-growing but long-lived shrub.

Fuchsia
Height: 1–10 feet (30 centimetres–3 metres). Flowering period: summer–autumn.[120]

Fuchsias are a well-established favourite in the garden. They provide great value for summer bedding, window boxes, hanging baskets and terrace containers. They will grow in any aspect except deep shade. They have a long flowering season and their growing habits range from upright bushes to trailers and standards.

Fuchsia flowers come in all sorts of attractive shapes and sizes, including singles, semi-doubles and doubles. Colours range from pink, purple, white and red through to multicoloured mixtures. The numerous variegated forms are very useful when inter-planted with green foliage in summer bedding schemes. Certain species can be used in permanent shrub borders or as ornamental hedges – this can be seen in hedgerows in West Kerry – flowering from midsummer to late autumn.

There are 105 known species of fuchsia, which are native to South and Central America and New Zealand. Most fuchsias today are man-made hybrids of which there are thousands of types. The first fuchsia was found in the Dominican Republic about 200 years ago and the plant was named after the German Dr Fuchs.

With so many varieties to choose from it is difficult to decide which plants to grow in the garden. It is best to buy them in flower so you can decide whether you like them or not. *Fuchsia magellanica* is a hardy form that flowers in summer. 'Mrs Popple' has scarlet flowers; 'Lena' is low growing with semi-double flowers that have rose-magenta petals; 'Tom Thumb' is a dwarf variety with single crimson and mauve flowers, ideal for a rockery; 'Annabel' is an upright bush with white double flowers.

The majority of fuchsias are tender and therefore prone to frost damage. The smaller the flower, the hardier the plant is. Fuchsias will nearly always re-shoot from the roots, even when the top of the plant is completely killed. Plant fuchsias with the roots slightly deeper than in the pot to give extra protection against frost. When grown in pots or containers pinch out the faded flowers and the developing seed case behind them. This ensures that the plant's energy is diverted into producing more flowers and will prolong the flower display.

Fuchsias grown outdoors are practically trouble free; those grown in a greenhouse or conservatory require a bit more attention. They need good light and sunshine but too much heat can scorch the leaves and flowers. Feed once a fortnight with a liquid fertiliser and check water requirements daily. They like a moist atmosphere with a high humidity in the air.

Look out for attacks of greenfly and whitefly. These aphids can be manually squashed or treated with an insecticide to control them. Apply the spray in the evening, and ideally in the open, and leave the plants in the shade for a while to recover – otherwise the leaves may scorch. All tender species must be brought into the greenhouse for the winter. In September reduce watering to allow the older wood to mature; by the end of the month they should be kept almost dry. Treat pots with Provado to prevent attack by vine weevils – they love fuchsias.

Do not prune fuchsias hard until spring. Then when the new shoots emerge from the base, prune off the old wood. Re-pot and replace some of the old compost. Fuchsias can be trained into a standard by allowing one stem from a young plant to grow upwards, pinching out side shoots as they appear. Once the stem has reached the desired height, pinch out the growing tip to create a bushy fuchsia head.

Ginkgo (maidenhair tree)
Height: 80–100 feet (24–30 metres).
Flowering period: spring.[121]

The *ginkgo biloba* is the world's oldest living species of tree, the sole survivor of the Ice Age. Fossil records show that the tree was growing when dinosaurs roamed the earth. The trees can live a long time, some over 600 years, so it is a tree that you plant for your children and generations to come. It is a deciduous tree from China and is extinct in the wild. It is hardy and will thrive in a variety of soils – its main requirement is adequate drainage. Ginkgos love full sun and young trees should be staked at first and watered during dry spells until they reach about 20 feet (6 metres). The tree is slow growing, conical when young and broadening out with age. The tree is dioecious – the flowers are either all male or female so both male and female trees must be planted to produce seed. The female tree produces yellowish plum-shaped fruit that has a foul smell. The flowers are inconspicuous and appear in spring. The male tree produces cones and the female the fruit and seed. The tree can grow up to 100 feet (30 metres) tall. It has fan-shaped leaves that are bi-lobed and they have a light-green colour in spring that turns a pure, dazzling yellow in the autumn. The leaves of the tree are widely used in alternative medicine. The tree is often grown as a bonsai.

Grevillea
Height: 10–65 feet (3–20 metres).
Flowering period: summer.[122]

This species of evergreen trees and shrubs are native to Australia and are members of the protea family. They vary in size from small ground-cover plants to medium-sized shrubs up to 10 feet (3 metres) tall. However, some species, like *Grevillea robusta* (silky oak), can grow up to 65 feet (20 metres) tall in mild gardens. They have needle-like foliage and flowers that are described as spider flowers – they radiate from the centre like a spider's legs. The flowers are red, pink or yellow and mostly occur in summer. They vary greatly in hardiness – some species will not stand any frost while others can tolerate it. They like an acid to neutral soil in full sun.

Griselinia
Height: 10 feet (3 metres).

Griselinia is a genus of evergreen trees and shrubs with glossy green leaves from New Zealand and South America.

Griselinia littoralis can grow to a medium size tree up to 30 feet (9 metres) tall. It is very seldom allowed to grow into a tree but is used widely for hedging in coastal gardens because it can tolerate salty winds and withstand heavy clipping. It is not very hardy and will not

survive severe frost. It thrives in fertile, well-drained soil in full sun.

Griselinia littoralis 'Variegata' has green leaves with a creamy-white margin. Single plants of established hedges can die off so remove roots and stems of infected plants, drench the soil with Armillatox disinfectant and replant with a different variety of hedging, such as escallonia.

Griselinia littoralis 'Bantry Bay' is a very attractive tender shrub that needs a sunny, sheltered corner. The amount of variegation on the leaves varies – as much as three-quarters of the leaf can be creamy yellow in colour. This plant makes a very nice specimen shrub or small tree, growing to 10 feet (3 metres) tall. This plant was first produced in Garnish Island about fifty years ago. It is a sport from the green-leaf griselinia. The plant has a tendency to revert back to green so remove any shoots with green leaves as they appear.

Hamamelis can brave the cold weather in the depths of winter to produce flowers with an intoxicating scent. The flowers are tucked in clusters along the naked branches of the shrub. Hamamelis resembles the common hazel, which was used for water divining and had a reputation for healing powers. These properties gave the plant its common name, witch hazel. It is a versatile shrub that can give height to the back of a border and create a splash of colour in winter. The leaves become a cloak of orange and purple in the autumn.

Hamamelis mollis is a popular type with golden-yellow flowers, which was introduced from China about a hundred years ago. *Hamamelis mollis* has been used to breed a new race of hybrids under the collection name *Hamamelis x intermedia*. 'Diane' has intense red flowers; 'Pallida' has large sulphur-yellow flowers with a delicate sweet scent. Grafting is the only way to propagate witch hazels, which unfortunately increases the cost of production. Autumn is the best time to plant them. They are slow growing, often painfully slow in the first few years. Once established they grow into large shrubs up to 12 feet (3.6 metres) high, often more spreading than tall. Although they prefer a neutral-to-slightly-acidic soil, they will grow in a lime soil provided there is a good depth of rich soil. Plant them at the level they were growing in the pots because grafted plants will often produce suckers if planted too deeply.

Flowering period: late spring (flowers are not prominent).[123]

Hamamelis (witch hazel) Height: 12 feet (3.6 metres). Flowering period: winter.[124]

Hebe
Height: 1–6 feet (30–180 centimetres) Flowering period: late spring–early summer.[125]

There are over a hundred species of hebe. They are evergreen shrubs and mostly native to New Zealand. They range in size from ground-cover plants to small shrubs up to 6 feet (1.8 metres) tall. The flowers can be spikes or clusters of small tubular blooms that range in colour from white through to purple. Hebes can be used in rockeries, used as small hedging plants or grown in containers. They like a moist but well-drained soil in sun with shelter from cold winds. Prune plants after flowering to keep them bushy and compact. *Hebe* 'Red Edge' has grey-green leaves with a red margin and pale-lilac flowers in early summer. *Hebe pinguifolia* 'Pagei' is a low-growing ground-cover plant that produces a profusion of white flowers from late spring to early summer. *Hebe x franciscana* 'Variegata' is a compact shrub with green leaves that have a large creamy-yellow margin.

Heliotropium (heliotrope)
Height: 2 feet. Flowering period: summer.[126]

Heliotropium arborescens is a plant guaranteed to enhance any garden all through the summer. It is a bushy, short-lived shrub that is native to Peru. It has lance-shaped, wrinkled dark-green, sometimes purple-tinged, leaves. It produces lavender-blue flowers in dense flower heads that bloom all through summer. In frost-prone areas grow in a greenhouse. In warmer gardens grow at the front of a border. The plant likes a moist, well-drained soil in full sun. The easiest way to grow this plant is in a large pot placed in the greenhouse for the winter and placed outdoors for the summer.

Hibiscus
Height: 10 feet (3 metres). Flowering period: late summer–early autumn.

The hardy hibiscus is a shrub that will bring a touch of the tropics to the garden in late summer and early autumn. It is one of the few flowering shrubs in the garden at that time of the year. The hardy hibiscus is a deciduous shrub that comes into leaf in summer – don't be fooled into thinking that the plant has died, because it can survive a few degrees of frost. The flowers are mainly funnel-shaped and come in a range of colours, such as red, pink, purple, blue, yellow and white. The plant flowers in late August or early September on shoots of the current year's growth so it has to make rapid growth over a period of three months to produce the flowers. To produce this rapid growth the summer must be warm with lots of sunshine and adequate rainfall. In cold, wet summers the plant may produce flower buds that will drop off before opening. Hardy hibiscus has

a long dormant period: it should be planted towards the back of a border so that smaller shrubs or bulbs can be planted in front of it to divert attention from the bare stems early in the year.

Hibiscus syriacus is an erect deciduous shrub that can grow up to 10 feet (3 metres) tall. It has a number of varieties: 'Blue Bird' produces blue flowers with red centres; 'Diana' has large white flowers; 'Red Heart' has white flowers with large dark-red centres; 'Pink Giant' has large pink flowers; and 'Woodbridge' is a very good plant with a red flower.

Grow hardy hibiscus in a well-drained, humus-rich soil in full sun. Water if the weather is very dry to maximise growth during its short growing season. Hibiscus do not need pruning but if pruning is required to control the size of the plant, spring is the time to do it. The plant can be trained into a standard to make a magnificent focal point in a sheltered garden. Train a young hibiscus up a strong cane. Remove all the side shoots until the plant reaches the desired height. Cut the growing tip to produce a bushy head. Pruning must be carried out each spring to keep the head bushy. *Hibiscus trionum* is a fast-growing annual, with a yellow flower and brown centre, that flowers from summer to early autumn.

Hydrangeas have large blooms that bring flamboyant colour to the garden in late summer and autumn. They are easy to grow, dependable and improve with age. The mophead and lacecap varieties are the best-known varieties. The mophead has spherical blooms, while the lacecap produces flattened flower heads. The flower colour of hydrangeas depends upon the pH of the soil and the availability of aluminium in it. Acid soils with a pH less than 5.5 will produce blue flowers. If the pH is high you will never get blue flowers, even if there is plenty of aluminium in the soil. However you can grow fabulous pink flowers. Soils with a high pH tend to lock up the aluminium, making it unavailable to the plant. If the soil is neutral, adding special blueing compounds that contain aluminium sulphate will increase the blue colour of the flowers. It may take a few years before the flower colour changes. Growing blue hydrangeas in a container makes it easier to control the pH. White-flowering varieties are not affected by soil pH. There are many varieties to choose from and most grow to about 5 feet (1.5 metres) tall and wide. There are many cultivars

Hydrangea
Height: 5–20 feet (1.5–6 metres).
Flowering period: summer.[127–29]

of *Hydrangea macrophylla* (common hydrangea) producing red, pink and blue flowers that are either mophead or lacecap. *Hydrangea paniculata* produces beautiful cone-shaped flowers that are mostly white. There are several varieties of this shrub or small tree that can grow to 20 feet (6 metres) tall. If pruned hard in spring it never gets out of hand and is ideal for the small garden. *Hydrangea petiolaris* is a climbing hydrangea, which will cover a shady wall, even a north-facing wall, using its self-climbing shoots that attach themselves to the wall like ivy. It produces small white flowers that only last for a few weeks in summer and does not flower well until the plant has matured. *Hydrangea seemannii* is an evergreen climbing plant that produces white flowers in summer. Hydrangeas like a moist, fertile soil in dapple shade against a north- or west-facing wall with some protection from cold winds, which burn the new foliage in spring. Pruning is not essential but may be done each spring as new buds appear. Since most hydrangeas flower on the previous year's growth, do not remove all of these stems. Remove about a third of the older, less productive stems, cutting them back to ground level to encourage new shoots to grow from the ground. Leave old flower heads on the shoots during the winter to give frost protection to the new delicate growth in spring. If they are not pruned they will continue to flower but the size of the flower heads will be reduced.

Ilex (holly)
Height: 20–70 feet (6–21 metres).
Flowering period: berries, winter.[130]

The ilex is one of our most beautiful native plants, with its waxy, variably shaped leaves offering year-round colour and interest. The flowers are insignificant and are followed by bright red berries on the female plants in winter. A male plant must be present in the garden or nearby to produce berries. They will grow in moist, well-drained soil. Variegated hollies need full sun to produce the best leaf colour. Planting or transplanting is best done in late winter or early spring. Free-standing specimens can be pruned to shape: start the pruning in the early years after planting. Hollies make excellent hedges or windbreaks and should be trimmed in late spring. *Ilex altaclerensis* 'Golden King' is a female plant, despite its name, that can grow up to 20 feet (6 metres) tall, has mottled green leaves with a broad golden margin and has sparsely produced red berries. *Ilex aquifolium* 'Silver Queen' is a slow-growing male plant with a creamy margin on the leaves. *Ilex aquifolium* 'Ferox' (hedgehog holly) is a large male plant

that can grow up to 50 feet (15 metres) tall; its leaves are covered with a large number of spines. Hollies can be slow to establish themselves and can take a number of years to grow into a sizeable shrub.

Indigofera garardiana, now called *Indigofera heterantha*, is a deciduous shrub that flowers in summer into the autumn. The plant produces arching branches with elegant, pinnate grey-green leaves and masses of pea-like purple-pink flowers. It can grow up to 10 feet (3 metres) tall in a moderately fertile, moist but well-drained soil in full sun. Grow it in a shrub border or trained against a warm, sunny wall.

Indigofera
Height: 10 feet (3 metres). Flowering period: summer–early autumn.[131]

These gorgeous deciduous trees are native to the higher mountains of Europe. The tree is grown for its flowers, which appear early in spring in rich, dangling sprays of yellow. These sprays can be up to 20 inches (50 centimetres) long depending on the variety. The heartwood of the tree is a dark-reddish colour, hard and durable and when polished looks like ebony. It is often used by woodturners and with other coloured woods for inlaying. All parts of the plant are poisonous, especially the seeds, so care should be taken if grown where young children are present. The tree makes a nice specimen plant in a small garden or can be trained to form a pergola in a large garden. Laburnums can grow up to 25 feet (7.5 metres) tall. The tree likes a moist, well-drained soil that is deep enough to accommodate their long roots. Plant young trees from autumn to spring and stake them. Several varieties of this tree are cultivated, differing in the size of the flowers. *Laburnum alpinum* 'Pendulum' has weeping branches and grows 6 feet (1.8 metres) tall. *Laburnum anagyroides* (common laburnum) can grow 25 feet (7.5 metres) tall. 'Aureum' has yellow leaves. *Piptanthus laburnifolius* (evergreen laburnum) is a semi-evergreen shrub with yellow flowers.

Laburnum
Height: 25 feet (8 metres). Flowering period: late spring–early summer.[132]

These are shrubs, perennials and annuals native to the Mediterranean region, Australia and California. They are grown for their saucer-shaped five-petal flowers in shades of red, pink and pure white, often striped with darker veining. The flowers are produced from midsummer into the autumn. They like a well-drained soil in full

Lavatera (mallow)
Height: 2–10 feet (0.6–3 metres).

Flowering period: midsummer–autumn.[133]	sun, with shelter from cold winds in frost-prone gardens. *Lavatera arborea* (tree mallow) grows up to 10 feet (3 metres) tall and bears purplish flowers throughout the summer. *Lavatera trimestris* cultivars are compact varieties, about 2 feet (60 centimetres) tall. 'Mont Blanc' has a pure-white flower.
Leptospermum (tea tree) Height: 10 feet (3 metres). Flowering period: late spring–early summer.[134–35]	Most species of these evergreen trees and shrubs are natives of Australia and New Zealand. The common name comes from the use of some leptospermums to make tea. They are grown for their neat aromatic foliage and small profusely borne flowers. The flowers are shallow and cup-shaped, with five petals, in shades of red, pink and white. The flowers are produced in late spring to summer. Many of the leptospermums are suited to planting in seaside gardens, where they enjoy the good drainage and mild winters. They will not survive severe frosts. After flowering, lightly trim the plant to keep it bushy. They like a sunny position and well-drained soil. There are many decorative garden cultivars and much of them have been developed from the species *Leptospermum scoparium*. This compact shrub grows about 10 feet (3 metres) tall and produces white flowers. Cultivars of this species include 'Red Damask', which has double dark-red flowers, and 'Silver Sheen', which has silver-green-coloured leaves and white flowers.
Ligustrum (privet) Height: 15 feet (4.5 metres). Flowering period: late spring–summer.[136]	Ligustrum is an evergreen shrub that can grow up to 15 feet (4.5m) tall. It produces white flowers in late spring and early summer, followed by black berries. The plant is so widely used in hedges that it is often referred to as privet hedge. It grows quickly and tolerates heavy trimming – it needs to be trimmed at least twice a year. It likes a well-drained soil in full sun or partial shade. The variegated species *Ligustrum sinense* 'Variegata' has yellowish leaves with a white margin.
Liquidambar (sweet gum) Height: 40 feet (12 metres).	This deciduous tree is grown for its attractive maple-like leaves that produce gorgeous shades of red, orange or bronze in the autumn. It can be grown as a specimen tree in large gardens and can grow up to 40 feet (12 metres) tall. It produces inconspicuous flowers in

late spring. Mature trees have a nice rough grey, furrowed bark. Best grown in moist, deep, well-drained acid or neutral soil. *Liquidambar formosana*, native to China, has red-tinted leaves in spring that turn red in autumn. *Liquidambar styraciflua* 'Argentovariegata' has green leaves with a white margin.

Flowering period: late spring (flowers are not prominent)[137–38]

*L*iriodendron tulipifera is a large deciduous tree from North America that can grow up to 100 feet (30 metres) tall. This is an excellent plant to grow as a specimen tree in large gardens. The tree produces large saddle-shaped leaves. The leaves are light green in colour and turn yellow in the autumn. The common name, tulip tree, refers to the small pale-green tulip-shaped flowers that are produced on mature trees, usually more than ten years old. The plant likes a slightly acid, moist, well-drained soil in full sun. *Liriodendron tulipifera* 'Aureomarginatum' has pale-green leaves with a yellow margin.

Liriodendron **(tulip tree)** Height: 100 feet (30 metres). Flowering period: summer.[139–40]

*L*uma apiculata is an evergreen shrub or small tree from Chile and Argentina. It is also known as *Myrtus luma*. It can grow up to 30 feet (9 metres) tall. Its small aromatic leaves respond well to pruning so it can be used as a hedge. It also makes a wonderful specimen tree if left unpruned. With age it develops a nice cinnamon-brown peeling bark. It is frost hardy and thrives in full sun to light shade and well-drained soil. In summer and early autumn the plant is covered with small white fluffy flowers, followed by dark-purple berries. The plant can produce seedlings around the garden when grown in ideal conditions. *Luma apiculata* 'Glanleam Gold' has a variegated leaf. The centre of the leaf is glossy dark-green, surrounded by an irregular patch of lighter greyish-green with a white margin. The leaves have a pink tinge when young. The plant produces white flowers. This plant was first produced in Ireland in Glanleam Gardens on Valentia Island in the 1960s.

Luma Height: 30 feet (9 metres). Flowering period: summer–early autumn.[141]

*A*magnolia in full flower is one of the most striking sights in the garden during spring. No matter what size your garden is there is a magnolia to suit you. A trip to your local garden centre will

Magnolia Height: 10–20 feet;

(3–6 metres).
Flowering
period:
spring.[142-43]

quickly reveal the great number of varieties available. The best time to plant magnolias is April to early May so that the new plant has the advantage of a full growing season to establish itself before winter sets in. Magnolias have been grown in Japan and China for as long as people have gardened. They were introduced into England in the 1700s and caused an immediate sensation with their large flowers on bare stems in spring. *Magnolia stellata* is a variety suitable for the small garden. It is a compact, deciduous shrub that covers itself with pure-white star-shaped flowers in early spring. It grows up to 10 feet (3 metres) tall. Several named varieties of *Magnolia stellata* are available with a pink tinge on the flowers. The best-known and most widely grown magnolia is *Magnolia x soulangeana*. This produces a large white-and-pink tulip-shaped flower. This is a substantial tree that grows up to 20 feet (6 metres) tall with a similar spread. *Magnolia* 'Galaxy' is a large variety that can grow up to 40 feet (12 metres) with large purple-pink flowers.

Magnolias may take a number of years before they flower. They grow extremely well in acid or lime-free soil but will tolerate neutral to limy conditions if plenty of organic matter is added to the soil. In the first year it is essential to water your new tree on a regular basis. Mulch the plant in spring with compost. Magnolias should be planted where they have shade from early morning sun to prevent leaf and flower damage by frost.

Mahonia
Height: 10 feet
(3 metres).
Flowering
period: late
autumn–early
spring.[144]

Mahonia is an evergreen shrub that has interesting leaves, an architectural shape and striking, scented winter flowers. The plant comes from the Far East and America: the plants from the Far East produce fragrant flowers in winter while the American species are smaller plants and flower in late spring to early summer.

The plant has long, distinctive leaves that radiate out from the central stem. The leaves have spines like a holly. Mahonias produce long spires of yellow flowers. They are strong, hardy shrubs that can reach a height of 10 feet (3 metres). The lower leaves can be removed and the plant trained into a standard. The plant produces new leaves each spring to form a dense mass of foliage. The fallen leaves with their spiky ends, like thorns, can be a problem when hand-weeding around the plant. The plant likes a humus-rich, moist, well-drained soil in partial shade. In exposed gardens provide shelter from wind,

which can dehydrate the foliage and kill the emerging flowers. There are about seventy different species of mahonia to choose from. *Mahonia japonica* grows up to 6 feet (1.8 metres) tall with pale-yellow flowers from late autumn to early spring, followed by black berries. *Mahonia x media* 'Charity' is a popular variety that produces erect dark-yellow flowers from late autumn to late winter. *Magnolia nervosa* is a late-flowering variety that flowers in late spring and early summer.

Malus is a genus of medium-sized deciduous trees that are easy to grow and flower in late spring to early summer. They produce clusters of bowl-shaped flowers that cover the branches in white or shades of pink and purple. The flowers are followed by bright-red or yellow fruit (crab apples), which can be the size of a golf ball, to produce a magnificent display in autumn.

Malus (crab apple) Height: 20 feet (6 metres). Flowering period: Late spring–early summer.[145]

A Malus is an ideal specimen tree for the small garden. It can grow up to 20 feet (6 metres) tall and likes a moderately fertile, moist but well-drained soil in full sun, although it will tolerate some shade. The purple-leaf forms give the best colour in full sun. *Malus* 'Evereste' is a conical tree that retains a good shape, producing white flowers. *Malus x purpurea* grows 15 feet (4.5 metres) tall and has purple leaves and pink flowers. *Malus floribunda* is a dense tree that can grow up to 30 feet (9 metres) tall and has pale-pink flowers.

Melianthus major is a dramatic tropical-looking shrub that is grown for its large blue-grey serrated leaves. The leaves produce a peanut-butter smell when rubbed. The plant comes from South Africa, where it is evergreen. In this country the plant is a half-hardy evergreen shrub if planted against a south-facing wall with protection from cold winds. It will grow 4 to 6 feet (1.2 to 1.8 metres) tall. In colder gardens it usually dies down to ground level in winter, like a herbaceous plant. It will shoot again from the base.

Melianthus (honey bush) Height: 4–6 feet (1.2–1.8 metres). Flowering period: summer.[146]

In warmer gardens, along the south coast of Ireland, it produces fascinating brick-red flowers in summer. It flowers on the previous year's growth. It can be grown in a border or as a specimen plant. It is particularly suited to a coastal garden. In frost-prone areas grow the plant in a greenhouse as a foliage plant and stand the pot or plant outside in summer. When grown outdoors the plant likes a moderately fertile, moist but well-drained soil in full sun with shelter from cold winds. Give the plant a winter mulch to protect against frost and to protect it from excessive wet in the winter.

Metrosideros (New Zealand christmas tree)
Height: 70 feet (21 metres).
Flowering period: summer.[147]

Metrosideros excelsa is an evergreen tree from New Zealand that can grow up to 70 feet (21 metres) tall in its native habitat. Although a large tree, it responds well to pruning to control its size.

The leaves are glossy dark green on top and silvery white underneath. The flower buds are also a silvery-white colour and stand out against the dark foliage. It produces clusters of crimson flowers in summer. The flowers are made up of a mass of stamens rather than the colourful petals found on most flowers. The tips of the stamens are gold in colour, very similar to the bottlebrush flower, except this flower is spherical in shape.

Metrosideros is a coastal plant that will not tolerate frost. Grow the plant in a humus-rich, moist but well-drained, neutral to acid soil in full sun. The plant likes a warm, sheltered position in the garden. In cold gardens it is best to move the plant to the greenhouse in winter for a few years before planting out in a permanent position. *Metrosideros kermadecensis variegata* is a smaller tree with green leaves and a white margin.

Myrtus (myrtle)
Height: 5–10 feet (1.5–3 metres).
Flowering period: summer or autumn.[148]

This group of small evergreen trees and shrubs are grown for their foliage and flowers. They may be grown in a shrub border or against a warm, sunny wall. They need long, hot summers to produce flowers. They like a fertile, moist but well-drained soil in full sun with shelter from cold, drying winds.

Myrtus bullata, also known as *Lophomyrtus bullata*, is a large shrub or small tree from New Zealand that can grow up to 20 feet (6 metres) tall. The leaves are blistered between the veins and have a bronze-to-red tinge when young that changes to a glossy dark green when mature. Produces cup-shaped white flowers in summer, followed by dark-red berries. *Myrtus communis subsp. tartentina* is a compact small shrub that grows up to 5 feet (1.5 metres) tall. It flowers in the autumn with pink-tinged petals.

This is a group of plants that are grown for their foliage. *Osmanthus heterophyllus* 'Goshiki' is a striking evergreen slow-growing shrub that can reach a height of 8 to 10 feet (2.4 to 3 metres). The leaves are variegated with various colours. The new growth has a pink tinge that changes to flecks of greenish yellow and cream as it matures. The leaf has spines that are softer than a holly. Mature plants produce small white blooms in the autumn. Grow in fertile, well-drained soil in sun or partial shade.

Osmanthus
Height: 8–10 feet (2.4–3 metres). Flowering period: autumn.[149]

Tree peonies have woody stems that produce large fragrant flowers similar to herbaceous peonies. The Chinese first produced tree peonies, which spread to the western world at the start of the last century. The plants declined in popularity due to a high failure rate with many gardeners. Recently there has been a renewed interest in tree peonies that can produce flowers in a range of colours from snowy white through delicate pink to rich maroon. The flowers are exceptionally perfumed and will fill the garden with a delightful scent. Mature plants can produce dozens of large blooms on woody stems that are 6 to 8 feet (1.8 to 2.4 metres) tall. They also have very attractive foliage. Tree peonies will thrive in a well-drained fertile soil in partial or dapple shade. Late spring frosts can damage flower buds so plant a tree peony where it is sheltered from morning sun. The thawing effect of the sun on frozen buds causes the problem, resulting in little or no flowers. Heavy rain is another problem for tree-peony flowers. The fully open flowers, especially the double-flowered varieties, tend to fill with water and flop over. Feed them once a year with well-rotted manure or compost. No pruning is necessary except to remove any dead wood in spring when the new foliage appears. *Paeonia delavayi* is one of the most reliable varieties, producing red flowers with yellow centres.

Tree peony
Height: 6–8 feet (1.8–2.4 metres). Flowering period: late spring–early summer.[150]

These deciduous trees are natives of China. They are valued for handsome foliage and beautiful blossoms. *Paulownia tomentosa* is a very fast-growing tree when young and can produce 8 feet (2.4 metre) of growth in a year. The tree will grow up to 40 feet (12 metres) tall. The huge leaves of this tree range from 5 to 12 inches (12 to 30 centimetres) long and 8 inches (20 centimetres) wide. The

Paulownia **(foxglove tree)** Height: 40 feet (12 metres).

Flowering period: spring.[151]	tree produces clusters of fragrant lilac, foxglove-like flowers in spring before the new leaves emerge. The flower buds are produced in the autumn and can be killed by frost in winter. Paulownias like a moist well-drained soil in full sun.
Perovskia Height: 4 feet (1.2 metres). Flowering period: late summer–early autumn.[152]	*Perovskia atriplicifolia* (Russian sage) is a striking small Himalayan deciduous shrub with grey-green foliage. During late summer and early autumn this upright plant produces sprays of lavender-blue flowers. It grows to about 4 feet (1.2 metres) tall and performs best in full sun. It likes a well-drained soil, preferring a sandy soil that drains well. The plant should be cut to the ground each spring, before growth begins, to ensure a lush growth for the next season. The variety 'Blue Spire' has larger flower heads and white stems in winter.
Philadelphus (mock orange) Height: 8–10 feet (2.4–3 metres). Flowering period: early–midsummer.[153]	This super deciduous shrub is grown for its large white, deliciously fragrant flowers with a scent like that of orange blossom. Philadelphus species vary in size – most are medium-sized shrubs that grow about 10 feet (3 metres) tall. The shrub is easily grown in any type of well-drained soil in sun or partial shade. The plant flowers in early to midsummer. After flowering, cut back the shoots that flowered to keep plants in shape. On established plants cut back about one-quarter of the old shoots to the ground to promote new growth. *Philadelphus* 'Beauclerk' is a slightly arching shrub that grows to 8 feet (2.4 metres) and produces a white flower with a slight pink-flush centre. *Philadelphus* 'Virginal' has large double white flowers and grows to 10 feet (3 metres) tall. *Philadelphus coronarius* 'Aureus' has golden-yellow leaves that need shade from the sun to prevent them from burning.
Phlomis Height: 2–5 feet (60 centimetres–1.5 metres).	*Phlomis fruticosa* (Jerusalem sage) is an evergreen shrub that grows to a height and spread of 5 feet (1.5 metres). It has soft foliage that is grey in colour and densely hairy. It produces dark-yellow flowers in early summer. A native of the Mediterranean region, it likes a sunny spot with protection from cold winds. It is reliably hardy in all but the coldest gardens, although hard frost can cause damage to the

shoot tips. It grows best in well-drained, limy soils. It can become leggy and bare at the base unless pruned annually after flowering is finished. It is a plant that flowers best when young so propagate a new plant every few years. *Phlomis purpurea* is a native of Spain and Portugal. It produces purple to pink flowers and grows about 2 feet (60 centimetres) tall. *Phlomis lanata* is a small, compact variety with yellow flowers suitable for a rock garden.

Flowering period: early–midsummer.[154]

This group of evergreen and deciduous shrubs come from the Far East and North America. The plants like a fertile, moist but well-drained soil in sun or partial shade. *Photinia x fraseri* 'Red Robin' has glossy dark-green leaves when they mature; the new leaves have a bright-red colour. The new leaves can be burned by late-spring frost. It can grow up to 15 feet (4.5 metres) tall and can be used for hedging. *Photinia davidiana* 'Palette', once called *Stranvaesia davidiana*, is a slow-growing shrub with variegated leaves that are marked creamy white. It produces small white flowers in midsummer.

Photinia
Height: 15 feet (4.5 metres). Flowering period: midsummer.[155]

Pieris is an evergreen shrub with bright-coloured foliage and attractive flowers in spring. The new coloured leaves are very striking against the dark-green leaves of the previous year. As an added bonus they produce flowers in shades of pink or white. It is an acid-loving plant so it will not tolerate lime. It can be grown in a container filled with lime-free compost and since it is a small plant it is ideal for container growing.

Pieris
Height: up to 12 feet (3.5 metres). Flowering period: spring.[156]

Pieris 'Forest Flame' is a popular variety that produces bright-red leaves in spring. The new leaves then turn to pink and then creamy white before becoming green. The plant also produces white drooping flowers that are slightly fragrant and it can grow up to 12 feet (3.6 metres) tall. There are a number of varieties to choose from – the main difference between them is in the colour of the young leaves, which vary from bright red to burgundy.

Pieris japonica 'Little Heath' only grows 2 feet (60 centimetres) tall. It has vivid-red young shoots that mature to give a variegated cream and green leaf and is an ideal plant for a container. Like most acid-loving plants, pieris like a soil with lots of humus added. Frost on young shoots in April can be a problem so grow them where they are sheltered from the morning sun. They do well under a canopy of mature trees and contrast well with camellias and rhododendrons. They do not need pruning but, if space is limited, pruning individual branches after flowering will control the size of the plant.

Pittosporum
Height: 6–30 feet (1.8–9 metres). Flowering period: late spring–early summer.[157–58]

These are small trees or large shrubs that vary a great deal in their leaves and flowers. Some kinds have pretty foliage and others have very fragrant flowers. The small flowers are produced from late spring to early summer. Most of them are native to New Zealand and some make good hedges in seaside gardens.

Pittosporum tenuifolium is one of the hardier species and can grow up to 30 feet (9 metres) tall. Many varieties of this plant are grown in Irish gardens. The most stunning is 'Irene Paterson', which grows up to 6 feet (1.8 metres) tall. The new growth is white in colour and becomes speckled as it matures. It can be trimmed at any time in summer and almost instantly produces a fresh crop of white leaves. 'Abbotsbury Gold' has foliage that changes to a yellow colour in autumn and winter. 'Tom Thumb' has purple-coloured foliage. Often sold as a small shrub, it can grow up to 6 feet (1.8 metres) tall. *Pittosporum* 'Garnettii' is a large shrub that can grow up to 15 feet (4.5 metres) tall. It has greyish-green leaves with pink spots and a creamy-white margin.

These plants grow best in ordinary well-drained soil with shelter from cold winds in frost-prone gardens. They will not survive severe frost.

Pseudowintera
Height: 5 feet (1.5 metres).[159]

This small group of evergreen trees and shrubs are native to New Zealand. They are grown for their handsome foliage. The yellow-green leaves are blotched with red and pink.

Pseudowintera colorata is a small bushy shrub that grows to 5 feet (1.5 metres) tall. *Pseudowintera* 'Mount Congreve' has more red colouration on the leaves.

The plant grows best in a humus-rich, well-drained, neutral to acid soil in full sun or partial shade. Prune only when necessary to restrict size. They grow best in a sheltered border.

These are a group of deciduous trees and shrubs grown for their fruit, known as pears. *Pyrus salicifolia* 'Pendula' is a small weeping pear with delicate weeping branches and silvery-grey foliage. The plant is covered with white flowers in late spring to early summer. The flowers are followed by small, inedible green pears. The plant makes an ideal specimen tree for the small garden. It is hardy and slow growing. It likes a fertile, well-drained soil in full sun. The plant can grow up to 15 feet (4.5 metres) tall. Remove misplaced or crossing branches and cut back branches touching the ground in late winter or early spring.

Pyrus (pear)
Height: 15 feet (4.5 metres). Flowering period: late spring–early summer.[160]

If you have a large garden and plan to plant a tree, none has more history, character and strength than the oak. There is so much pleasure in growing your own oak tree from an acorn that you have collected or found. The young oak tree should be planted in its final location as soon as possible because it resents disturbance due to its rapidly developing tap root. The common oak (*Quercus robur*) has produced many interesting varieties suitable for the smaller garden – *Quercus robur fastigiata* grows upwards with a smaller spread. *Quercus ilex* is an evergreen variety that responds well to pruning and can tolerate salt spray in coastal gardens; it can grow up to 80 feet (24 metres) tall. *Quercus rubra* has red leaves in the autumn while 'Aurea' has golden-yellow leaves in spring. *Quercus suber* (cork oak) has a thick bark used to make corks and grows 70 feet (21 metres) tall. Oaks like a deep, fertile, well-drained soil. They make beautiful specimen trees in a large garden.

Quercus (oak)
Height: 50–120 feet (15–36 metres).[161]

These are among the most colourful of all garden plants. They are mostly evergreen shrubs that can reach tree-like proportions. They form a great profusion of colour as branches become obscured by beautiful flowers from late spring to late summer. They are found growing all over the world. The different species range from enormous trees that can grow up to 100 feet (30 metres) tall through to alpine shrubs a few inches tall.

Rhododendron
Height: 3–20 feet (0.9–6 metres); some species, 100 feet (30 metres).

At present there are over nine hundred varieties known to exist, which can be further divided into more than eight thousand species, so there is no shortage of plants to choose from. Rhododendrons are now available in a range of colours that covers the visible spectrum and some of them are strongly scented.

Rhododendrons need an acid soil with a pH of 5 or less. If the soil pH is higher, around pH 6, it is possible to grow rhododendrons in the open ground, provided they are treated with an appropriate acidifier to help prevent the leaves turning yellow. A simple pH testing kit, available at garden centres, will determine whether your garden soil is acidic or not. In gardens where the pH is higher than 6, it is best to grow rhododendrons in a raised bed or container. Plastic sheeting should be placed under the raised bed to prevent seepage of lime into the soil. The raised bed can be made with brick, stone or sleepers. Fill the bed with a lime-free compost enriched with well-rotted compost and some conifer pine needles.

Rhododendrons are shallow rooted so it is important to plant them at the depth they were growing in the pot. Keep them well watered, especially during the summer when the flower buds for the following year are forming. It is best to use rainwater, as tap water can have a high pH level. Do not dig or hoe around the plant, to avoid disturbing the roots. Once planted, rhododendrons need very little attention and if grown under ideal conditions will not need feeding or pruning. To control weeds and to keep the roots cool and moist apply a layer of wood bark around the plants.

Rhododendron 'Blue Tit' is a compact dwarf shrub that grows 3 feet (1 metre) tall and produces blue flowers. *Rhododendron* 'Fragrantissimum' grows 6 feet (1.8 metres) tall, producing white flowers with a strong scent. *Rhododendron* 'St Breward' grows 3 feet (90 centimetres) and has red flowers. *Rhododendron* 'Goldkrone' grows 5 feet (1.5 metres) tall and has golden-yellow flowers.

Azaleas

Azaleas are closely related to rhododendrons. Azaleas are grouped under the general title of rhododendron but most gardeners look on them as a separate group of plants. Japanese azaleas are small evergreen shrubs that are free flowering. They will grow to about 3 feet tall and like a sunny position. Deciduous azaleas are larger shrubs that produce a profusion of funnel-shaped flowers in a range of colours; some of the flowers are scented. Azaleas like the same growing conditions as rhododendrons. *Rhododendron mollis* is a deciduous azalea that produces orange-red flowers before the leaves appear in late spring.

This is a vigorous evergreen shrub grown for its attractive glossy leaves, flowers and large red berries that last all year round – birds do not eat them. To obtain berries a male and female plant must be planted in the garden. They produce clusters of pink buds in winter that open in spring to reveal scented star-shaped flowers, which are followed by red berries on the female species. Skimmias are suitable for a shrub or mixed border. They will grow in dapple or deep shade in any fertile, humus-rich soil. They need little pruning other than to shape them, if necessary, after flowering. *Skimmia japonica* is a commonly grown variety – it is best to buy them in flower and with berries to determine that you have a male and female species.

Skimmia
Height: 6–20 feet (1.8–6 metres). Flowering period: spring.[166]

This is a group of tender and hardy trees and shrubs. Some are deciduous and the rest are evergreen. *Sophora microphylla* 'Goldilocks' is a tropical-looking plant from New Zealand. Although tender looking, this evergreen, with its elegant fern-like foliage, is totally hardy. In early spring it is covered with clusters of yellow flowers that can last for a month. It is a large tree that can grow up to 25 feet (7.5 metres) tall. It can be pruned to keep the plant in shape and to control its size. Pruning should be carried out immediately after flowering because the flowers appear on the previous year's stems. It will grow in most garden soils but avoid excessively wet soils. It needs plenty of sun – they flower best after a long, hot summer. *Sophora japonica* (Japanese pagoda tree) is a deciduous tree from China that can grow up to 60 feet (18 metres) tall. It produces white flowers in late summer and early autumn when the tree is ten to fifteen years old. *Sophora prostrata* 'Little Baby' is a small evergreen shrub that grows about 7 feet (2 metres) tall. The branches are twiggy, growing in a zig-zag fashion, and turn a beautiful brown colour in the autumn. It has very small leaves and produces yellow flowers in spring. Some sophoras may be frost tender and may be trained into a climber against a south- or south-west-facing wall.

Sophora
Height: 7–60 feet (2.1–18 metres). Flowering period: early spring.[167–68]

This group of hardy deciduous shrubs and small trees are grown for their ability to thrive by the sea and will survive even when fully exposed to harsh salty winds. They have long arching branches that are coloured purple-brown and covered with attractive needle-like

Tamarix
Height: 15 feet (4.5 metres).

Flowering period: late summer.[169]

leaves to give a feathery appearance. *Tamarix ramosissima* can grow up to 15 feet (4.5 metres) tall and produces rose-pink flowers in late summer. The plant flowers on the current year's shoots so it can be pruned hard in early spring, cutting branches back to one-third of their length to control its size and stop it swamping its neighbours. It can become top heavy and unstable if it is not pruned. It can be trained into a nice standard by removing the side shoots until the desired height is reached and pinching out the growing tip to produce a bushy head on top. They like a well-drained soil in full sun. Shelter the plant from cold, drying winds in cold inland gardens.

Taxus (yew)
Height: 30–70 feet (9–20 metres). Flowering period: spring; red berries in autumn on female plants.[170–71/342]

Taxus baccata (English yew) is an evergreen tree that grows very slowly and lives for many hundreds of years. The tree has been planted in many churchyards and makes an excellent specimen tree or can be trained into topiary shapes or grown as a hedge. The wood of the tree is used for turning wooden bowls and as a veneer by furniture makers. In the past it was used to make longbows. All parts of the tree are highly poisonous. Yew trees will grow in any well-drained soil in sun or deep shade. *Taxus baccata* 'Fastigiata' (Irish yew) is a striking slow-growing tree that forms a dense, compact conical shape. It needs no clipping or trimming to keep its shape. It makes a nice specimen plant and can be used to add height and winter structure to the garden. The Irish yew was discovered over two hundred years ago in Co. Fermanagh as a sport from a normal yew: it is still growing there. The female plant produces red berries. *Taxus baccata* 'Fastigiata Aurea' has golden-yellow leaves. *Taxus baccata* 'Repens Aurea' is a prostrate form with yellow leaves that forms a spreading ground cover.

Viburnum
Height: 6–10 feet (1.8–3 metres). Floweing period: late winter–spring.[172]

This is a large group of evergreen, semi-evergreen and deciduous shrubs that are grown for their flowers and scent. Many of them are winter flowering and provide valuable colour in the garden then. Viburnums will grow in any moderately fertile, moist but well-drained soil in full sun or partial shade. They can be grown in a shrub border. The flowers are mainly white, often pink in bud, and are usually flattened heads like a lacecap hydrangea. Some species produce attractive berries that may be red, blue or black. *Viburnum*

tinus is a compact, bushy evergreen shrub that produces small white flowers from late winter to spring, followed by blue-black berries. *Viburnum setigerum* is an erect deciduous shrub that can grow 10 feet (3 metres) tall and produces white flowers and red berries.

This small group of deciduous shrubs are grown for their profusion of small flowers, many of them like miniature foxgloves. The funnel-shaped flowers come in a range of colours – mainly pinks and reds but also white and yellow. They will grow in any soil. Full sun is appreciated but they will tolerate a little shade. Some varieties have variegated foliage that looks attractive through the year. Weigelas should be pruned hard after flowering to maintain vigour. Thin out old shoots to ground level and prune stems that have flowered back to within a few inches of old wood after flowering. *Weigela florida* 'Variegata' is a popular variety that has green leaves with a white margin and produces pink flowers in late spring to early summer. *Weigela florida* 'Foliis Purpureis' has purple foliage and deep-pink flowers; it grows about 3 feet (90 centimetres) tall. *Weigela middendorffiana* produces bell-shaped yellow flowers with orange and red markings; it grows 5 feet (1.5 metres) tall.

Weigela
Height: 5–8 feet (1.5–2.4 metres). Flowering period: late spring–early summer.[173-74]

Bulbs for all seasons

With a bit of planning it is possible to have bulbs in flower nearly all through the year. Bulbs do not take up much space so they can be planted in small gardens or grown in containers on a patio. They die down when not in bloom so where space is limited they can be grown under deciduous trees and shrubs. A bulb that has died down out of sight is often described as being dormant. This period is a very important time in the life-cycle of the bulb. During this dormant period the bulb ripens and produces flower buds for the following year's growth.[175]

It can be confusing when you discover that the word bulb is often used as a blanket term for any plant that has an underground food-storage organ. As well as true bulbs such as daffodils, tulips and onions, there are three other forms: corms (crocus and gladioli), tubers (dahlias and anemones) and rhizomes (iris).

Seasons of bloom

Bulbs can be divided into two main groups: spring-flowering bulbs and summer-flowering bulbs. The spring-flowering bulbs are planted in the autumn and are quite hardy; they include daffodils, tulips,

crocuses, fritillarias and irises. Most summer-flowering bulbs are tender and are planted in spring after the last frost of the year. In frost-prone areas most of these bulbs must be dug up in the autumn and stored indoors over the winter; lilies are the exception, as they can survive the winter outdoors. Summer-flowering bulbs include dahlias, begonias, crocosmia, lilies, gladioli, dahlias and alliums. Autumn-flowering bulbs include cannas, colchicums and nerines. For winter colour grow some snowdrops and muscari. Bulbs are excellent for providing a display of flowers in window boxes and in containers on the patio. Plant species with different flowering times to give colour most of the year.

Purchasing bulbs

Most bulbs are sold in the dormant state. Buy spring-flowering bulbs in late summer and summer-flowering bulbs in spring. Buy bulbs soon after they become available in garden centres to get the best, healthiest bulbs. Choose bulbs that are big and firm, a bit like buying vegetables in the supermarket. Reject any bulbs that have signs of disease, rot or mould – these may be cheaper to buy but they may not flower. Cheap bulbs are often smaller in size and will produce smaller flowers. Some bulbs, like snowdrops, are best bought 'in the green', which means with the foliage attached to the bulbs.

Cultivation

Plant bulbs as soon as possible after buying them. Bulbs like a neutral, well-drained soil in full sun. The Dutch have a saying that 'bulbs do not like wet feet'. If the soil is heavy and wet dig in lots of grit and coarse gravel to improve drainage. If the soil is poor mix some fertiliser with the soil – most soils require no fertiliser to produce the first year's blooms. On very dry, light soils mix in some well-rotted compost with the soil to prevent the roots drying out.

After the flowers have faded cut off the dead flower heads to stop them going to seed and allow the green foliage to die back naturally, a process that takes about six weeks. Avoid the urge to tie up the leaves with string – during this period the leaves need sun to produce food to recharge the bulb for next year's blooms. If the dying foliage seems unattractive the best solution is to camouflage the foliage with hosta or other leafy perennials. Apply a potash-rich liquid fertiliser, like tomato feed, to the plants after the flowers have faded – this will feed the bulb for the following year. When the leaves have died down they can be cut off. Some bulbs, like tulips and hyacinths, may only last for one year. If the variety is not marked as a perennial it is best to treat the bulbs as annuals and discard them after flowering. Some bulbs are forced indoors to produce early blooms: planting these bulbs outdoors after they have died down may not produce flowers in subsequent years because the bulbs have been through an exhausting process – daffodils and crocuses would be the exception.

Bulbs must be planted deep enough. A planting depth equal to twice the height of the bulb is a good rule of thumb. Space bulbs at two to three times their width. If the soil is wet place a layer of grit at the base of the planting hole. Plant the bulbs with the pointed end upwards – if the bulb is not pointing in the right direction the flower will still find its way upwards. Plant corms and tubers with their growth buds upwards: they are not as distinct as on true bulbs. Cover the bulbs with soil and apply a layer of mulch to protect against frost and stop the soil drying out. To keep bulbs flowering well, lift and divide them every three to four years. Dig up the clump and tease the bulbs apart and replant; discard any diseased bulbs.

Plant bulbs in groups, either in small clusters or large beds – a single flower standing on its own is not very dramatic. Plant low-growing bulbs in front of taller varieties. It is possible to plant small bulbs in a layer right on top of larger bulbs. Planting muscari bulbs on top of tulips, which flower at the same time, will produce an interesting double-decker effect. What you can do with spring bulbs is limited only by your imagination – a few hours' work in the autumn can produce months of exciting colour in the garden next spring. Mixing bulbs that flower from March to April with perennials that bloom in summer will give the maximum amount of colour in a herbaceous bed and the flowering perennials will camouflage the dying leaves of the bulbs. The sale of bulbs has grown enormously in recent years – they are like nature's fast food, coming pre-packed with the baby flower inside ready to grow. The following are some bulbs worth growing in your garden.

Agapanthus provides an impressive display of blooms through summer and early autumn. The plant is native to South Africa, where it grows in the shade of trees. In Ireland they need a warm, sheltered position where they can bathe in sunlight for most of the day. Agapanthus has flower heads known as umbels, which are large and rounded and made up of many tubular flowers that open wide at the mouth. Their colours range from shades of blue through to violet and there are also pure white forms. Different varieties of agapanthus can grow from 20 to 40 inches (50 to 100 centimetres) in height.

Plant the rhizomes just deep enough to cover them with well-drained soil enriched with well-rotted garden compost. Water well in dry weather. In frost-prone gardens cover the plant with a layer of mulch in winter or grow the plant in containers, where it likes being pot-bounded. When clumps become overcrowded divide and replant the fleshy roots in mid- to late spring. Slugs and snails can be a problem when the new shoots appear in spring.

Agapanthus campanulatus is a clump-forming perennial with narrow strap-shaped green leaves. 'Albus' has white flowers, while 'Royal Blue' has intense rich-blue flowers.

Agapanthus **(African lily)** Height: 20–40 inches (50–100 centimetres). Flowering period: late summer–early autumn.[176–77]

Alliums have become very popular plants for the garden. They like a well-drained soil in full sun. They produce striking spherical, drumstick flower heads in a range of colours like purple, yellow, pinks and white in summer. Some alliums are ideal for the herbaceous border, others for rock gardens. Alliums dry very easily if cut when the flower is fading and hung upside down in a cool, airy garage.

Allium giganteum can grow up to 5 feet (1.5 metres) tall, producing large spherical mauve-coloured flowers in early summer. *Allium cristophii* produces lilac-pink flowers on stems 2 feet (60 centimetres) tall. The seedheads that follow in the autumn are excellent for indoor dried-flower arrangements. *Allium* 'Globemaster' has deep-violet flowers on stems 32 inches (80 centimetres) tall. *Allium moly* has yellow star-shaped flowers on stems 12 inches (30 centimetres) tall. *Allium flavum* produces flower stems about 10 inches (25 centimetres) tall with up to sixty bell-shaped bright-yellow flowers.

Allium **(ornamental onion)** Height: 8 inches–5 feet (20 centimetres–1.5 metres). Flowering period: summer.[178–79]

Anemone
Height: 6–12 inches (15–30 centimetres). Flowering period: winter–spring.[180]

Anemones are grown for their open saucer-shaped flowers with a central cluster of stamens. The winter- and spring-flowering anemones are ideal for naturalising in a wild corner of the garden or for producing early colour in a rock garden. There are species like the Japanese anemones that flower in late summer to mid-autumn. *Anemone blanda* grows 6 inches (15 centimetres) tall, producing large daisy-like pink, blue or white flowers from late winter to early spring. The little rhizomes naturalise easily to form a colourful carpet of colour under deciduous trees and shrubs. *Anemone coronaria* grows 12 inches (30 centimetres) tall, with red, blue or white flowers in spring. Two varieties that are commonly grown are 'De Caen' (single flowered) and 'Saint Brigid' (double flowered); both of these should be planted in spring. Before planting soak the tubers in water for a couple of hours.

Aurum Italicum
Height: foliage, 12–16 inches (30–40 centimetres). Flowering period: late spring.[181]

This tuberous perennial is a native of the Mediterranean, often found growing in the wild in Italy, Spain and Southern France. It has beautiful spear-shaped green leaves with white veins that appear in the autumn and last all over winter. In late spring it flowers with green and white bracts. The foliage withers in the summer when spires of bright orange-red berries appear, which last until the new leaves appear again. It may be grown in herbaceous beds, under trees and shrubs and will tolerate partial shade.

Begonia
Height: 10–12 inches (25–30 centimetres). Flowering period: summer–autumn.[182–83]

The tuberous-rooted begonia, with its velvety flowers that range in colour from bright reds and oranges to whites, yellows, deep pinks and bicolours, is often considered as the queen of bedding plants. The flowers are produced from summer to autumn. They are ideal for adding colour in summer to pots, window boxes, hanging baskets and borders in sun or partial shade. The flowers range from big blossoms, 6 inches (15 centimetres) in diameter, to small multi-flowered versions to double-flowered and pendant types that are popular in hanging baskets. The tuberous begonias grown today bear little resemblance to the original plants from South America. The plants grown now are the creation of hybridisers who have taken a good plant and made it even better. Botanically the plants are grouped together as *Begonia tuberhybrida*. Begonias are often sold

by colour. The average plant height is 10 to 12 inches (25 to 30 centimetres). They grow best in light shade, as direct sunlight causes burning of the flowers and leaves. Begonias are not frost hardy. In the autumn dig up the bulbs before the first frost and store them in a cool, dry place. In spring plant the tubers, with the hollow side facing upwards, indoors to get early blooms. Plant them 2 to 3 inches (5 to 8 centimetres) deep in containers with drainage holes. Place the tubers near the surface and just barely cover with a layer of potting compost. Place a layer of cling film over the container. Keep the compost moist but not wet – a warm, humid setting is ideal for promoting growth. When the shoots are 6 inches (15 centimetres) tall, transplant the begonias outdoors when the threat of frost is over. Plant them in well-drained soil, enriched with compost, in partial shade and sheltered from wind. Stake upright-flowering plants and try to avoid damaging the tuber.

Camassia
Height: 2–3 feet (60–90 centimetres). Flowering period: summer.[184]

This plant from the damp regions of North America is relatively unknown. It has a very natural look and will fit in perfectly between perennials in a border or grown on its own. It produces light-blue or white star-shaped flowers on stems up to 3 feet (90 centimetres) tall. It grows best in humus-rich, well-drained soil that does not dry out in spring and early summer. Covering the bulbs with a layer of compost will help to keep the soil damp. It grows in full sun or partial shade. Plant the bulbs in autumn. When the clumps become too crowded lift the bulbs in early autumn, divide and replant immediately. Species of *Camassia leichtlinii* are the most commonly grown plants.

Canna
Height: 2–7 feet (60 centimetres– 2.1 metres). Flowering period: summer– autumn.[185–88]

Cannas are tender tropical plants that have large banana-like foliage and large colourful flowers. They are excellent for late-summer bedding and will flower until the first frost. Their brightly coloured flowers resemble a cross between an orchid and a gladiolus. The flowers produced from late summer onwards come in a range of colours, such as red, orange, pink and yellow. Flowers are often bicolour with blotches, spots and streaks of different colours. The leaves are large and can grow up to 18 inches (45 centimetres) long and 12 inches (30 centimetres) wide. They are also very attractive and come in shades of purple, red and green and striped. Cannas can range in height from a few feet to as much as 10 feet (3 metres) tall. They are very strong, sturdy plants that require no staking.

Cannas are easy to grow. Newly purchased rhizomes should be potted up in any potting compost in late March and placed in a greenhouse. The earlier the rhizome is started into growth the sooner it will flower. Plant out into the garden in June and they should start to flower from August and continue until the arrival of frost. When planting out prepare the site well. The planting hole needs to be enriched with lots of well-rotted compost – it is impossible to over-feed cannas. The ideal location for cannas is a warm, damp, sheltered place. Cannas may also be grown in pots or containers and placed on your patio in the summer. If planting in pots or containers, again the message is lots of rotted manure. Plants in pots can be removed to the greenhouse in the winter. Cannas are tender plants that will not survive severe frost. Lift the rhizomes when the leaves are blackened by frost. Cut off the leaves and flowers and store the rhizomes in slightly moist peat in a frost-free place. Canna rhizomes do not normally enter a totally dormant stage – if they dry out they may die; if kept too wet they will rot. In gardens with little frost the rhizomes can be left in the ground and covered with a mulch for the winter. Do not cut the flower stalks but allow them to die down naturally.

The variegated cannas are the most popular. *Canna* 'Durban', sometimes sold under the name 'Tropicana', has stunning colourations: pink veins on a dark-purple leaf with an orange flower. *Canna* 'Striata' has yellow veins on a green leaf with an orange flower. *Canna* 'Black Knight' has bronze foliage with dark-red flowers. *Canna* 'Stuttgart' has green foliage with large white patches and apricot flowers. *Canna* 'Lucifer' is a dwarf variety that grows 2 feet (60 centimetres) tall with green leaves and red flowers.

Colchicum **(autumn crocus)**
Height: 7–10 inches (18–25 centimetres).

Colchicum is one of the favourite autumn-flowering bulbs. It will brighten up the garden with its deep-pink to purple blooms. They are perfect for the front of a border or in a rockery; they look best when planted in clumps. They are also called autumn crocuses because they flower in the autumn but the foliage does not emerge until spring and this is why they are often called 'naked ladies'. Grow

them in a fertile, well-drained soil that is not too dry. Plant the corms in summer, as soon as they are available, in groups of at least ten corms, about 4 inches (10 centimetres) deep. *Colchicum speciosum* has large goblet-shaped flowers on stems 7 to 10 inches (18 to 25 centimetres) long. They should not be confused with the genuine crocus, which has three stamens and flowers in spring. Colchicum has six stamens.

Flowering period: autumn.[189]

Crinum is a plant that will give a subtropical feel to a sunny part of the garden. It is not the easiest bulb to grow, as it needs mild conditions and protection from frost. It produces pink or white flowers on stems up to 4 feet (1.2 metres) tall in early autumn. Plant the bulbs in late spring in rich, moisture-retentive but well-drained soil in a location with shelter from north and east winds. Plant the bulbs with their necks above ground level where they will not be disturbed to grow into a clump. *Crinum x powellii* 'Album' has pure white flowers on stems up to 5 feet (1.5 metres) tall.

Crinum Height: 4–5 feet (1.2–1.5 metres). Flowering period: early autumn.[190]

Crocuses are very hardy bulbs that provide some of the earliest colour at ground level in late winter and early spring. Most species stand about 3 inches (8 centimetres) tall; the Dutch hybrids are slightly taller. The flowers come in shades of yellow, blue, purple, lilac and white in single and bicolours. They have narrow leaves with a silvery-grey stripe down the middle. The effect of crocuses is especially beautiful when they are planted in large numbers. For a massive effect 100 to 150 corms should be planted in well-drained soil in full sun or partial shade. They may be grown in rock gardens or as an edging to flower and shrub borders. The flowers only open when the sun shines or there is a lot of light – they close up in rainy weather and at night.

Crocus Height: 3–4 inches (8–10 centimetres). Flowering period: autumn–spring, depending on variety.[191]

The pretty pink or white flowers and attractive foliage of cyclamen make a charming sight in a shaded rock garden, under a tree or around the base of a shrub. They are one of the few bulbs that will grow under conifers. They will grow in almost any well-drained soil in a shady position. Since many of them come from woodlands the

Cyclamen Height: 3–4 inches (8–10 centimetres).

Flowering period: spring and autumn–winter.[192]

soil must contain sufficient humus – they should be covered once a year with a light mulch of well-composted leaves. Flowers may be produced at any time of the year, depending on the species, most of them flowering early in the year, while others wait until late summer. The leaves have a lovely shape and are often beautiful marked. Plant the tubers in late summer and early autumn. The tubers do not divide or produce offsets – cyclamen propagate themselves rapidly by self-seeding. Seedlings usually flower after two years.

Cyclamen hederifolium is a hardy variety that produces white or pink flowers on stems 4 inches (10 centimetres) tall in early to mid-autumn. The leaves are variegated and form an attractive carpet through the winter and spring. When planting, barely cover the tubers but add a one-inch layer of leaf-mould annually after flowering. *Cyclamen persium* is a tender species suitable for growing in greenhouse or as a houseplant.

Eremurus (foxtail lily)

Height: 4–8 feet (1.2–2.4 metres). Flowering period: summer.[193]

This plant is grown for its enormously tall flower clusters; its average height can be 4 to 8 feet (1.2 to 2.4 metres), depending on the species. The flowers are produced in summer. The tuberous roots have a very strange shape – thick, fleshy roots fan out in all directions from a central hub. Grow the tubers in fertile, sandy, well-drained soil in full sun. Mulch with a layer of compost in winter. The leaves of the plant wither back during the flowering period so plant the tubers among low-growing shrubs to cover the decaying foliage. The Ruiter and Shelford hybrids of eremurus produce flowers in shades of salmon, yellow and orange on flower stems up to 4 feet (1.2 metres) tall. *Eremurus robustus* has pink flower clusters up to 40 inches (1 metre) long on stems 7 feet (2.1 metres) tall.

Erythronium (dog's-tooth violet)

Height: 4–12 inches (10–30 centimetres).

Erythroniums are attractive spring-flowering plants with marble-patterned leaves and pendant flowers in shades of white, yellow, pink and purple. They are low-growing plants, usually 4 to 12 inches (10 to 30 centimetres) in height. Since the plant is a native of woodland habitats it likes a moist, humus-rich soil that does not dry out in summer. Cover the plant with a layer of mulch in summer to prevent this. Plant the corms in late summer. The corms are shaped like the canine teeth of a dog, hence the common name, dog's-tooth

violet. *Erythronium dens-canis* is the only European species and the most commonly grown. It produces a single flower on each flower stem in shades of white or pink. *Erythronium* 'Pagoda' has four to five nodding yellow flowers on each stem.

Flowering period: spring.[194]

Eucomis (pineapple lily)

This is a tender plant that comes from South Africa. Eucomis is only winter hardy in frost free, warm gardens. It is very suitable as a pot plant that is brought indoors for the winter months in frost-prone gardens. Grow the plant in a fertile, well-drained soil in full sun in a sheltered position at the base of a warm wall and mulch in winter. The bulbs look better when planted in a group rather than left to grow singly. The flower spike produced in late summer and early autumn is an amazing sight. Each spike can range in size from 12 to 24 inches (30 to 60 centimetres) tall and is made up of hundreds of small flowers that open from the bottom up. The top of the flowering spike has a turf of green leaves, similar to those of a pineapple. *Eucomis bicolour* has pale-green flowers with a purple margin to the petals.

Height: 12–24 inches (30–60 centimetres). Flowering period: late summer.[195]

Fritillaria

There are fritillarias for almost every garden situation. The combination of delicate flower structure, rich colouring and a nodding head makes each stem a thing of beauty. There are about 100 species and they share their botanical name, *fritillus*, with the butterfly.

The flowers come in a range of colours, such as white, yellow and different shades of purple, with some flower stems producing a number of flower heads. Some fritillarias have checkerboard markings, which act like the landing lights for aircraft, to guide the pollinating bees into the flower bell. The flowers are produced in spring on stems up to 12 inches (30 centimetres) tall.

They all like a fertile, well-drained soil – the only exception is *Fritillaria meleagris*. *Fritillaria meleagris* (snake's head) is a native of moist meadows in Europe so it likes a moist soil with lots of humus added. It produces a bell-shaped pendant flower in purple or white. *Fritillatia pallidiflora* produces pale-yellow flowers on stems 16 inches (40 centimetres) tall. *Fritillaria michailovskyi* has deep brown-purple flowers with a yellow edge. *Fritillaria imperialis*, commonly known

Height: 1–3 feet (30–90 centimetres). Flowering period: spring–early summer.[196–99]

as crown imperial, makes a colourful splash with its large yellow, red or orange flowers on stems 2 to 3 feet (60 to 90 centimetres) tall in spring. Each cluster of flowers has a crowning turf of leaves to add to the beauty of the flower.

This plant comes from Turkey and likes a well-drained soil. The problem with this bulb is that it has a hollow centre that holds water and in cold, wet soils will rot. The bulbs should be planted on their sides with plenty of sharp sand or grit worked into the soil. Most fritillarias grow well in a rock garden or raised alpine bed. They also look good at the front of a herbaceous border, providing early spring colour.

Galanthus (snowdrop)
Height: 4–7 inches (10–18 centimetres).
Flowering period: winter–spring.[200]

The first sight of snowdrops peeping through the ground is like a breath of fresh air and a sign that winter is coming to an end. The small white bell-shaped flowers are always a welcome sight in the garden in the bleak days of January and February. Snowdrops are very hardy and the colder the weather the longer the flowers will last. They look their best in light shade under deciduous trees and shrubs or planted in drifts through a border. They can be naturalised in grass or grown in containers for the patio. Like most bulbs, snowdrops like a well-drained soil that does not dry out in summer. The ideal conditions are those that occur in the natural woodland habitat of snowdrops, which is humus-rich and slightly moisture retentive. Snowdrops are slow to establish themselves when planted as dry bulbs. It is best to plant them with green leaves attached – this is called planting 'in the green'. Once established, the snowdrops will multiply each year. Divide the clumps every three years to avoid overcrowding. Lift the plants after flowering, with the green leaves attached, and carefully tease the clump of bulbs apart by hand – try to avoid damage to the roots. Replant the bulbs immediately. Do not use fertilisers: it is best to use leaf-mould, which is similar to the woodland growing environment of snowdrops. Snowdrops may all look alike but there are over a hundred different species and cultivars. The variations appear in the green markings on the flower petals and the texture and colour of the foliage. *Galanthus nivalis* (common snowdrop) produces white flowers on stems 4 inches (10 centimetres) tall.

This plant, from South Africa, is grown for its white, pendant bell-shaped flowers that hang from a flower spike up to 4 feet (1.2 metres) tall. The flower spike may contain up to twenty flower heads. These flowers have a very pleasant fragrance and are produced from summer to autumn. The plant looks at its best at the back of a herbaceous border, among shrubs or grown in containers. *Galtonia candicans* is the most common variety grown in gardens. Plant the bulbs in spring, placing five bulbs together, and leave undisturbed once established.

Galtonia (summer hyacinth)
Height: 4 feet (1.2 metres). Flowering period: mid-summer–early autumn.[201]

Gladioli are one of the four most popular summer-flowering bulbs. They are grown for their range of colour in the garden, as a cut flower and for exhibition. They do have some drawbacks: they need staking and the flower spikes only last about two weeks. The gladioli now grown in gardens are all hybrids; they are easy to hybridise so new plants appear every year as old ones decline in popularity. Plant gladioli in clumps in a border in spring in well-drained soil with humus added. To produce a succession of blooms through the summer, make three or four plantings of bulbs at intervals of two weeks. *Gladiolus communis subsp. byzantinus* is a vigorous perennial that produces long spires of loosely arranged funnel-shaped wine-red flowers from late spring to early summer. It can grow up to 3 feet (90 centimetres) tall and is one of the first gladioli to flower. *Gladiolus* 'Halley' produces white-flushed pale-yellow flowers on spires up to 20 inches (50 centimetres) in early summer.

Gladiolus
Height: 1–5 feet (30 centimteres–1.5 metres). Flowering period: late spring–autumn.[202]

Hedychiums are grown for their foliage and trumpet-shaped, often fragrant, flowers. In mild areas these plants may be grown outdoors. In cold gardens they can be grown outside during the summer and brought into the greenhouse before winter. When they are grown outdoors they need a warm, sunny position that is protected from cold winds. Grow them in a humus-rich, moist but well-drained soil. Some hedychiums will survive in a warm position in a frost-prone garden if given a deep winter mulch. When they are grown indoors pot them in equal parts of loam and leaf-mould with a bit of sand added.

Hedychium densiflorum is a clump-forming perennial with lance-

Hedychium (ginger lily)
Height: 2–3 feet (60–90 centimetres). Flowering period: late summer–early autumn.[203]

shaped glossy green leaves on reed-like stems. In late summer slender stems shoot up bearing dense spires of small fragrant yellow or orange flowers. The plant is a native of the Himalayas. *Hedychium gardnerianum* produces pale-yellow flowers with red stamens. The flowers are produced from late summer to early autumn.

Iris
Height: 8 inches to 5 feet (20 centimetres–1.5 metres). Flowering period: mid-spring–summer.[204]

Irises are grown for their colourful flowers, which are produced on strong stems above the foliage from mid-spring to summer. The flowers have three large outer petals, which are called falls. In some species the falls have conspicuous tufts of hair like a beard or crest and these are known as bearded irises. Another group has perfectly smooth falls and are called beardless irises.

Both these groups grow from rhizomes that should be planted from late summer to early autumn. Plant the rhizomes, with the tops just visible above the ground, in fertile, well-drained soil in full sun. Make sure the soil around them does not dry out for the first few weeks after planting.Most irises need a long, hot summer to flower well. Irises can range in height from 8 inches (20 centimetres) up to 5 feet (1.5 metres).

Iris pseudacorus 'Variegata' has attractive foliage with yellowish-white stripes on the leaves. This variety is suitable for a wet part of the garden and will grow in a pond. The flowers are yellow in colour and after the flowers fade the leaves lose their variegation, reverting to green. *Iris* 'Edens Charm' has white petals with a yellow streak. Another group of irises grows from bulbs and many of these flower early in the year, from late winter to spring. They are the smallest variety of irises and are ideal for a rock garden or under deciduous trees.

Lilium (lily)
Height: 2–7 feet (0.6–2.1 metres). Flowering period: early–late summer.[205-7]

Every garden that has well-drained soil can grow these striking plants. They can be grown in heavy clay soils by digging in lots of coarse gritty sand and leaf-mould. Poor sandy soils may need enriching with humus to help retain some moisture. If you want to grow lilies that do not suit the soil in your garden grow them in containers. Plant lilies in groups in a mixed herbaceous border, among shrubs or in tubs on a patio. The bulbs can be planted in the autumn or spring. Plant the bulbs immediately after buying them to

reduce the chance of them drying out. Lilies like to have their flower heads in full sun with their roots in partial shade. Planting them among low-growing shrubs will provide these conditions and when the flowers fade the decaying foliage will be hidden. The tall-growing varieties need staking.

There are hundreds of hybrids to pick from. *Lilium candidum* (Madonna lily) has pure-white trumpet-shaped flowers that appear in midsummer. The flowers are highly scented. When planting the bulbs plant them with the bulb tip just below the surface of the soil; they also tolerate drier soil than the other lilies. All other lilies are planted two to three times the height of the bulb deep in the soil. *Lilium* 'African Queen' has yellow- or orange-coloured flowers on stems 5 to 6 feet (1.5 to 2 metres) tall. *Lilium* 'Star Gazer' has red petals marked with darker spots.

Muscari are such hardy and easy-to-grow plants that no garden should be without them. When planted *en masse* they produce a splash of blue colour in spring time. There is a famous planting of muscari in the Keukenhof Gardens in Holland that is known as the blue river: this is a dense planting of muscari that winds through shrubs. Muscari can be planted in a mixed border or woodland garden, naturalised in grass or grown in a rock garden. The bulbs like a moderately fertile, moist but well-drained soil in full sun. The bulbs should be planted in the autumn.

Muscari armeniacum is the most popular variety, often grown as a pot plant for cut flowers. It produces small, scented bell-shaped cobalt-blue flowers on stems up to 3 inches (8 centimetres) tall. The flowers last for a long time.

Muscari botryoides 'Album' produces fragrant white flower clusters and has become popular in recent years. *Muscari latifolium* is a gorgeous species that has flower clusters with two different types of flower. At the top of the stem are light-blue flowers; below these dark-purple flowers are produced. Most muscari need no special care and once planted will flower and spread freely so division may be necessary every few years. Plants may be divided in late summer.

Muscari (grape hyacinth)
Height: 6–10 inches (15–25 centimetres). Flowering period: spring–early summer.[208]

Narcissus (daffodil)
Height: 3–18 inches (8–45 centimetres). Flowering period: spring–summer.[209–11]

The big yellow trumpet daffodil is one of the best-loved and most recognisable flowers grown in gardens. Daffodils come in many colours other than the basic yellow and many are bicoloured. The flowers are available in numerous shapes and sizes and are cheap to buy. Daffodils will grow in almost any soil or situation, though their preference is for soil that stays moist but well drained during the flowering season. Full sun or partial shade is usually desirable but most cultivars will grow in shade provided it is not too dense. Dead-head as flowers fade and allow leaves to die down naturally, which takes about six weeks. Apply a high-potash fertiliser after flowering to increase the size of the bulb for the following year. Bulbs are best planted in the autumn. There are thousands of cultivars to pick from. *Narcissus* 'Tete-a-Tete' is a dwarf variety ideal for the rock garden; it grows 6 inches (15 centimetres) tall.

Nectaroscor–dium (honey lily)
Height: 3 feet (90 centimetres). Flowering period: summer.[212]

This is a plant from France and Italy that grows up to 3 feet (90 centimetres) tall. It produces numerous bell-shaped flowers that hang down from the top of the stem. The flowers are cream in colour with purple stripes on the inside and it flowers in summer. It will grow in any moderately fertile, well-drained soil in full sun or partial shade. After the flowers fade seedpods are produced on the tips of the stems, which may self-seed if conditions are right.

Nerine
Height: 16–24 inches (40–60 centimetres). Flowering period: early–late autumn.[213–14]

Nerines are colourful South African bulbs that brighten up the autumn garden when many other plants are way past their best. *Nerine bowdenii* is the most hardy variety. It produces masses of pink trumpet-shaped blooms on naked stems in autumn. Up to eight flowers are produced on each stem, which grow 16 to 24 inches (40 to 60 centimetres) tall. Each flower has six petals that arch backwards. The long leaves do not appear until the following spring. Nerines should be planted at the foot of a south-facing wall where they can bake in the sun, although I have seen clumps growing at a north-facing wall doing very well. Plant the bulbs in autumn or spring in any well-drained soil. Plant the bulbs so that their long necks are just covered with soil. Cover the bulbs with a layer of compost in winter to protect them from frost. If you have heavy clay soil grow the nerines

in pots or containers using a soil-based compost, such as John Innes, with some grit added to improve drainage. *Nerine sarniensis corusca* produces crimson to orange-red flowers. *Nerine undulata* has pink flowers with a crinkled edge to its petals.

These bulbs are grown for their star-shaped white flowers that are produced in early summer. Ornithogalum can be divided into two groups: those that are winter hardy and those that are not. Varieties like *Ornithogalum* 'Arabicum' are not winter hardy and are planted in spring. It produces white cup-shaped flowers with conspicuous black centres on stems up to 2 feet (60 centimetres) tall. The plant requires a sunny position and can be grown in pots; the pots can be placed out in the garden among shrubs or foliage plants in late spring. The flowers are ideal for cutting and will last a long time. Remove the pots to a frost-free glasshouse in winter. *Ornithogalum umbellatum* is a hardy species that has white flowers on stems 6 inches (15 centimetres) tall in late spring.

Ornithogalum (star of Bethlehem) Height: 6 inches–2 feet (15–60 centimetres). Flowering period: late spring.[215]

Puschkinia scilloides is the only member of this hardy genus that comes from Turkey. It produces clusters of bell-shaped flowers that are white in colour with a blue stripe at the centre of each petal. The flowers are produced in late spring on stems 4 to 6 inches (10 to 15 centimetres) tall. The plant looks most effective at the front of a border or in a rockery against a background of dark foliage to show off its white flowers. Plant the bulbs in autumn in a well-drained soil in full sun or partial shade. The plant is sometimes sold as Russian snowdrop.

Puschkinia Height: 4–6 inches (10–15 centimetres). Flowering period: late spring.[216]

The kaffir lily is a plant from South Africa that flowers in the autumn. It is an amazing plant at that time of the year – even though the clump of green leaves may look battered due to wind, elegant blooms appear on the stems. Frost at that time of the year will only affect flowers that are open – other flowers further up the stem will continue to open in the following days. The flowers are like miniature gladioli. A flower spike may contain five to twenty pink or red flowers that are ideal for cutting. *Schizostylis coccinea* 'Major'

Schizostylis **(kaffir lily)** Height: 2–3 feet (60–90 centimetres). Flowering period: autumn.[217]

has large red flowers. *Schizostylis coccinea* 'Sunrise' has pink flowers. Plant the rhizomes in spring in moist soil with plenty of well-rotted compost added to retain moisture. The plant likes full sun with shelter from cold, drying winds. Mulch in spring with a layer of compost.

Tigridia (tiger lily)
Height: 18 inches (45 centimetres). Flowering period: midsummer–early autumn.[218]

This plant from Mexico produces exotic-looking flowers from midsummer to early autumn. The common name comes from the spots on the petals, which look like the spots on a tiger.

A number of flowers are produced on a central flower stem that grows up to 18 inches (45 centimetres) tall. Each separate flower only lasts for a day. The flower colours range from white and yellow to pink and red. The plant is only semi-hardy so it needs a warm, sunny position with shelter from cold winds. Since the flower colours are very strong it is best to grow it on its own in a small group.

Plant the bulbs in well-drained soil in late spring when the soil starts to warm up. During the growing season feed the plant with a liquid fertiliser every two weeks. In cold gardens lift the bulbs in the autumn, before the first severe frost, and store them in damp peat in a frost-free place. Keep the peat just moist enough to prevent the bulbs' shrivelling up. In warmer gardens the plant will survive outside if protected with a layer of mulch in winter. *Tigridia pavonia* is the most commonly grown variety.

Trillium
Height: 12–18 inches (30–45 centimetres). Flowering period: spring–summer.[219]

Trilliums are often considered difficult plants to grow. Given the right conditions they will thrive to give a spectacular display of flowers from spring to summer. They are a woodland plant so they like a moist, well-drained soil with lots of well-rotted compost mixed into the soil. They like partial shade to prevent the soil drying out in summer. Plant them in large clumps to give maximum effect. Trilliums produce a short stem, about 12 inches (30 centimetres) tall, with three leaves and a cup-shaped flower with three petals.

Trillium grandiflorum is the most popular species. It grows 16 to 18 inches (40 to 45 centimetres) tall with snow-white flowers that gradually change to pink with age. *Trillium luteum* has green leaves with patches of paler green to give a marbled effect and lemon- to butter-yellow flowers.

Tulips are found in every garden and public park. Tulips bulbs are widely available, cheap to buy and produce flowers in a wide range of colours and forms. The large-flowered varieties are very popular for formal displays in public parks and can be grown in scattered clumps in a herbaceous border. The smaller tulips, which grow about 8 inches (20 centimetres) tall, are ideal for the rock garden, as they do not need staking.

There are thousands of varieties to choose from. They range from single to double blooms through to frilled and peony types. The bulbs grow best in fertile, sandy soil in a sunny, open location and should be protected from excessive moisture and strong winds. The bulbs should be planted in November – they root better when soil temperatures have cooled down. After flowering, most tulip varieties can be lifted and stored in a dry place until the following autumn. Some varieties can be left in the ground. *Tulipa* 'Red Riding Hood' has broad leaves that are streaked with maroon marbled markings. The flowers are large, cup-shaped and brilliant red in colour. It grows about 8 inches (20 centimetres) tall, which makes it ideal for the rock garden. *Tulipa* 'Queen of Night' has dark maroon-coloured flowers – the nearest growers have got to producing the black tulip.

Tulipa **(tulip)** Height: 6–36 inches (15–90 centimetres). Flowering period: spring–early summer.[220]

The calla lily is grown for its unusual white or brightly coloured flowers. The leaves are green or speckled and spear shaped. The flowers are funnel shaped and come in a variety of colours that range from white to pink, yellow and various other colours. The plant flowers in summer. It likes a humus-rich, moist soil in full sun or partial shade. It is suitable for border beds or containers. In frost-prone gardens protect the bulbs with a deep mulch.

Zantedeschia **(calla lily)** Height: 12–16 inches (30–40 centimetres). Flowering period: summer.[221]

Climbers

Climbers are great plants for the small garden: they give height without taking up too much space. They can be used to cover walls, tree stumps and other garden structures or allowed to climb up through trees and shrubs. Climbers provide a wide range of flowers, fruit and foliage. Climbers may be self-clinging or twining, which need wire support if grown on a wall.

The main types of support used to grow climbers are walls, wooden trellis, wire-mesh such as chicken wire supported by stakes, pergolas and arches.

Selecting climbers

Choose climbers that will not grow too big for their location. If you want to grow a number of climbers together so that they intermingle, pick ones that have the same pruning requirements. For a south-facing wall select climbers that like sun, such as wisteria, passion flower or a vine. Some climbers, like *Hydrangea petiolaris* and Virginia creeper, will thrive in sun or shade. For a shaded location use ivy. Clematis like to have their roots in the shade with the flower heads in full sun.

Cultivation

When planting climbers against a wall or fence place the plant at least 18 inches (45 centimetres) from the base of the wall. The soil near the wall can get very dry in summer and receive little rainfall. Water well after planting and apply a mulch around the plant. Climbers with aerial roots or adhesive pads should be spread out along the base of the wall and allowed to stick to the wall themselves. Climbers that need support must be tied to a wire support or chicken wire attached to the wall. When the climber is planted remove the stake that came with the plant, fan the stems outwards and tie them to the supporting wire. As new shoots appear tie them into the support. When planting a climber to grow up through a tree, plant the climber away from the main trunk of the tree and use canes to guide the stems up to the lowest branches of the tree.

Berberidopsis
Height: 15 feet (4.5 metres). Flowering period: summer–early autumn.[222]

Berberidopsis corallina is a climber from Chile that flowers from summer to early autumn. It is an evergreen weakly twining plant with dark-green leaves. The plant produces dark-red spherical flowers in a cluster. It likes a humus-rich, neutral to acid soil in partial shade with shelter from cold winds. It needs no regular pruning but can be pruned in spring to fit into its available space.

Billardiera (climbing blueberry)
Height: 6–10 feet (1.8–3 metres). Flowering period: summer.[223]

Billardiera longiflora is a tender evergreen twining climber from Australia. It produces bell-shaped pale-green flowers in summer that are followed by large purple-blue berries that will survive until winter. It is not very hardy and will not survive severe frost. It likes a humus-rich, neutral to acid soil in a sunny position with shelter form cold winds.

Clematis
Height: 6–40 feet (1.8–12 metres). Flowering period: early spring–mid-autumn.[224–28]

When we think of climbing plants clematis is the name that springs to mind. There are clematis that will flower in almost every month of the year and flowers come in all colours except bright red and orange. Clematis are divided into three main groups. Group one contains the spring-flowering varieties, such as *Clematis montana* and its cultivars. Group two contains the early summer-flowering kinds, such as 'Nelly Moser'. Group three contains the late-summer varieties, such as 'Duchess of Albany', 'Jackmanii' and 'Ville de Lyon'. Clematis can be grown to cover a wall, trellis or pergola or they can be grown through shrubs or trees. Clematis like a neutral to slightly alkaline well-drained soil. They like their roots damp and shaded from the sun with the flower heads exposed to the sun. When planting mix some well-rotted manure or compost into the soil. Plant the root ball about 4 inches (10 centimetres) deeper than it was in the pot. This reduces drying out of the root ball, which encourages new shoots below ground and reduces clematis wilt. Clematis wilt is a problem with newly planted clematis. If shoots die cut out the dead shoots and new shoots will grow the following year. To produce the maximum flush of flowers water the plants well and feed with a liquid fertiliser such as tomato feed during the growing season. Group one and two clematis require little or no pruning. Prune group one clematis after

flowering by trimming long stems back. Prune group two clematis in early spring before growth starts: cut long stems back to a pair of buds on each stem. Prune group three clematis in early spring: cut all stems back to 6 to 8 inches (15 to 20 centimetres) above the ground. Feed clematis immediately after pruning.

Clematis armandii is a vigorous group-one evergreen climber that produces white saucer-shaped flowers with cream-coloured anthers. When cut and brought indoors the flower will fill the house with a beautiful almond scent. Since the plant is evergreen and flowers in late winter to spring, it needs a sheltered spot on a south or south-west facing wall to avoid severe weather damage, which can result in loss of flowers.

Clematis montana is a vigorous deciduous climber that can reach a height and spread of 40 feet (12 metres). It produces white flowers. *Clematis montana* 'Tetrarose' has bronze leaves and lilac-rose flowers. This is a group-one clematis, producing flowers in late spring.

Clematis 'Nelly Moser' is a group-two plant, producing large mauve-pink flowers with crimson stripes. *Clematis* 'Jackmanii' is a late-flowering group-three plant that produces dark purple-blue flowers. *Clematis* 'Ville de Lyon' is another late-flowering variety that has bright carmine-red flowers.

Clianthus
Height: 12 feet (3.6 metres). Flowering period: spring–early summer.[229]

This is an evergreen trailing or climbing shrub that is a native of New Zealand. It is a tropical-looking climber that will survive in mild gardens. *Clianthus puniceus* (lobster claw) has graceful pinnate green leaves and unusual red flowers that resemble a lobster's claws. It likes a well-drained soil in full sun or partial shade with shelter from cold, drying winds. It is not very hardy but will survive frost to about -7°C. When cut back by frost it often sprouts again from the base in spring – if it was protected by a deep mulch. Prune after flowering: cut back the flowering stems by about a third. *Clianthus puniceus* 'Albus' produces white flowers.

Cytisus battandieri (pineapple broom)

This is a vigorous deciduous tree or shrub that can be trained as a climber. This Moroccan shrub was first introduced in 1922 and for a long time it was thought to be a tender plant. It is best grown in full sun with shelter from cold winds. It has silvery-grey leaves

Height: 18 feet (5.4 metres).
Flowering period: summer.[230]

and produces golden-yellow flowers that form large upright cones in summer. The flowers have a strong scent of pineapple. The plant can grow up to 18 feet (5.4 metres) tall with a similar spread. It may be pruned after flowering or in early spring to remove branches that are crossing each other; do not cut back into the old wood. It thrives in well-drained, neutral to acid soil. Like all cytisus plants it resents root disturbance.

Dregea
Height: 10 feet (3 metres).
Flowering period: late summer.[231]

This is a twining woody semi-evergreen climber found in the tropical forests from South Africa to China. *Dregea sinenis* has heart-shaped green leaves and produces fragrant creamy-white flowers in late summer. The flowers are followed by long slender seed pods. The plant is a native of China and likes a well-drained soil in sun or partial shade. Tie the young shoots onto support wires until they start to twine themselves. Prune after flowering to control size and remove dead wood in spring.

Fremonto–dendron
Height: 20 feet (6 metres).
Flowering period: late spring to mid-autumn.[232]

Fremontodendron 'California Glory' is a vigorous evergreen shrub from California that can be trained as a climber. It has dark-green leaves and produces saucer-shaped yellow flowers from late spring to mid-autumn. It grows in poor to moderately fertile, dry soil in full sun, ideally on a south-facing wall. Prune branches that are growing outwards or towards the wall in late winter or early spring. Contact with the foliage may irritate the skin.

Hedera (ivy)
Height: 15–30 feet (4.5–9 metres).
Flowering period: autumn.[233-34]

Ivies are ideal climbers as a backdrop for other plants or for covering a wall. They vary greatly in size and vigour and should be carefully selected to suit the space available. Variegated ivies are useful for brightening up a dark wall. Ivies are often blamed for knocking down old buildings. They will not damage solid, sound walls but they will dislodge loose mortar and walls.

Hedra hibernican (Irish Ivy) is an exceedingly vigorous dark-green-leaved ivy. It can produce new shoots over 10 feet (3 metres) in a single growing season. If left to grow freely there is no limit to the height and spread that it can grow to, so it should only be planted in a spot that is not going to be a source of regret in future years. *Hedera helix* 'Goldheart' is a popular ivy with a splash of golden-

yellow at the centre of the leaves. It is a medium vigorous plant that needs pruning each year to control its size. *Hedera colchica* 'Paddy's Pride' is a slow-growing ivy with cream edges to its large leaves and the centre of the leaves made up of two shades of green. This ivy is non-clinging so it needs to be supported. It grows to a height of 15 feet (4.5 metres) and flowers in the autumn.

Ivies will grow in a wide range of conditions but grow best in fertile, humus-rich soil. The green-leaf ivies will grow in shade but the variegated varieties prefer sun.

This is a spreading evergreen shrub from China with arching branches that makes a very nice wall climber. It has spiny, glossy dark-green leaves like holly leaves. It produces an abundance of narrow, pendulous catkin-like flowers that can be up to 12 inches (30 centimetres) long. The individual flowers are tiny and densely packed, greenish-white in colour. The flowers are produced from late summer to early autumn and are fragrant, with a hint of honey scent.

Itea ilicifolia
Height: 10–15 feet (3–4.5 metres). Flowering period: late summer–autumn.[235]

The plant will grow in a fertile, moist but well-drained soil in full sun or partial shade. If grown in full sun the soil needs to be quite moist. In cold or exposed gardens the plant needs shelter from cold winds.

Jasmines are deciduous and evergreen shrubs or climbers that are grown for their fragrant flowers. They produce mainly white or yellow flowers. *Jasmimum nudiflorum* (winter jasmine) is a hardy climbing variety with yellow flowers in winter to early spring. The plant is deciduous and the flowers often appear before the leaves. It can be trained onto a wall, trellis or pergola using ties. It needs to be pruned as soon as the flowers have faded. *Jasminum officinale* (common jasmine) is a vigorous twining climber that produces very fragrant white flowers from summer to early autumn. The plant is deciduous but may be semi-deciduous in frost-free winters. It can grow up to 40 feet (12 metres) tall. There are variegated species of this plant with creamy-white margins or leaves marked with yellow. Jasmines grow best in well-drained soil that has been enriched with leaf-mould and a bit of sand.

Jasminum (jasmine)
Height: 40 feet (12 metres). Flowering period: winter–early spring; or summer–autumn.[236]

Lonicera (honeysuckle)
Height: 6–20 feet (1.8–6 metres). Flowering period: late spring–autumn.[237]

Honeysuckles are semi-evergreen or evergreen shrubs and woody-stemmed twining climbers grown for their flowers, which are often fragrant. The flowers are mainly tubular or funnel-shaped and range in colour from cream and light yellow to scarlet and purple-rose. *Lonicera periclymenum* (woodbine honeysuckle) is a medium-sized deciduous climber that flowers throughout the summer. The flowers are purple or yellow on the outside with a cream colour inside. It produces red berries in the autumn. Many varieties of it are available, such as 'Belgica', which has flowers coloured red on the outside and yellow inside and blooms in early summer. The variety 'Serotina' flowers in midsummer; the flowers are purple-red on the outside and yellow inside. Honeysuckles will grow in almost any soil but thrive in well-drained, humus-rich soil in full sun or partial shade. Pruning can be done when the flowers fade; varieties that flower in late summer can be pruned in spring.

Mitraria coccinea
Height: 6 feet (1.8 metres). Flowering period: late spring–autumn.[238]

Mitraria coccinea is an evergreen spreading shrub that makes a very attractive wall climber. The plant is a native of Chile and Argentina so it is a tender plant that will not survive frost. In gardens where frost is severe grow it in a cool greenhouse. The plant produces spectacular red flowers over a long period of time from late spring to autumn. The flowers are followed by small reddish fruit, which contain tiny seeds in a gelatinous mixture. In frost-free gardens grow the plant in a moist, well-drained, humus-rich, acid soil in light dapple shade. Keep the roots cool and shaded but allow the flower heads to grow into sunlight. It needs shelter from cold, drying winds. The plant requires very little pruning: trim or lightly cut back shoots to reduce size in spring. When growing *Mitraria coccinea* in a greenhouse use a lime-free compost and water freely during the growing season; apply a balanced liquid fertiliser once a month.

Parthenocissus (Virginia creeper)
Height: 20–30 feet (6–9 metres).[239]

This is a deciduous tendril hardy climber that is grown for its foliage. It sticks to walls using tiny sucker pads so it does not need any support and is useful to cover a large wall with the minimum of effort. It will grow in any fertile, well-drained soil in sun or shade. The plant really stands out in the autumn when it will turn a wall to flame when the leaves change to a bright-red colour.

Parthenocissus henryana (Chinese Virginia creeper) has green leaves with a conspicuous white vein down the centre. This variegation is most pronounced on a shady wall. *Parthenocissus tricuspidata* (Boston ivy) is another variety, which produces brilliant red to purple foliage in the autumn.

The passion flower is a dramatic and unusual plant. When Spanish priests first saw this flower growing in the forests of Brazil, they described it as follows: 'the flower represents the symbols of Christ's Passion, each bloom opens flat to reveal an outer circle of ten white petals (the Disciples, minus Judas and Peter), within these occur a ring of fine purple-blue filaments (the crown of thorns) and in the centre are conspicuous anthers (the nails), while the wounds are represented by five yellowish stains'.

Passiflora (passion flower)
Height: 12–30 feet (3.6–9 metres). Flowering period: mid–late summer.[240]

The hardy species can be used to cover a wall or trellis. The tender species need a warm glasshouse to survive. The plant needs a well-drained, moderately fertile soil in full sun with shelter from cold winds. The plant grows rapidly each year, using its tendrils to attach itself to supports or to climb up through a tree or shrub. *Passiflora caerulea* (blue passion flower) is a fast-growing climber that can reach a height of 30 feet (9 metres); it produces creamy-white flowers with purple filaments. It will flower in late summer if the summer has been warm. After the flower it produces large orange fruit, which are edible but do not have an outstanding flavour.

This is a very vigorous climber that will grow over everything in its path – for this reason it is often called 'mile-a-minute'. It can grow 10 to 15 feet (3 to 4.5 metres) in a year. For this reason think carefully before you plant it. It is perfect for screening an unsightly shed or other garden eyesore but its ultimate size should not be forgotten.

Polygonum baldschuanicum (Russian vine)
Height: sky is the limit. Flowering period: late summer–autumn.

In late summer to autumn the plant is covered with long sprays of white to pale-pink flowers.

Pyracantha (firethorn)

Height: 6–12 feet (1.8–3.6 metres). Flowering period: early summer; berries: autumn.[241–42]

The pyracantha is enjoying a huge surge in popularity. This is easy to understand, as pyracanthas are some of the most versatile evergreens. They can be planted as an ornamental and vandal-proof hedge or they can be trained to cover a garden wall or fence.

In late spring the branches are covered in a mass of small white flowers, like hawthorn blooms. In autumn the plant is covered with berries in vibrant colours such as orange, yellow and red, which will last until they are eaten by birds in winter. Pyracanthas will grow happily in most fertile, well-drained soils in full sun or partial shade. Work plenty of well-rotted manure or garden compost into the soil before planting. One of the most popular ways of growing pyracanthas is to train them into a formal shape such as an espalier on a wall or fence. Wires are attached to a wall or fence posts. Leave a vertical gap of 18 inches (45 centimetres) between the wires so you can train the plant along the wires. To train a newly planted pyracantha, tie its strongest branches to the wire on either side of the main stem and remove any small, unwanted branches. In subsequent years continue to tie branches onto the support wire to extend the framework. In June, when the berries have set, remove unwanted growth on the top and prune away unwanted growth down the sides so that the berries can be seen and enjoyed more easily.

Pyracanthas are prone to scab, which shows up as brown or greyish patches on the leaves with the berries often splitting and falling off. To control scab, spray with a fungicide such as Nimrod-T in spring, just before the new leaves are emerging, spray again when most of the flowers have fallen off and give the final spray a month after this. In recent years new disease-resistant cultivars have been introduced that require no spraying. *Pyracantha* 'Mohave' can grow up to 12 feet (3.6 metres) tall with red berries. *Pyracantha* 'Golden Dome' grows about 6 feet (1.8 metres) tall with golden-yellow berries.

Rhodochiton atrosan–guineum

Height: 10 feet (3 metres).

This is a tender fast-growing climber that comes from Mexico. It will climb up along trellis or wire support, where it will twine itself around the support, or it may be grown in a hanging basket where it will trail down. It has bright-green heart-shaped leaves that show off the unusual flowers to good effect. The flowers are bell shaped and pink in colour, with an almost-black tube hanging down like the hammer in a bell. It can grow up to 10 feet (3 metres) tall

and will grow in sun or partial shade. It is frost tender so it is best to collect the seeds and sow them in spring to produce new plants for the following year. Plant out the young plants in May, when the danger of frost is over, in fertile, humus-rich soil. Whether you grow it as a climber or in a hanging basket, it will give you a long season of flowers from summer to autumn.

Flowering period: summer–autumn.[243]

Climbing roses and ramblers are used to cover walls, trellis, garden buildings or pergolas. The only difference between the two is how they grow and their pruning requirements.

Climbing roses can produce strong stems from any part of the plant. They grow much taller than ramblers and can be fanned out along a wall to produce a burst of colour on the higher branches. Some climbers flower on short stems produced the previous year in summer while some flower at intervals from summer to autumn. When a climber is planted, tie the long stems onto horizontal wires to form a fan shape. Train young flexible side shoots horizontally along the wires as they grow. When established, prune the side shoots annually in spring, reducing their length by about two-thirds and cutting the stem at a bud. Tie the newly pruned stems to their support.

Climbing roses
Height: 10–15 feet (3–4.5 metres). Flowering period: summer–autumn.[244]

Ramblers produce a number of strong stems from their base each year and these will flower the following year. Ramblers only produce one flush of flowers in summer. To prevent your rambler becoming a tangled mess, cut out the oldest stems at ground level in the autumn. Retain the young stems and tie them onto wires or other suitable supports. Prune the side shoots back to two to four buds from the main stem.

Roses thrive in a fertile, humus-rich, well-drained soil in full sun. Apply a mulch in autumn and feed the roses with a rose feed when the flower buds are forming.

Rosa 'Albertine' is a rambling rose that grows up to 15 feet (4.5 metres) tall, producing a sweetly scented salmon-pink flower in midsummer. *Rosa* 'New Dawn' is a climber that grows 10 feet (3 metres) tall, producing fragrant pale-pink flowers from summer to autumn. *Rosa* 'Climbing Iceberg' produces clusters of numerous white flowers from summer to autumn.

Plant roses in the autumn or spring – there is a huge selection to pick from. Do not plant roses in soil that has already grown roses: they will die. Replace the soil completely or plant the rose away from where a previous rose grew.

Solanum
Height: 20 feet (6 metres). Flowering period: summer–autumn.[245]

Solanum crispum (Chilean potato plant) is a fast-growing evergreen or semi-evergreen climber. When the plant is in full bloom it is hard to think that it belongs to the same genus as the potato. In summer the plant is covered with great clusters of purple starry flowers with prominent yellow stamens, making it one of the finest summer-flowering climbers. The plant is loose, bushy and scrambling so it needs to be tied to a solid support. It can grow up to 20 feet (6 metres) tall with a similar spread. It also looks effective when allowed to scramble over a fence or garden building. It will grow in any type of soil that is free draining, though it does best in a slightly alkaline soil in full sun. We have it growing on a north-facing wall and it is doing very well.

The variety 'Glasnevin' is the one to grow: it flowers more profusely and is also slightly hardier than *Solanum crispum* but it will not survive severe frost. It has deep purple-blue flowers that can last from late spring to autumn in mild gardens. It is a very vigorous climber in mild gardens and can become untidy so it needs severe pruning in autumn to control its size. *Solanum jasminoides* 'Albus' has white flowers with yellow anthers.

Vitris (vine)
Height: 20–40 feet (6–12 metres). Flowering period: summer.[246]

Ornamental vines are grown for their foliage. They are deciduous tendril climbers that need supports to cling onto. They like a humus-rich, well-drained, neutral to alkaline soil in full sun. They can be trained against a wall or grown over a trellis, pergola, fence or through a large tree or shrub. When grown against a wall, pinch off some of the shoot tips in spring and summer to produce bushy growth. Prune back the whole plant to the supporting wires when all the leaves have fallen off.

Vitris coignetiae is a hardy climber that can grow 30 to 40 feet (9 to 12 metres) tall, using its tendrils to cling onto supporting wires. It has large green leaves that turn to flame colours such as yellow, orange and red in the autumn. *Vitris vinifera* 'Purpurea' has purple leaves that turn a dark purple in the autumn.

isteria is a vigorous deciduous climber that can take a number of years before it blooms. It is one of the great joys of the summer garden to see a wisteria in full flower.

The long dangling tresses of flowers in various shades of lilac, pink and white make wisteria a favourite climber. Wisteria is capable of reaching a height of 70 feet (21 metres) if grown up through a tree so it is obviously not a plant for a small garden unless it is drastically pruned. Wisteria can be trained into a multitude of shapes, from a formal espalier against a wall to a canopy over a pergola. Wisteria thrives in a fertile, moist but well-drained soil in full sun or partial shade.

There are nine species of wisteria to choose from, including many North American natives. The most spectacular are the varieties of the Japanese wisteria (*Wisteria floribunda*) and the Chinese (*Wisteria sinensis*). The former is the hardier of the two and climbs by spiralling anticlockwise around its support.

Wisteria is an easy plant to grow but difficult to get to flower. The plant needs to be pruned twice a year to direct its energy into producing flowers. If you remember the half-crown, or two and six, that is your secret to the pruning of wisteria: prune in February and again in late June. When planting against a wall disentangle the stems from the support cane in the pot. Select the longest and strongest stem and tie it to the supporting wires. Then prune off all the remaining shoots at the base. When the main shoot reaches its desired height cut off its top. This will encourage the development of side branches. At the end of June cut back any side shoots to within 6 inches (15 centimetres) of the main stem and tie in the new growth to the supporting wires. In the following spring and every spring thereafter shorten the new stems that grew since last summer to leave two or three dormant buds. These short side shoots will produce lots of spring flowers. It may seem drastic to remove so much of the plant each year but if you ignore this pruning you will sacrifice a good display of flowers.

Wisteria floribunda (Japanese wisteria) produces fragrant lilac-blue, pink or white flowers, depending on the variety. *Wisteria sinensis* (Chinese wisteria) produces similarly coloured flowers that are bigger.

Wisteria
Height: 28 feet (8.5 metres). Flowering period: late spring–summer.[247]

Architectural and exotic plants

Architectural plants can be used to give height and interest from all angles of the garden. They are plants with varied foliage shapes and textures combined with good branching structure to make them the cornerstones of the garden. Although most of them do not flower, they can provide interest all through the year. They can be used as focal points at key locations or used at the back of a border to give a dramatic effect. The choice of plants is wide so try to pick plants that have distinctive shape, that are evergreen or have nice bark colouration so that your garden does not become dull in winter. Try plants like bamboos, ferns, palms, phormiums and grasses to create focal points.

More and more Irish people are going on holidays to warm climates, where they see exotic plants growing freely. When the holiday is over they return home full of memories of the beautiful foliage and glorious flowers they have seen, wondering if it is possible to create a tropical paradise in Ireland. A surprising number of hot-climate plants can be grown outdoors in our country and almost everything you see growing abroad is available from local garden centres. Our winters are getting milder and with a bit of protection in winter many of these plants will survive here. So with a little effort

and a dash of imagination you can create your own tiny tropical paradise. Even in a small country like Ireland a plant that would be considered exotic in one part of the country could be considered a weed in another part. The echium plant from the Canary Islands would be considered exotic in the middle of the country while along the south-coast of Ireland and Howth it could be classified as a weed, it self-seeds so freely.

Winter Protection

We all want to grow more tender plants that will survive our cold, wet winters. Most gardeners who grow exotic plants will wonder in the late autumn whether this winter our gardens will be devastated by weeks of sub-zero temperatures, what plants should be moved to the greenhouse and what plants require protection. The fun of growing exotic plants that we know are not totally hardy is in using our skills to nurse them through the winter. Plants growing in pots can be moved to the greenhouse or a warm, sheltered part of the garden. Tender plants growing in the ground must be insulated. The material used must allow air to circulate and moisture to evaporate. The material can be a temporary covering during cold spells or left in place throughout the winter. Horticultural fleece is cheap and easy to cover a plant with and it can give about two degrees of frost protection. Bubblewrap is often advocated as a useful material for protection but in my experience the plant cannot breathe with it and most likely will die. Bubblewrap is very good to insulate a cold greenhouse. We use fibreglass, the material to insulate attics, which allows the plant to breathe, but wear gloves and a mask when using it. It can be used to insulate the crown of tree ferns and tender palms. Small plants can be protected by placing terracotta chimney-flue liners over them. They can be stacked together to protect a tall trunk. Large multi-stemmed plants present a problem: the individual stems can be bandaged with horticultural fleece or the stems can be tied together with twine and wrapped in horticultural fleece. Succulents can be protected with plastic domes, which are sold in garden centres. Excessive wetness kills these plants: make the soil around the plants very free draining by placing a layer of grit around the plant. These plants need good air circulation around them to evaporate the excess moisture.

Palms and cycads

We normally associate palm trees and cycads with the sunny tropical islands and tropical forests. They can be grown as specimen plants outdoors in mild frost-free gardens. In frost-prone gardens they are best grown in pots and transferred to a greenhouse for the winter. The palms usually have an upright trunk and can grow to a large tree. The leaves are usually palmate or pinnate in shape. In warm climates they produce small flowers that are followed by fruits, such as dates or coconuts.

Cycads have a tuber-like trunk that produces a number of stems that spread outwards from its base near the ground. The foliage is pinnate and is usually tough and rigid. They are slow growing and will eventually reach a height of about 6 feet (1.8 metres). Palms and cycads like a well-drained, neutral to acid soil in full sun or partial shade. Most require shelter from cold winds.

Chamaerops humilis
Height: 6–10 feet (1.8–3 metres).
Flowering period: summer.[260]

This plant is a native of Europe, where it grows wild in the western Mediterranean. It is a small bushy palm, producing many stems from the base. It can grow from 6 to 10 feet (1.8 to 3 metres) tall. It is not very hardy and may survive short spells just below 0°C. In cold gardens it is best grown in a pot and moved to greenhouse in winter.

Cycas revoluta (Japanese sago palm)
Height: 3–6 feet (90 centimetres–1.8 metres).[264]

This multi-stemmed cycad from Japan has stiff, arching dark-green leaves on its branches. It will only survive short periods of frost so it is best grown in a pot and moved to a greenhouse in winter. Grow it in a mixture of garden soil, compost and gravel and use a slow-release fertiliser. In the greenhouse the plant is susceptible to red spider mite. To control it use moderate humidity and wash the leaves with soapy water or use biological controls. Cycas can be damaged by chemical pesticides.

This palm from the Canary Islands can grow up to 50 feet (15 metres) tall. It has a stout, straight trunk with spreading, arching leaves. In mild gardens it makes a nice specimen plant – covering the trunk with fibreglass in the winter will protect it from frost. Grown outdoors it likes a moist, well-drained soil in full sun, with some mid-day shade. It produces creamy-yellow flowers in summer, followed by fruit.

Phoenix canariensis (Canary Island date palm) Height: 50 feet (15 metres). Flowering period: summer.[285]

This is a very hardy palm that will survive outdoors in this country. It forms a single stem, which is covered with fibre. It forms a canopy of large fan-like evergreen leaves. Although very hardy, the leaves can be shredded by high winds and the palm can lose its attractiveness. The plant is small enough to be grown in a limited space such as a patio, where it can be grown in a pot. It can grow to a height of 70 feet (20 metres), although it will take about twenty years to reach a height of 12 feet (3.6 metres). In warm gardens it can produce dense clusters of yellow flowers in summer.

Trachycarpus fortunei (chusan palm) Height: 70 feet (20 metres). Flowering period: summer.[292]

Ferns

Ferns are grown for their attractive foliage and, since they like damp, shaded areas, they are ideal plants for our wet climate. They may be evergreen or deciduous and produce leaf-like structures that are called fronds. Ferns are a very old family of plants – they were thriving on Earth for millions of years before flowering plants evolved. They do not produce flowers or seeds: they reproduce from spores that form on the underside of the fronds. Ferns have become very popular in recent years and are grown for shape, texture and the colour of the fronds. Once established, they require little maintenance. Most of them prefer partial to deep shade. Do not plant ferns where they will be exposed to the sun at mid-day. All ferns like growing in soil that contains lots of compost and a mulch of compost in the autumn will help to keep the soil moist and free draining. Some of them, like *Matteuccia* and *Osmunda*, like damp soil; others, like *Asplenium*, *Polypodium* and *Polystichum* tolerate relatively dry soil. Deciduous ferns produce bright foliage in spring that starts to fade by late summer and will die back after the first frost.

Asplenium scolopendrium (hart's tongue fern)[273] This fern will grow in wet or dry conditions and prefers an alkaline soil. It is an evergreen fern with a creeping rhizome. It produces bright-green fronds up to 16 inches (40 centimetres) long.

Athyrium filix-femina 'Frizelliae' (lady fern)[279] This fern has short fronds about 6 inches (15 centimetres) long with rounded lobes along each side of the midribs. The lobes form a spiral along the midrib. It is a deciduous fern.

Athyrium nipponicum 'Pictum' (Japanese painted fern)[278] This is a very attractive deciduous fern, with soft shades of metallic silver-grey with hints of red and blue markings on the fronds, which are about 14 inches (35 centimetres) long. This is one of the showiest ferns for a shady position in the garden.

This is another species of tree fern that comes from the South Island of New Zealand. It is a fast-growing, large tree fern that can reach a height of 25 feet (8 metres). It is a tender plant that will not survive frost – the level of frost that it will survive has not been tested in this country yet. It is best to grow it in a large pot filled with mixture of garden soil, sharp sand and lots of coarse leaf-mould. Remove the plant to the greenhouse until it gets too big. Then plant it out in fertile, moist, well-drained soil in dapple shade. Unlike the dicksonia, the cyatheas should never have water poured on their crowns because this can cause the crown to rot. However, keep the roots well watered. The plant has a fibrous trunk of erect rhizomes that produces fronds 3 to 6 feet (90 centimetres to 1.8 metres) long. It does not produce as many fronds as *Dicksonia antarctica*.

Cyathea smithii 263

This is an evergreen fern in mild gardens. It can grow up to 2 feet (60 centimetres) and has dark-green holly-like leaves on the fronds. It is a fern that will not survive severe frost.

Cyrtomium falcatum (**Japanese holly fern**) 277

This tree fern from Australia and Tasmania is the most common one grown in this country. It is reasonably hardy and can survive a few degrees of frost. Tree ferns are extremely old plants – fossils of them hundreds of millions of years old have been found, so they could have been used as food by dinosaurs. They were extremely popular in Victorian times, when special greenhouses were built to grow them. Many ferns grow from horizontal rhizomes but the tree fern has an erect rhizome, which forms the trunk and is very hairy at the base. The hairs are actually roots. Tree ferns develop very small roots underground and they do not thicken with age, as do the roots of woody plants. The trunk can grow up to 10 to 13 feet (3 to 3.9 metres) tall, with a diameter of 16 inches (40 centimetres). The trunk grows about an inch or so each year so tall specimens can be hundreds of years old. At the top of the trunk dark-green fronds up to 7 feet (2 metres) are produced. These fronds produce a spreading canopy that can be 20 feet (6 metres) wide on mature tree ferns. This canopy provides shelter for more delicate ferns to flourish underneath.

Dicksonia antartica thrives in filtered sunlight in well-drained

Dicksonia antartica (**tree fern**) 266/281

soil with lots of organic compost added and lots of water. The plant should be watered at the top, in the crown, and the trunk should be kept moist as well as the surrounding soil. The plant will benefit from a dilute feed of liquid fertiliser. Tree ferns are generally expensive to buy so it is worth protecting them from frost. The crown at the top of the trunk is the most vulnerable part of the plant. Protect the top part of the plant with fibreglass and push some of it into the crown. Tree ferns grow very well in south Kerry, where the mild winters and high rainfall are similar to their natural habitat in Australia and New Zealand. There are fine collections of tree ferns in Glanleam Gardens and Derreen Gardens, where the ferns have produced numerous young plants by self-sporing themselves.

Matteuccia struthiopteris **(shuttlecock fern or ostrich-feather fern)**[291]
This is a deciduous fern that produces fronds up to 4 feet (1.2 metres) tall. The dark-green fronds grow in a vase shape. This fern spreads by creeping rhizomes that spread out in every direction, producing new plants around the parent fern. In summer it produces dark-brown fronds, which contrast beautifully with the green fronds produced in spring.

Osmunda regalis **(royal fern)**[290]
This is a deciduous fern that produces bright-green fronds up to 6 feet (1.8 metres) tall. It looks very attractive in spring when the new fronds unfold like a bishop's crosier. It has very long fronds with lance-shaped leaves that spread slowly. It thrives in moist, fertile, humus-rich, acid soil in full sun or partial shade. It will grow in full sun if the soil contains sufficient water. The fibrous roots of osmundas have been used as a source of osmunda fibre, which was used as potting compost for orchids and may explain the decline of this fern. *Osmunda regalis* 'Purpurascens' produces attractive purple fronds in spring.

Polystichum setiferum **(soft shield fern)**[289]
This is a low-growing semi-evergreen fern with fronds that grow in an arc-shape. It has lance-shaped leaves on the fronds, each frond ending in a sharp point. This is a dwarf fern that likes a humus-rich, well-drained soil in deep or partial shade. This fern is ideal for a rock garden.

Bamboos and Grasses

Bamboos and grasses have become popular foliage plants in recent years. A huge range of ornamental grasses is now available and they can be used right across the garden. They are available in a wide variety of colours, shapes, textures and sizes. They may form low, compact mounds, tall screens or densely spreading mats. The foliage colours include various shades of green, blue and red, as well as variegated varieties with coloured stripes. Grasses can add motion and sound to the garden. They are the ultimate designer's architectural plant, adding see-through effects, gentle rustling, autumn colour and winter shapes.

They grow in almost any garden soil, seldom need watering once established and are rarely bothered by pests or diseases. They prefer well-drained soil that has been enriched with compost. They can be used in borders as individual eye-catchers, large or small, or repeated in groups to create a natural look with paths rambling through them.

Grasses that die back completely in winter can be rejuvenated by cutting the entire plant back to within a few inches of the ground in early spring. Evergreen varieties that survive the winter should not be cut back: clean up the plant in early spring by removing any dead growth. On plants a few years old, new growth may only appear at the sides of the clump, leaving a bare centre. When this happens the plant should be divided and replanted, removing the dead growth; this is best done in spring. Some grasses self-seed themselves around the garden, which can be a problem. The term 'ornamental grasses' is used to include grasses, rushes and bamboos.

Some varieties, such as the bamboos, can be rampant and spread too much. These plants can be planted in a hole with the sides lined in plastic to prevent the roots spreading. Most of these rampant varieties can be grown in a container, which will give an evergreen, exotic touch to a patio or balcony. When growing in pots use a good compost mixture made up of garden soil, sharp grit and leaf-mould. Use a glazed pot to show off the plant. Add a slow-release fertiliser to the compost mix; in subsequent years use a liquid fertiliser to boost the plant. Water the plants well, especially bamboos.

Carex
Height: 2–3 feet (60–90 centimetres). Flowering period: summer.

Carex flagellifera is an imposing evergreen grass that is suitable for a border or containers. It is a cascading grass that grows about 3 feet (90 centimetres) tall, with metallic bronze leaves. *Carex elata* 'Aurea' (Bowles' golden sedge) is a dense clump-forming grass with yellow arching leaves up to 2 feet (60 centimetres) long.

Cortaderia (Pampas grass)
Height: 6–7 feet (1.8–2.1 metres). Flowering period: late summer.[262]

Cortaderia is a giant grass: be careful where you plant it because it will quickly form enormous clumps. *Cortaderia selloana* 'Albolineata' will grow about 6 feet (1.8 metres) tall and is slow growing and compact, with a white margin to the leaves and silvery-white plumes. *Cortaderia selloana* 'Sunningdale Silver' will grow about 7 feet (2.1 metres) tall with a spread of 4 feet (1.2 metres). This plant forms clumps of thin, very sharp-edged arching leaves with silvery-white plumes in early summer that remain attractive until winter.

Elegia carpensis (horsetail restio)
Height: 3 feet (90 centimetres). Flowering period: summer.[268]

This plant is a native of the fynbos regions of South Africa – *carpensis* means from the cape. It produces thick dark-green stems from underground rhizomes that are divided in sections like bamboo plants; these stems can grow up to 10 feet (3 metres) tall. At each node along the stem it produces a circle of needle-like branches. Young stems have a large leaf-like structure around the stem at each node. As the stems grow older these leaves become stiff and paper like. It will grow in fairly poor, sandy soil with lots of water. The plant looks lush and green where there is lots of water. The plant is tender and will not survive frost.

Equisetum (horsetail)
Height: 6 feet (1.8 metres).[270]

This grows like a rush, producing long stems up to 6 feet (1.8 metres) tall that are rigid and dark green with attractive nodes along the stem. The nodes have blackish rings around them and the stems are hollow between the nodes. A word of warning on this plant: it can spread very rapidly to become a weed that is difficult to eradicate. The plant should be grown in a pot, which can be sunk into the ground, keeping the top of the pot above ground level, to prevent the rhizomes escaping into the garden. This is an ancient plant that has remained from millions of years ago. It does not flower but reproduces from spores, like the ferns. It thrives in a bog-type

environment and will grow in up to 6 inches (15 centimetres) of water so it can be placed in a garden pool.

This is an upright, rigid bamboo that can grow to 15 feet (4.5 metres) tall. It forms a dense clump, which spreads slowly. The canes are purple-green in colour with purple-brown leaves. Thin out some of the canes in late spring to create a see-through effect – bamboo clumps look great as semi-transparent screens rather than dense clumps – which makes it easier to appreciate the individual canes and the views through them to other parts of the garden. The canes that remain will grow thicker and taller and have better colouration.

Fargesia nitida
Height: 15 feet (4.5 metres).[271]

This is a small low-growing grass that is ideal for the rock garden, where it likes the dry soil. It is a dense tufted grass with blue needle-like leaves that grow about 6 inches (15 centimetres) long. If the plant becomes waterlogged in winter it can rot at the centre and look unsightly. Comb through the plant in winter to remove dead foliage.

Festuca glauca **(blue festuca)**
Height: 6 inches (0.15 metres). Flowering period: summer.

This is an evergreen grass with pointed grey-blue leaves that grow upright. It produces one-sided seed heads in summer that begin white and then turn golden. It grows about 2 feet (60 centimetres) tall.

Helictotrichon sempervirens **(blue oat grass)**
Height: 2 feet (0.6 metres). Flowering period: summer.[274]

This leafless rush makes a spectacular spiralling mound of green stems to form a tangled mass. Like all rushes, this plant likes a wet, boggy soil and can be grown in a garden pool.

Juncus effusus **'Spiralis' (cork-screw rush)**
Height: 1.5 feet (0.45 metres). Flowering period: summer.

Miscanthus sinensis 'Zebrinus' (zebra grass)
Height: 5 feet (1.5 metres). Flowering period: autumn.[280]

This is a deciduous grass that produces dense clumps of foliage with cream-white or pale-yellow horizontal bands on the leaves in late summer. It grows up to 5 feet (1.5 metres) tall and produces a mass of feathery flowers in the autumn. Cut the grass down to within a few inches of the ground in early spring.

Ophiopogon planiscapus 'Nigrescens'
Height: 12 inches (0.3 centimetres). Flowering period: summer.[282]

This is an evergreen perennial with purple-black arching grassy leaves that grows about 12 inches (30 centimetres) tall. It spreads into a small clump after a number of years and looks very well against white rocks in a rock garden. In summer it produces small bell-shaped pale-mauve-coloured flowers that are followed by black berries.

Phyllostachys aurea (golden bamboo)
Height: 6–30 feet (1.8–9 metres). No Flowering period.

This upright clump-forming bamboo has green canes at first that mature to a golden colour. It can grow from 6 to 30 feet (1.8 to 9 metres) tall. The leaves are golden green in colour. It thrives in a woodland garden and can also be used to create a screen. *Phyllostachys nigra* (black bamboo) has green canes that turn black in their second or third year of growth.

Stipa gigantea (golden oats)
Height: 8 feet (2.4 metres). Flowering period: summer.

This is a dense evergreen grass with green leaves up to 28 inches (70 centimetres) tall. The plant produces an array of flower spikes in summer that can be 8 feet (2.4 metres) tall and turn gold when ripe. The plant looks very effective against a dark background of evergreen shrubs.

Succulents

Succulents are plants that have adapted to extreme conditions of drought. They have little or no leaves, the stems and roots are swollen to store water. Succulents like the cacti have spines or needles in stead of leaves to reduce water loss. Many of them produce brightly coloured flowers. They like a well drained soil and are frost tender.

Agave americana 'Marginata'
Height: 2–3 feet (60–90 centimetres). Flowering period: summer.[250]

Despite its name this succulent comes from Mexico. It is a variegated plant with rigid, fleshy green leaves with a yellow margin along the sides. The sides of the leaves have small spines with a sharp spine at the top: this terminal spine should be cut off with secateurs to avoid injury to eyes and limbs. Always wear gloves and safety glasses when working with this plant.

The plant is frost tender so grow it in a pot and move it to the greenhouse in winter. Grow it in well-drained compost and cover with a layer of gravel – try to use a terracotta pot, which allows the compost to breathe. If the plant has room to mature it can flower after a number of years, producing a flower spike up to 20 feet (6 metres) tall, covered with greenish-yellow flowers. The downside is that the plant dies after flowering but new suckers will appear shortly afterwards to replace the dead plant.

Aeonium
Height: 2–3 feet (60–90 centimetres). Flowering period: summer.[248–49]

This group of plants are quick-growing, small to medium-sized succulents that form rosettes of waxy leaves. They are natives of the Canary Islands, Madeira and North Africa. They are frost tender and will only survive short periods of frost outdoors so remove to the greenhouse in winter. They need full sun to give the best leaf colouration. *Aeonium arboreum* has light-green leaves. *Aeonium arboreum* 'Schwartzkopf' (black aeonium) has dark-purple leaves that appear almost black.

Beaucarnea recurvata (ponytail)

This is a frost-tender evergreen plant from Mexico. It has a large trunk base that can grow to the size of a football with age. From this base it produces trunks with little or no branches. It produces

Height:
12–20 feet
(3.6–6 metres).
Flowering
period:
summer.[255]

long, slender leaves at the top of the trunk. In frost-prone gardens move to the greenhouse in winter.

Beschorneria
Height: 5 feet
(1.5 metres).
Flowering
period:
summer.[256-57]

This is a group of perennial succulents that come from Mexico. *Beschorneria yuccoides* 'Quicksilver' forms a compact rosette of lance-shaped leaves that have a blue-green colour and can grow up to 2 feet (60 centimetres) long. After a while it branches at the base to form clusters of rosettes. In summer it produces a flower stalk up to 10 feet (3 metres) long. The flower stalk is bright red in colour with yellow-tinted green flowers. The plant likes a well-drained soil, enriched with humus and full sun. The plant is frost tender but can survive a few degrees of frost for a short period.

Tender Plants

The following tender plants will grow and flower, in pots, outside in the garden during the summer but most of them must be removed to a greenhouse in winter time to avoid damage by frost.

Brugmansia
(angel's
trumpet, tree
datura)
Height: 8–12
feet (2.4–3.6
metres).
Flowering
period:
summer–
autumn.[258-59]

Brugmansia is an evergreen shrub from South America. They are grown for their large, usually scented, trumpet-shaped flowers. In frost-prone gardens, grow the plant in a pot in the greenhouse and place it outside for the summer. Brugmansias may not flower the first year after planting but after that will produce waves of flowers followed by rest periods. The flowers are beautiful and come in a variety of colours, such as white, yellow, pink and red. Some flowers have an amazing scent, especially at night – for example, daturas.

We grow our brugmansias in the greenhouse, moving them out in May to a warm, sheltered spot in full sun. They will grow in full sun or partial shade. On a hot day, in full sun, they need to be watered daily – watch out for the leaves drooping. Once watered they will pick up within a few hours. Water sparingly during the winter. Prune to encourage bushy growth or limit the size of the plant.

Brugmansia sanguinea is a 12-foot (3.6 metres) high shrub from Peru. It has leaves up to 7 inches (17 centimetres) long and the flowers can be 6 inches (15 centimetres) long. The flowers are drooping trumpets, brilliant orange-red at the mouth with yellow veins and fading to yellow at the base. The flower has no scent. The plant flowers from late spring to autumn and often flowers in the greenhouse during winter. *Brugmansia sauveolens* is a native of Brazil. It has yellow or pink flowers, which are highly scented.

Brugmansias are susceptible to white fly and red spider mites when grown in the greenhouse: spray with liquid Derris to control red spider mite.

Clivia
Height: 18 inches (45 centimetres). Flowering period: spring–summer.[261]

The clivia is a member of the amaryllis family and has many common characteristics of the amaryllis. It is a native of South Africa. The plant is frost tender so it is best to grow it in a pot and move it to a greenhouse in winter. It has thick, fleshy roots that are well equipped to store water. On a mature plant the swollen roots can completely fill the pot, pushing all the compost out over the sides. When this happens the plant should be repotted – use a slightly larger pot because the plant does best when the roots are constricted. Clivias should be grown in semi-shade with the compost kept evenly moist during spring and summer. *Clivia miniata* produces yellow- or orange-coloured lily-like flowers. The flowers are produced in clusters at the top of a thick stem. Once the flowering stem has emerged, watering can be increased and the plant can be fed with a liquid fertiliser. The flowers are produced from spring to summer on stems up to 18 inches (45 centimetres) tall and can last for weeks. A mature plant will produce a number of offshoots each year and these can be removed and potted up to produce new plants.

Echium
Height: 16 feet (4.8 metres). Flowering period: summer.[267]

Echium pininana (tree echium) is a stunning plant for any sheltered border, providing a tropical touch to any garden in late spring or early summer. The plant is a native of the Canary Islands, where its flower heads can be seen growing above the laurel forests. It is a biennial plant that grows about 4 feet (1.2 metres) tall, with silvery, hairy leaves in the first year. In the second year the plant suddenly spurts into growth to produce a single flower spike up to 16 feet (4.8

metres) tall that is covered with blue funnel-shaped flowers. After flowering the plant dies and scatters its seeds, which will germinate and grow in mild gardens. In colder regions the seeds should be collected and grown in the greenhouse. Echiums can be grown in an open position in sun, in moderately fertile, well-drained soil. If the soil is too rich the plant tends to grow too much foliage and produce very few flowers. Since they are tall plants they need shelter from strong winds. Echiums are frost tender so in frost-prone gardens protect them with horticultural fleece when frost is expected. There are forty different species of echiums and they produce flowers in a range of colours, such as purple, yellow, white and red. Some species are so tender they will only survive in a greenhouse.

Epiphyllum (orchid cacti) Height: 12 inches (30 centimetres). Flowering period: summer.[269]

Epiphyllums are a group of tender cacti from Mexico that require a minimum temperature of 10°C for most of the year, which should increase to 15°C in early spring. The plant has long, scalloped-edge stems that will hang down if grown in a hanging basket. Most species produce large creamy-white flowers with a scent that will fill your conservatory with their fragrance. There are many hybrids that produce flowers in colours such as yellow, red and pale pink. Grow them in rich, porous, sandy soil in bright light and feed every two weeks with a high-potash fertiliser when the flower buds form. Allow the soil to almost dry out between watering; in winter keep soil fairly dry.

Fascicularia bicolor Height: up to 18 inches (45 centimetres). Flowering period: autumn[272]

This evergreen plant comes from Chile. It is a hardy member of the Bromeliad family and grows about 18 inches (45 centimetres) tall. Fasciculus is the Latin for bundle and a bundle of leaves is a good description for this plant which has a tight mass of narrow, prickly leaves that grow into a clump. The plant really comes into its own in autumn and winter when the green leaves change to an astonishingly vivid scarlet-red colour. A turquoise blue flower is produced at the centre of the leaves. The plant likes a poor, sharply drained soil in full sun. It will withstand low temperatures, even light frost, provided the soil does not become too wet. It is completely maintenance free and will spread into a large clump after a few years. It looks very attractive in a rock garden or raised bed.

15

64

200

Top to bottom, left to right: 1: Herbaceous borders in summer, 2: Herbaceous bed in winter, 3: Herbaceous bed in spring after shedding stalks, 4: Acanthus 'Lady Moore', 5: Aconitum carmichaelii 'Arendsii', 6: Alstroemeria, 7: Alstroemeria dwarf variety 'Little Miss Isabel', 8: Aquilegia, 9: Asters, 10: Astilbes, 11: Campanulas, 12: Cerinthe major, 13: Chrysanthemum 'Ruby Mound', 14: Cimicifuga simplex 'Brunette', 15: Cirsium rivulare.

16: Cosmos atrosanguineus, 17: Crocosmia 'Solfatare', 18: Crocosmia 'Lucifer', 19: Dahlia 'Mi Wong', 20: Dahlia 'Zoro', 21: Dahlia 'Bishop of Llandaff', 22: Delphinium, 23: Dicentra spectabilis 'Alba', 24: Dierama pulcherrimum, 25: Digitalis purpurea albiflora, 26: Eryngium bourgatii, 27: Euphorbia griffithii 'Fireglow', 28: Filipendula, 29: Francoa appendiculata, 30: Galega.

31: Gaura 'Crimson Butterflies', 32: Gazania, 33: Geranium 'Johnson's Blue', 34: Geranium 'Ann Folkard', 35: Geum coccineum, 36: Helleborus orientalis, 37: Helleborus niger, 38: Hemerocallis 'Bela Lugosi', 39: Heuchera 'Amber Wave' 40: Hosta, 41: Anemone x hybrida 'Honorine Jobert', 42: Kitaibela vitifolia, 43: Kniphofia 'Ice Queen', 44: Ligularia dentata 'Desdemona', 45: Lobelia tupa.

6: Lupins, 47: Lychnis chalcedonica, 48: Lysimachia punctata 'Alexander', 49: Meconopsis betonicifolia, 50: Mon-
da, 51: Myosotidium hortensia, 52: Paeonia, 53: Papaver orientale 'Cedric Morris', 54: Penstemon 'Sour Grapes', 55:
enstemon 'Evelyn', 56: Penstemon 'Rubicon', 57: Persicaria polymorpha, 58: Persicaria virginiana 'Painter's Palette', 59:
hlox paniculata 'Hampton Court', 60: Polygonatum multiflorum 'Striatum'.

61: Pulmonaria, 62: Pulsatilla vulgaris, 63: Rodgersia aesculifolia, 64: Rudbeckia, 65: Salvia patens 'Cambridge Blue', 66: Scabiosa, 67: Sedum spectabile 'Brilliant', 68: Solidago 'Golden Wings', 69: Thalictrum aquilegiifolium, 70: Tradescantia andersoniana 'Purewell Giant', 71: Verbascum chaixii f. album, 72: Verbena bonariensis, 73: Abutilion megapotanicum, 74: Abutilion 'Ashford Red', 75: Abutilion pictum 'Thompsonii'.

365

351

339

341

76: Acacia baileyana 'Purpurea', 77: Acer davidii 'Serpentine', 78: Japanese maple, 79: Acradenia frankliniae, 80: Aralia spinosa, 81: Arbutus unedo, 82: Aucuba japonica, 83: Berberis thunbergii 'Rose Glow', 84: Berberis thunbergii 'Aurea', 85: Silver birch, bark, 86: Buddleja davidii 'Black Knight', 87: Buddleja 'White Profusion', 88: Callistemon brachyandrus, 89: Callistemon pallidus, 90: Camellia 'Golden Spangles'.

91: Camellia x williamsii 'Donation', 92: Ceanothus, 93: Chaenomeles japonica, 94: Choisya ternata, 95: Choisya 'Aztex Pearl', 96: Cordyline australis 'Purpurea', 97: Cotinus coggygtia, 98: Coprosma repens 'Pink Splendour', 99: Cornus kousa, 100: Cornus alternifolia 'Argentea', 101: Corokia cotoneaster, berries, 102: Correa pulchella, 103: Corylus avellana 'Contorta', 104: Corokia cotoneaster, 105: Crinodendron hookerianum.

106: Daphne cneorum, 107: Davidia involuctata, 108: Davidia involuctata (close-up), 109: Deutzia, 110: Drimys winter
111: Eleagnus, 112: Embothrium coccineum, 113: Enkianthus, 114: Escallonia laevis 'Gold Brian', 115: Eucalyptus gunnii, 116: Euonymus, 117: Fatsia japonica, 118: Forsythia, 119: Fothergilla, 120: Fuchsia 'Annabel'.

121: Ginkgo biloba in autumn, 122: Grevillea robusta, 123: Griselinia littoralis 'Bantry Bay', 124: Hamamelis, 125: Hebe 'Red Edge', 126: Heliotropium arborescens, 127: Hydrangea (red flower), 128: Hydrangea (white flower), 129: Hydrangea (lacecap), 130: Ilex aquifolium 'Ferox', 131: Indigofera heterantha, 132: Laburnum, 133: Lavatera, 134: Leptospermum 'Red Damask', 135: Leptospermum 'Silver Sheen'.

136: Ligustrum japonica, 137: Liquidambar styraciflua 'Argentovariegata', 138: Liquidambar styraciflua 'Argentovariegat' bark, 139: Liriodendron tulipifera 'Aureomarginatum' leaf, 140: Liriodendron tulipifera 'Aureomarginatum' bark, 141: Luma apiculata 'Glanleam Gold', 142: Magnolia x soulangeana, 143: Magnolia stellata, 144: Mahonia x media 'Charity', 145: Malus, 146: Melianthus major, 147: Metrosideros excelsa, 148: Myrtus bullata, 149: Osmanthus heterophyllus 'Goshiki', 150: Paeonia delavayi var. ludlowii.

151: Paeonia delavayi, 152: Paulownia, 153: Perovskia atriplicifolia, 154: Philadelphus, 155: Phlomis fruticosa, 156: Photina x fraseri 'Red Robin', 157: Pieris 'Forest Flame' flower foliage, 158: Pieris 'Forest Flame' foliage, 159: Pittosporum tenuifolium 'Abbotsbury Gold', 160: Pittosporun tenuifolium 'Irene Paterson', 161: Pseudowintera colorata, 162: Pyrus salicifolia 'Pendula', 163: Quercus rubra, 164: Rhododendron 'Blue Tit', 165: Rhododendron 'Fragrantissimum'.

166: Skimmia japonica, 167: Sophora microphylla 'Goldilocks', 168: Sophora 'Little Baby', 169: Tamarix ramosissima, 170: Taxus baccata 'Fastigiata', 171: Taxus baccata 'Fastigiata Aurea', 172: Viburnum opulus, 173: Weigela florida 'Foliis Purpureis', 174: Weigela middendorffiana, 175: Bulbs at Chelsea Flower Show, 176: Agapanthus 'Royal Blue', 177: Agapanthus 'White', 178: Allium giganteum, 179: Allium cristophii, 180: Anemone coronaria 'Mr Fokker'.

181: Aurum italicum, 182: Begonias. 183: Begonia 'Anniversary', 184: Camassia leichtlinii, 185: Canna 'Striata', 186: Canna 'Durban', 187: Canna 'Stuttgart', 188: Canna 'Black Knight', 189: Colchicum, 190: Crinum x powellii 'Album', 191: Crocus, 192: Cyclamen, 193: Eremurus, 194: Erythronium, 195: Eucomis bicolour.

96: Fritillaria michailovskyi, 197: Fritillaria meleagris, 198: Fritillaria pallidiflora, 199: Fritillaria imperialis 'Aurora', 00: Galanthus, 201: Galtonia candicans, 202: Gladiolus communis subsp. byzantinus, 203: Hedychium, 204: Iris 'Professor Blaauw', 205: Lilium candidum, 206: Lilium 'African Queen', 207: Lilium 'Star Gazer', 208: Muscari armeniacum, 09: Narcissus 'Professor Einstein', 210: Narcissus 'Rip van Winkle'.

211: Narcissus 'Emperor of Ireland', 212: Nectaroscordium, 213: Nerine, 214: Nerine bowdenii, 215: Ornithogalum 'Arabicum', 216: Puschkinia scilloides, 217: Schizostylis, 218: Tigridia pavonia, 219: Trillium, 220: Tulipa 'Red Riding Hood', 221: Zantedeschia (Calla Lily), 222: Berberidopsis corallina, 223: Billardiera longiflora, 224: Clematis 'Ville de Lyon', 225: Clematis 'Multi-Blue'.

35

353

71

86

226: Clematis 'Nelly Moser', 227: Clematis 'Jackmanii', 228: Clematis 'Early Sensation', 229: Clianthus puniceus,
230: Cytisus battandieri, 231: Dregea sinenis, 232: Fremontodendron 'California Glory', 233: Hedera trained into
shape, 234: Hedera helix 'Goldheart', 235: Itea Ilicifolia, 236: Jasminum officinale, 237: Lonicera, 238: Mitraria coccine
239: Virginia Creeper in autumn, 240: Passiflora caerulea.

241: Pyracantha 'Mohave', 242: Pyracantha 'Golden Dome', 243: Rhodochiton atrosanguineum, 244: Rosa 'New Dawn', 45: Solanum jasminoides 'Albus', 246: Vitris vinifera 'Purpurea', 247: Wisteria, 248: Aeonium arboreum 'Schwartz-opf', 249: Aeonium arboreum, 250: Agave americana 'Marginata', 251: Araucaria (Monkey Puzzle), 252: Artichoke ower, 253: Artichoke fruit, 254: Astelia, 255: Beaucarnea recurvata.

256: Beschorneria 'Quicksilver', 257: Beschorneria leaves, 258: Brugmansia sanguinea, 259: Brugmansia sauveolens, 260: Chamaerops humilis, 261: Cliva miniata, 262: Cortaderia selloana, 263: Cyathea smithii, 264: Cycas revoluta, 265: Dicksonia antartica with fibreglass insulation, 266: Dicksonia antartica, 267: Echium pininana, 268: Elegia carpensis, 269: Epiphyllum laui, 270: Equisetum.

271: Fargesia nitida, 272: Fascicilaria bicolor, 273: Hart's tongue fern, 274: Helictotrichon sempervirens, 275: Hippeas-
um 'Clown', 276: Hippeastrum, 277: Japanese holly fern, 278: Japanese painted fern, 279: Lady fern, 280: Miscanthus
nensis 'Zebrinus', 281: Dicksonia antartica with new fronds, 282: Ophiopogon planiscapus 'Nigrescens', 283: Orchid,
34: Pelargonium 'Lord Brute', 285: Phoenix canariensis.

286: Phormium 'Platts Black', 287: Phormium tenax 'Jester', 288: Phyllostachys aurea, 289: Polystichum setiferum, 290: Royal fern in spring, 291: Shuttlecock fern in summer, 292: Trachycarpus fortunei 293: Xanthorrhoea (Tree Gras 294: Yucca 'Variegata', 295: Vegetable garden, 296: Basket of vegetables, 297: Aubergine, 298: Beetroot, 299: Runner beans' flower, 300: Cabbage 'Hispi'.

301: Broccoli, 302: Brussels Sprouts, 303: Carrots, 304: Celery, 305: Cucumber, 306: Leeks, 307: Lettuces, Iceberg and 'Lollo Rossa', 308: Onions, 309: Parsnips, 310: Peas, 311: Peppers, 312: Chillies, 313: Spinach, 314: Strawberries, 315: Tomato (Removing a side shoot).

316: Tomatoes, 317: Apples, 318: Cherries, 319: Grapes, 320: Pears, 321: Plums, 322: Peaches, 323: Basil, green and purple, 324: Bay tree, 325: Chervil, 326: Chives, 327: Dill, 328: Garlic, 329: Variegated lemon balm, 330: Mint.

331: Oregano, 332: Parsley, 333: Rosemary, 334: Sage, 335: Sweet Cicely, 336: Tarragon, 337: Thyme, 338: White statu with spring bulbs, 339: Garden entrance, 340: Driftwood, 341: Patio area, 342: Yew tree, 343: Lawn with herbaceous beds, 344: Grass path, 345: Griselinia hedge.

6: Lonicera nitida 'Baggensen's Gold', 347: Beech hedge in winter, 348: Lonicera nitida 'Baggensen's Gold' clipped
o ball shape, 349: Herbaceous border with paved path, 350: Garden pool, 351: Cast iron water fountain, 352: Lion's
ad water spout, 353: Red water lily, 354: Water lily with mottled leaf, 355: Rockery, 356: Large limestone, 357:
aphne and Pulsatilla, 358: Dodecatheon clevelandii (American cow slip), 359: Stone trough, 360: Stone statue with
zy paving and stone wall.

361: Terracotta statue, 362: Concrete statue, 363: Terracotta pot, 364: Gate, 365: Pergola with cobblestone path, 366: Stone steps, 367: Greenhouse, 368: Stone chips with slate design, 369: Canker, 370: Coral Spot, 371: Grey Mould (Botrytis), 372: Rust, 373: Caterpillar damage, 374: Slugit, 375: Slug damage.

376: Adult vine weevil, 377: Vine weevil grub, 378: Provado, 379: Blackspot, 380: Propagator, 381: Modular tray, 382: 'net', 383: Cutting in pot, 384: Lettuce seedlings, 385: Filling compost bin, 386: Wormery, 387: Worms at work, 388: compost cone, 389: Compost, 390: Shredder.

This is a bulbous perennial from South America that is grown for its large funnel shaped flowers. The flowers are produced in winter and spring in shades of white, pink, salmon and red; they may be bicolour or striped. The flowers are produced on leafless stems up to 18 inches (45 centimetres) tall. Some flower stems may produce four or more flowers on each stem. Thousands of gardeners grow this plant as a potted plant.

Plant the bulbs in pots in autumn with the neck and shoulders above the soil surface. The soil should be well-drained sandy soil that has been enriched with leaf-mould. Water sparingly until the bulb starts to grow; over-watering will rot the bulb. Water regularly after the foliage emerges and feed every two weeks with a liquid fertiliser. After flowering, remove the flower head but leave the hollow stalk to die back naturally before removing. Also after flowering feed the plant to build up the bulb and develop the foliage. The aim should be to grow the biggest possible bulb. Keep the plant in a warm place, like a glasshouse, but out of direct sun which can scorch the leaves. In mid-summer place the plant outside in a shady position, keep the soil just moist – during this period next year's flowers develop inside the bulb. Move the plant back to the greenhouse in the autumn before frosts arrive. During the winter keep the soil fairly dry, making sure the bulbs do not shrivel up. In late winter move the plant to a warm place. Insects love to hide in the top of the bulb and can cause lasting damage so spray with an insecticide to kill any pests present. Only re-pot bulbs when they have totally outgrown their pot which may occur after 3-5 years. Each year scrape away the top few inches of soil and replace with fresh compost. To get the plant into active growth and to produce a flowering shoot, heat is required so place the plant in a well-lit warm position. The plant produces small side bulbs that can be removed and potted up, they will flower in about three years.

Hippeastrum (Amaryllis)
Height: 18 inches (45 centimetres)
275–76

Orchids are one of the largest family of flowering plants in the world. They are considered difficult plants to grow and care for. Although many plants require expert care, there are orchids which are relatively easy to grow. The genus cymbidium is the most familiar and widely grown orchid. They are often sold by flower shops as cut flowers and the blooms can last a long time, up to two months. Orchids do not like ordinary potting compost so use a ready made

Orchids
Height: 2 feet (60 centimetres)
Flowering period: spring[283]

orchid compost or make your own using a mixture of peat moss, bark, charcoal and perlite to produce a free-draining mixture. They should be grown in terracotta pots. Over watering is the easiest and most common way to kill an orchid, they like a humid environment so stand the pot on a tray of gravel and add water to the tray. In the summer when they are growing nicely they need nutrients, water and heat. In the autumn they need plenty of light and a reduction in water. In spring when they are flowering they like lots of light and very little water. They can produce roots above the compost, these are aerial roots and don't mean the plant is pot bound. When the plant becomes too big for its pot it can be repotted into a bigger pot or divided into a number of plants and potted up. Orchids should be repotted at the start of the growing season, except for the genus cymbidium which should be repotted after flowering in spring.

Pelargonium
Height: 1–2 feet (30-60 centimetres)
Flowering period: summer–autumn.[284]

Pelargoniums are often called geraniums but they should be distinguished from the true geraniums which are popular hardy perennials. Pelargoniums originate in South Africa and are frost tender. They are grown for their bright coloured flowers which are produced from late spring until the first autumn frost. When grown in pots indoors in the right conditions they can flower all through the year. The flower colours range from white to shades of pink, red, orange and purple. Many pelargoniums are grown for their attractive coloured leaves and aromatic foliage.

Pelargonium 'Vancover Centennial' produces orange-red flowers with bronze and brown leaves.

Pelargonium 'Lord Brute' produces dark red flowers with a pinkish margin.

Pelargonium crispum 'Variegatum' has green leaves with a cream margin and produces a lemon fragrance when brushed.

Pelargoniums can be grown all year round indoors; choose a sunny position. When grown outdoors they like a well-drained soil in full sun. Deadhead regularly to prolong flowering, remove any yellowing or brown leaves. During the growing season, water thoroughly, then let the compost almost dry out before watering again. Feed plants with a liquid fertiliser every few weeks.

Phormiums are grown for their magnificent evergreen foliage which gives contrast and colour variation in the garden. The foliage is often coloured or variegated. They soon become focal points as they mature. Some varieties can grow up to 10 feet (3 metres) tall and, since you cannot cut the top without ruining the look of the plant, consider carefully where you plant them. Phormiums grow best in well-drained soil in an open, sunny position. They like lots of moisture in summer but can tolerate dry conditions, so mix lots of compost with the soil when planting. They have a reputation for being slightly tender so give them a mulch in winter in very cold gardens. Grow them in a sheltered position because the leaves can be damaged and shredded in wind. Once established, they are reliable, low-maintenance plants. Cut off any scruffy looking dead, shredded or split leaves in spring. Plants three to five years old will produce flowers; the flowering stems can be up to 7 feet (2 metres) tall. The flowers are small and insignificant, the seed pods are much more noticeable and last for months. Phormiums are widely used in flower arranging to give height to the arrangement. There are two species of phormium. *Phormium tenax* has upright leaves while *phormium cookianum* has arching leaves; both have the same colour variations.

Phormium tenax (New Zealand flax) has rigid dark green leaves up to 10 feet (3 metres) long. *Phormium tenax* 'Dazzler' has arching bronze leaves with red, orange and pink stripes, and grows about 3 feet (90 centimetres) tall. *Phormium tenax* 'Jester' has deep pinky-red coloured leaves and grows 3 feet (90 centimetres) tall. *Phormium tenax* 'Platt's Black' has almost black leaves with a yellow margin along the leaf.

Phormium
Height: 3 – 10 feet (0.9 – 3 metres).[286–87]

The tree grass is a very slow growing tree, growing about 1 centimetre each year so it can take 100 years to grow 3 feet (90 centimetre) tall. It has a black trunk made up of masses of old leaf bases held together by a natural resin. This resin was used by European settlers, who found it in Australia, to make varnishes and lacquers. Long, thin, grass-like leaves grow at the top of the trunk. The plant can grow to a height of 13 feet (3 metres) and can have branches. They can be grown in pots using a well-drained soil and a sunny location. The bottom leaves that have turned brown are cut away to expose the trunk beneath. Mature plants produce a flower stalk that can grow up to 10 feet (3 metres) tall.

Xanthorrhoea
(Grass Tree)
Height: up to 13 feet (3 metres).[293]

The vegetable garden

Tired of vegetables from the supermarket that are tasteless and deteriorate within days of purchase? Remember how fresh vegetables, just pulled from your garden, used to taste? Growing your own vegetables is not difficult and you do not need a large amount of space. Apart from the wonderful taste of your own vegetables, you know exactly what has gone into and onto your food and you do not have to worry about the sell-by-date: you will have fresh vegetables at your fingertips. In recent years the sales of vegetable seeds have increased dramatically. This may be due to food scares such as BSE and public opinion against genetic engineering – people want to control what they eat. Many people believe that organic food is good for you and tastes better. People are getting more adventurous with their cooking and eating habits – the dinner of bacon and cabbage is on the wane. Vegetables and herbs are now grown in flower borders and containers.[295]

The traditional vegetable or kitchen garden was walled in, with high brick walls, containing a number of rectangular beds, each several metres wide, in which vegetables were grown in rows. The paths between the beds were often paved or gravelled. The garden could be one acre in size and would have had a number of gardeners to maintain it, producing food for a large number of people in a great house. The French designed kitchen gardens called *potagers*. The growing space in these gardens was framed by a clipped box hedge that formed a circle around a bed or lined a pathway. This system made the maintenance of the garden much easier: these permanent

beds did not have to be tilled every spring, since you did not walk on them. The soil was just loosened with a fork and raked smooth before planting; the hedges provided shelter for the young seedlings.

For too long vegetable gardens were banished to a plot in the backyard and treated like school children – placed in orderly rows and attended to only when they became wild. When vegetables are grown in a garden designed to accentuate their beauty, they will complement your garden and you will be surprised at how many people will enjoy and take time to investigate your vegetables.[296]

If you want to treat your vegetable garden as a painter would a canvas, your job is to attract the eye and keep it engaged. Many gardeners fail to see the beauty of vegetables: but look at the feathery fronds of asparagus, the glistening leaves of ruby chard, the pristine white heads of cauliflower, the flower stalks of garlic and onions – and best of all you can eat them. Garden designers have put great imagination into designing flower gardens but have paid little attention to designing an attractive vegetable plot within a garden. Just imagine how you could design a vegetable garden with a focal point at the centre and all paths leading to that centre with a bench where you can enjoy all the beautiful vegetables around you. The beds may be triangular or circular, with different vegetables in each bed so you cannot tell at a glance what's growing where and you have the urge to roam around and check things out. Mixing things up in the vegetable garden is also a good way to confuse pests. When a variety of vegetable is planted here and there in the vegetable garden it makes it much more difficult for pests to locate a particular plant. Mixing up your plants provides different growing conditions and you can create the microclimate that best suits particular plants – full exposure to sun for tomatoes and onions; sheltered areas for lettuce and spinach. With an interesting garden layout and well-defined beds and pathways, your vegetable garden can become one of the stars of your garden. A raised bed of different coloured and textured lettuces can become a thing of beauty. Imagine how a bed of yellow tomatoes, purple basil, red peppers and Swiss chard would look. If space is limited try to grow vegetables that the family will eat. Look on vegetables as food for the eye as well as for the body.

The traditional garden is rectangular in shape, divided into four squares – the size of the squares will depend on the available space you have. A vegetable garden 15 by 20 feet (4.5 by 6 metres), the size of the average sitting-room, is big enough to grow a wide variety of vegetables and is easy to maintain. The soil in the vegetable garden needs to be well drained with the soil broken up into a fine silt that allows rapid root growth and easy access to nutrients, water and air. Digging in lots of organic material, such as homemade compost, is best because it is weed free. Most vegetables thrive in soil with a pH between 6 and 7, which is slightly acid or neutral. Soils with lots of organic matter may need the addition of garden lime to raise the pH and it will make heavy clay soils easier to work with and improve drainage. If you want organically grown vegetables you can produce satisfactory results with homemade compost on its own. Homemade compost is available to buy in most cities at the present time. If you are starting with a new garden where the soil is poor, shallow or heavy clay and wet, make a raised bed, which will improve drainage and give better yield. In new gardens where the soil is poor, a mixture of topsoil and sub-soil, it may take a few years to get the right conditions to grow vegetables. However, once you get the conditions right, growing your favourite vegetables will become very easy. Once you have prepared the soil for vegetables, cover the whole bed or row with a sheet of black plastic to prevent the rain leaching out nutrients from the soil. In new gardens with heavy clay soil it is good practice to roughly dig the soil in late autumn or early spring – this will expose the soil to frost and hungry birds. The frost will break apart the big clods of soil that occur in heavy soils and the birds will feed on the exposed insect eggs.

Rotation

Rotation is a term often used with growing vegetables, meaning you should never grow vegetables in the same piece of ground year after year. You should rotate your crops each year to prevent a build up of disease and pests. The easiest way to do this is to divide your vegetable garden into four sections, however big or small. Make sure the paths between the beds are wide enough to walk on and have a hard surface, such as paving slabs, to stop your feet getting muddy. In section 1, grow all the brassicas; in section 2 the root crops such as carrots, beetroot, celery; in section 3 the alliums like onions and leeks; and in section 4 the salads like lettuces, spinach, tomatoes. Move the crops around to a different section in subsequent years so that the same plants will only grow in a section once every four years.

Vegetable seed

Most vegetables can be grown from seed. A lot of information is given on seed packets about sowing time, distance between plants and so on, so read them carefully. The seeds may be raised in the greenhouse or sown directly into the ground. When sowing directly into the ground it is best to cover the ground with plastic a few weeks previously to increase soil temperatures. Many vegetable plants can be purchased from your local garden centre and planted directly into the ground.

Aubergines
Sow seed in: early spring
Harvesting time: late summer.[297]

These can be grown in the greenhouse. Sow the seed in early spring and when the seedlings are 4 inches (10 centimetres) tall transfer them to 8-inch (20-centimetre) pots or growing bags. Pinch out the growing tip to produce bushy plants. Feed every two weeks with a liquid fertiliser. Thin out the small fruit to leave about six fruits on each plant.

Beetroot
Sow seed in: late spring
Harvesting time: late summer.[298]

Beetroot can be grown outdoors in the garden. Sow the seeds directly into the ground in late spring when the soil has warmed up. Sow the seeds in rows, 12 inches (30 centimetres) apart. When the seedlings are a few inches tall thin them out to leave 3 inches (8 centimetres) between the plants. In dry weather water the soil to prevent drying out. 'Red Ace' is a common crop variety with a good dark-red colour.

Beans
Sow seed in: spring
Harvesting time: summer.[299]

Broad beans, French beans and runner beans are the common types of beans grown in the garden. Broad beans need support: place two stakes at the end of each row and tie strings on to them at intervals of 12 inches (30 centimetres). Sow the seeds singly in spring, when the soil is warm and dry – the seeds can rot if the soil is too wet. They like a well-drained soil with compost mixed in. Pick the pods when they are about 3 inches (8 centimetres) long and cook them whole – do not allow them to become tough. If the pods get too big remove the beans from the shell.

French beans are sown outdoors when the danger of frost is over or they may be sown in pots in the greenhouse and transplanted out later. They also need support – dwarf varieties can grow 20 inches (50 centimetres) tall. Water in summer when the pods are developing. Pick the pods when they are young – if they are left too long they become stringy.

Runner beans can grow up to 10 feet (3 metres) tall so they need good support – they look great climbing up a wigwam made of canes. They also have attractive scarlet flowers. They like a deep, rich soil – do not sow beans in the same piece of ground each year. To produce an early crop sow seeds in pots in the greenhouse in late spring and plant out when the danger of frost is over. Pick the pods when they are 6–8 inches (15–20 centimetres) long. The more you pick, the more the plant will produce.

Brassicas

Sow seed in: spring
Harvesting time: summer–autumn.[300]

Brassicas include a range of vegetables such as cauliflower, cabbage, Brussels sprouts and broccoli. All of these can be grown from seed sown in the greenhouse in spring and planted out later in the garden or from plants bought at garden centres. They all like a fertile, well-drained soil that has been enriched with well-rotted compost. To avoid disease rotate them so that they grow in the same ground once every four years. If the soil is acidic, spread lime and dig it in

There are varieties of cabbage that will crop throughout the year. 'Greyhound' and 'Hispi' will produce small pointed heads from late spring to autumn. Savoy cabbage such as 'January King' will crop from autumn to winter. 'Red Jewel' has large, tightly packed hearts of ruby-red leaves. It is an excellent cabbage to bring colour to the vegetable garden and lasts a long time. It crops from late summer to autumn. Plant cabbage seedling 12 inches (30 centimetres) apart, firm the soil around each plant and water in dry weather.

Broccoli

Sow seed in: spring.
Harvesting time: summer–autumn.[301]

Broccoli is available in green or purple heads. 'Trixie' is a club-root resistant variety that produces green heads from summer to autumn. Seed should be sown in spring. 'Late purple sprouting' grows about 3 feet (90 centimetres) tall, producing purple heads from early summer on. Broccoli should be cut when the buds are small and tightly closed, before the whole head begins to loosen out

and produce yellow flower heads. Water plants regularly, especially during dry spells.

Brussels sprouts are slow-growing plants that take up to six months to mature. They are very hardy and will crop in winter when very few other vegetables are available in the garden. Transplant young seedlings outdoors in late spring or early summer, spacing them 18 inches (45 centimetres) apart. Plant them deeply and earth up the stems as they grow to provide stability – they can grown up to 30 inches (75 centimetres) tall. If they are grown in an exposed site they may be supported with a stake. Apply a liquid fertiliser in late summer if the plants are not growing vigorously. Remove any withered or diseased leaves from the stems as they appear.

Pick the lowest sprouts first by snapping them off the base – the sprouts further up the stem will continue to develop. Their flavour improves after they have been exposed to some frost. To avoid damage in winter the sprouts can be picked and placed in the freezer. 'Carus' is an F1 hybrid that produces a high yield of large, smooth sprouts with an excellent taste. Three or four plants will produce plenty of sprouts for the average family.

Brussels sprouts
Sow seed in: late spring
Harvesting time: winter.[302]

Cauliflower have creamy white heads or curds. They take a long time to mature – the summer varieties take four months while the winter ones take ten months. They do not like direct sun – the summer varieties can lose their white colour very fast. The winter and spring varieties are the best to grow and mature when there is little else in the garden. Sow seed of winter varieties like 'Walcheren winter 3-armado' in late spring in the greenhouse and transplant out in summer, 2 feet (60 centimetres) apart. It is important that the young seedlings start growth without any distribution, to prevent the plant bolting or going to flower. They need regular watering during the growing season.

Cauliflower
Sow seed in: late spring
Harvesting time: spring.

Carrots like a well-drained, sandy soil that has been well dug and broken up. If the soil is lumpy the carrots will produce deformed, forked roots. They like plenty of sunlight. Grow them in soil that was manured for a previous crop, such as brassicas, as they can also

Carrots
Sow seed in: late spring.[303]

Harvesting time: late summer– autumn.

produce forked roots if grown in freshly manured soil. Cover the soil with plastic a week before sowing to increase soil temperature and speed up germination.

Carrot seeds are tiny and difficult to handle. Sow them thinly in drills, in late spring, 0.5 inches (1 centimetre) deep and 9 inches (23 centimetres) apart, and cover them with soil. Place horticultural fleece over the bed to prevent carrot fly and leave in place until the seedlings are well up. Thin the seedlings to 2 inches (5 centimetres) apart when they are large enough to handle and replace the fleece for a few weeks. 'Early Nantes' is quick to mature with medium-length roots. The carrot fly is a common pest of carrots – the larvae of the fly tunnel into the roots to produce a rusty-brown colour on the outside. The problem can be solved by placing a frame covered with fleece, 2 feet (60 centimetres) high, around the bed of carrots. The carrot fly is low flying and cannot get over the fleece barrier.

Celery
Sow seed in: early spring
Harvesting time: autumn– winter.[304]

There are two types of celery: trench grown and self-blanching. Trench grown must be earthed up as the stems grow to blanch them so that they are white. They are grown in long rows and are harvested between mid-autumn and winter. Self-blanching is grown in blocks instead of long rows, so the plants shield each other from the light. Only the plants on the outside need shading with a collar of black plastic or cardboard. Blanching produces longer, crisper and more tender stems with a less bitter flavour than if they were exposed to light.

Sow seeds in the greenhouse in early spring – do not cover the seeds as light helps germination – and transplant them out in early summer. They like a rich soil that has been enriched with well-rotted compost. Plant the self-blanching plants 10 inches (25 centimetres) apart in each direction to form a block. They need adequate water during the entire growing season. Plant the trench-grown plants in a trench that is 6 inches (15 centimetres) below ground level; pile the earth from the trench on either side. Draw the earth up around the stems when they are 12 inches (30 centimetres) tall. Loosely tie black plastic or cardboard around the stems. Continue to earth up around the plants for about six weeks. Be careful not to earth up higher than the base of the green leaves. 'Lathom Self-Blanching' is a high-yielding variety with long stringless sticks of crispy celery.

ucumbers may be grown in the greenhouse or planted outdoors. 'Carmen F1 hybrid' is a greenhouse variety while 'Burpless Tasty Green F1 hybrid' is an outdoor variety. Sow the seeds in mid-spring in 3-inch (8-centimetre) pots; place three seeds in each pot and thin out to one plant when they germinate. Transplant indoor varieties to a large pot or grow bag and fix a vertical stake beside each plant. When the plant has reached the glasshouse roof pinch out the tip of the leading shoot to encourage the growth of lateral shoots. Water the plants frequently during hot weather and spray the inside of the glasshouse daily with water to increase humidity.

Grow outdoor varieties in a sunny position in well-drained soil that has been enriched with compost to retain moisture. Plant them 24 inches (60 centimetres) apart when all risks of frost are over and keep well watered. Pinch out the growing point when six leaves are produced and train the new shoots along a cane or support. Water around the plant to keep the soil continually moist. Feed them regularly with a liquid fertiliser. Harvest the cucumbers before they reach full size for improved flavour and vitamin content.

Cucumber
Sow seed in:
mid spring
Harvesting
time:
summer.[305]

eeks like a fertile, moisture-retentive soil with lots of compost mixed with it. They need a long growing season – they can take up to five months to harvest. The seeds may be sown directly into the ground in spring or sown in modules, a seed tray divided into sections, and placed in the greenhouse. Transplant the seedlings outdoors, spacing the plants 4 to 6 inches (10 to 15 centimetres) apart. Leeks can be harvested from autumn through to spring. Leeks do not store well when lifted out of the ground. 'Oarsman' is an F1 hybrid that produces long white stems.

Leeks
Sow seed in:
spring
Harvesting
time: autumn–
spring.[306]

ettuces are one of the easiest vegetables to grow, as they do well in almost any soil. They are quick growing and easy to care for. If planted at regular intervals they will provide a succession of delicious plants all summer long. To produce an early crop sow seeds in the greenhouse in spring using modules. When they are large enough to handle transplant them outside, spacing them 9 inches (23 centimetres) apart. Lettuces grow best in moist, well-drained soil with plenty of compost added in. Water them well after planting.

Lettuces
Sow seed in:
spring
Harvesting
time: summer–
autumn.[307]

There are a number of varieties to choose from, such as cos, iceberg and butterhead. 'All the Year Round' is a butterhead variety with pale-green leaves that is quick to mature and can be grown under cloches in the autumn. 'Triumph' is an iceberg variety with crispy, curled leaves. 'Lollo Rossa' is a loose-leaf variety with frilled, deep-red-coloured leaves. 'Little Gem' is a cos variety that is quick maturing with small, sweet, crisp leaves. Lettuces can bolt easily, producing long, thick stems that are bitter and useless for eating. This is often caused by poor soil and lack of water. Slugs can be another menace.

Onions
Sow seed in: early or mid spring
Harvesting time: autumn.[308]

Onions can be grown from seed or sets. The seeds take about a year to mature while sets will mature in about five months. Sets are easier to handle, quicker to grow and no thinning or transplanting is required. Onions grow best in full sun in well manured soil.

Plant the sets in early or mid-spring when the soil conditions are suitable. Never plant the sets in cold or wet soil. Space the sets in drills 4 inches (10 centimetres) apart and cover with soil so that only the tips are showing. Firm the soil around the sets and cover with horticultural fleece to prevent birds lifting the bulbs; the fleece will also provide shelter from wind and increase soil temperatures. Check the onion bed a week later and replant any sets that have been lifted out of the soil as the roots grow. Make sure that they have enough water: if the soil dries out the sets will bolt and go to flower. If flower heads appear remove them at once. When the outer leaves of the onions turn yellow and the leaves bend over, growth for the season is over. Lift the onions about two weeks later and dry them off in a sunny place. Hang the bulbs in a dry, cool place. 'Red Baron' produces red-skinned onions that are very attractive in salads.

Shallots are smaller than onions and grow in clusters of up to ten bulbs. They are used for flavouring or pickling rather than as a vegetable. Their growing and storage conditions are similar to onions.

Spring Onions
Sow seed in: late spring
Harvesting time: summer– autumn

Spring onions are used in salads. 'White Lisbon' is a widely grown cultivar that is used when young. Sow the seed outdoors in late spring in rows 4 inches (10 centimetres) apart. Thin them out if larger onions are required. Water in dry conditions. They are ready for picking after two months.

Parsnips are a hardy crop that like a deep soil free of stones. Sow the seed directly into the ground in drills half an inch (1 centimetre) deep and in rows 12 inches (30 centimetres) apart. They need a long growing season so sow them as soon as the soil is workable in spring, but not in cold or wet soil. Germination can be very slow if soil is not warm. Covering the bed with horticultural fleece will help to increase soil temperatures. Thin out the seedlings to 4 inches (10 centimetres) apart.

Parsnips can be grown in pots in the greenhouse and transplanted outside before the tap roots develop. They take about four months to mature. They can be left in the ground over winter and lifted as required – frost can improve their flavour. Parsnip canker produces reddish-brown rough patches around the top of the root. There is no cure for it so choose varieties that are resistant to it, such as 'Gladiator' or 'White Gem'. Adding lime to the soil to raise its pH and rotating the crop yearly can reduce the risk.

Parsnips
Sow seed in: spring in dry, warm soil
Harvesting time: autumn–winter.[309]

Peas are tall-growing plants that need supports to climb up through – use twiggy branches or string between posts. They can grow up to 6 feet (1.8 metres) tall, depending on the variety. They cling onto supports with tendrils. Peas like a well-drained soil enriched with well-rotted garden compost; they do not like cold, wet soil or drought.

Sow seeds in the greenhouse or outdoors when soil temperatures are above 10°C. The plants have nitrogen-fixing nodules in their roots, which increase the nitrate content of the soil. Sow the seeds 1 inch (2.5 centimetres) deep in spring in three staggered rows, 2 to 3 inches (5 to 7.5 centimetres) apart. They will germinate poorly if soil is cold and wet. When the seedlings are a few inches tall use twiggy sticks to encourage the plants to climb. When the plants are growing strongly put in final supports, like wire or plastic mesh or netting between solid supports. Give the plants a constant supply of water, especially during dry spells and at flowering time to encourage the pods to develop. Harvest the pods when the seeds are well developed – the pods at the base ripen first. 'Greensage' produces pods over 4 inches (10 centimetres) long with an average of eight to eleven peas per pod.

Peas
Sow seed in: spring, when soil temperature above 10°C
Harvesting time: summer.[310]

Peppers and chillies
Sow seed in: early spring
Harvesting time: summer–autumn.[311–12]

These are relatives of the tomato and need similar conditions so they are usually grown in a greenhouse. Sow the seeds in a greenhouse in early spring and transplant into 9-inch (23-centimetre) pots or grow bags. Support each plant with a 3-foot (90-centimetres) cane and tie the plants to the cane with a string. Apply a liquid fertiliser every two weeks after the first fruits appear. Spray the greenhouse with water daily to increase humidity and discourage red spider mites. Green peppers are ready for picking in late summer or you can wait until they ripen to red. 'Jumbo Sweet' is an F1 hybrid that produces giant peppers. 'Inferno' is a moderately hot chilli that produces a big crop over a long season.

Spinach
Sow seed in: spring
Harvesting time: summer.[313]

Spinach is a fast-growing plant with highly nutritious leaves that can be eaten lightly cooked or raw in salads. Sow seeds thinly in drills half an inch (1 centimetre) deep and cover with soil in spring. Spinach likes a rich, moist, well-drained soil. For a continuous crop, sow in succession every few weeks. Thin the seedlings to 2 inches (5 centimetres) apart when large enough to handle. The leaves can be harvested as required by removing a number of leaves from each plant. 'Scenic' is an F1 hybrid that produces a heavy crop of dark-green leaves.

Strawberries
Sow plants in: June to September
Harvesting time: summer–autumn.[314]

Strawberries are one of the most popular fruits that can be grown in the garden. They are low-growing plants that take up little space. They can be grown in the traditional terracotta strawberry pot, which has planting pockets on the side for the plants, and placed on the patio. There are different varieties of strawberries that fruit from June to August. Perpetual strawberries, such as 'Aromel', produce a succession of crops from early summer to mid-autumn. Summer fruiters, such as 'Elsanta', will produce one crop in summer. Alpine strawberries, such as 'Fraise des Bois', produce small dark-red berries from early summer to late autumn.

Strawberries like a sunny position and rich, well-drained soil with plenty of well-rotted compost added to it. Change the location of the plants every three years to prevent the build-up of pests and disease. Replace plants every two to three years and remove the old ones. Plant strawberry plants between June and September to get a good

crop of fruit the following year. Water the plants thoroughly after planting and during dry spells. When they have finished producing fruit in the autumn, clean up the strawberry bed. Remove unwanted runners and the old leaves, to allow more sun into the centre of the plant. Strawberries produce runners in midsummer and these can be pegged down into the soil to produce new plants.

Tomatoes
Sow seed in: spring
Harvesting time: summer–autumn.[315–16]

Tomatoes are tender plants that are usually grown in a greenhouse. Some varieties will grow outdoors in a sheltered, sunny position against a south-facing wall. Sow seeds in the greenhouse in spring and transplant to 9-inch (23-centimetre) pots or grow bags.

Tomato plants may be purchased in your local garden centre. Support each plant with a tall stake and tie the plant onto it. Remove side shoots regularly by pinching them out with your finger and thumb or cutting them with a knife. Pinch out the top of the stem when plants reach the glasshouse roof. Water plants regularly, and when the first truss of fruit forms feed the plant with a liquid tomato fertiliser every two weeks. Outdoor varieties can be planted out in the garden when the risk of frost is over. 'Tumbler' is a dwarf variety, producing cherry-sized fruit, that can be grown outdoors in a hanging basket or container; it needs no staking. 'Moneymaker' is a tall-growing variety, producing a heavy crop, that can be grown in the greenhouse or outdoors.

Fruit trees

A wide variety of fruit trees, such as apple, plum and cherry, can be grown in a small garden. These trees can be trained to grow along a wall as espaliers or fan shapes. An espalier has a single central stem with pairs of horizontal branches on each side tied onto support wires on a wall. These horizontal branches contain the fruiting spurs. Buy an espalier trained tree from your garden centre. A fan-trained tree has branches radiating out from the base in the form of a fan. The branches are tied onto support wires on a wall.

Apples
Planting time: autumn–spring.
Harvesting time: autumn.[317]

Apple trees may be trained into an espalier or fan shape to grow against a wall or, if space is available, they can be grown as a bush. The Coronet miniature apple tree is a small tree that grows to a maximum of 5 feet (1.5 metres) tall and 3 feet (90 centimetres) in diameter. It can be planted into the ground or grown in a pot. The plant is five years old when purchased so it is trained and requires the minimum of pruning. Some varieties of the Coronet tree produce two different types of apples on the same tree. Coronet apple trees are produced by Springfield Nurseries in Dungarvan. Apple trees are grafted onto a number of different rootstocks, which determine the size and vigour of the tree. Most apple trees need a second variety of tree that flowers at the same time for cross-pollination to occur.

Apple trees are planted between late autumn and early spring. They like full sunshine, good fertile soil and some shelter from cold winds. Make sure the graft union at the base of the stem is at least 4 inches (10 centimetres) above soil level to prevent suckers growing from the rootstock. If planting the trees against a wall place them 9 to 12 inches (23 to 30 centimetres) away from the base of the wall. Water well during dry spells in the first year of growth. Apply a mulch of well-rotted compost and sulphate of potash around the base of the tree in spring. Bush trees should be pruned in winter when they are dormant. Remove any dead, dying or diseased branches. Remove branches that are crossing over each other and branches that are growing into the middle of the tree to allow sunlight into the centre.

There are two kinds of cherries, sweet and sour. The sweet cherries are eaten fresh; the sour cherries are used to make jam and for cooking. Cherry trees are large trees so it is best to train them into a fan-shape against a wall. Pick a variety that is self-pollinating and grown on a dwarf rootstock. Sweet cherries need a warm, sheltered position to produce a good crop. They need a deep, well-drained soil. Sweet cherries are ready for picking in midsummer.

Cherries
Planting time: autumn. Harvesting time: mid-summer.[318]

Vines need a warm environment, such as a greenhouse, to produce and ripen their fruit. The vine may be planted inside or outside the greenhouse. Plant it at one end of the house in soil that has been enriched with compost. Set support wires up the side of the house and along the roof. Tie the main stem onto the support wires and cut back the lateral branches to five or six leaves.

Grapes
Planting time: autumn–spring. Harvesting time: autumn.[319]

Vines are fast growing – over a period of three to four years the main stem will have grown up the side of the greenhouse and along the roof. At this stage cut back the tip of the main stem. In winter cut back all lateral branches to the main stem. In spring allow two shoots to develop at each spur on the main stem and remove the rest. When the flower trusses develop in summer, allow one to grow on each lateral stem and remove the rest. Prune the lateral stem at two leaves beyond the flower truss. Any lateral stems that produced no flowers are cut back to five leaves from the main stem. Pinch out any sub-laterals that grow from the lateral stems. In summer when the fruit is starting to set, thin the berries to give them room to develop.

Peaches can be grown outdoors in mild gardens. They are best trained into a fan-shape on a south-facing wall, where they will get the maximum sun. They like a deep, fertile, slightly acid soil. They start growth very early so plant new trees before the middle of winter if possible. Water thoroughly during the growing season – the soil dries out very quickly near walls in warm weather. They produce blossoms early in spring when few insects and bees are around. They can be pollinated by hand, using a soft brush to transfer the pollen from one flower to another. To produce large fruits, thinning may be necessary. Thin the fruit out to one fruit per cluster. Peach trees bear fruit on shoots produced the previous year. Cut back each stem that

Peaches
Planting time: autumn. Harvesting time: summer.[322]

has produced fruit after the fruit has been picked. In spring remove any branches growing across each other and any damaged branches, cutting them back to just above a healthy shoot.

Peach-leaf curl is a common problem with fan-shaped trees. Spray the plant with Dithane 945 or any traditional copper fungicide. Spray the leaves before they fall and again from January to February, repeating the spray every ten to fourteen days. Make sure the spray runs down the bark and fills the crevices where the spores hide. The disease is spread by rain running into the buds as they swell. If grown as a fan-shaped tree against a wall, try covering the plant with plastic and leave both ends open for ventilation.

Pears
Planting time: autumn–spring.
Harvesting time: autumn.[320]

Pears need similar growing conditions to apples but they need more consistent heat to crop well. They produce blossoms earlier than apples so they need a more sheltered position. Like apple trees, you need two different varieties for cross-pollination.

Plums
Planting time: autumn–spring.
Harvesting time: autumn.[321]

Plum trees are usually vigorous trees that can produce a large amount of fruit on young trees. They take up a lot of space so grow them as bushes or fan-shapes trained against a wall. Choose a self-pollinating variety grafted onto a semi-dwarf rootstock. Plums grow best in full sun with shelter from wind. Plant plum trees any time from late autumn to early spring. They like a well-drained soil that has been enriched with compost. Plant a fan-shaped tree 9 inches (23 centimetres) from the base of a wall, spread out the branches of the fan evenly and tie onto support wires attached to the wall. The blossoms on fan-shaped trees can be protected against frost by covering them with fleece.

Herbs

People have used herbs for thousands of years as medicines, cosmetics, dyes, insect repellents and especially to add those wonderful flavours to meals. Herbs are not fussy about soil type but they do like a light, sandy well-drained soil in the sun. In these conditions they will produce the highest level of the aromatic oils that give them their smell and taste. Herbs can be grown in pots and containers placed near the kitchen door, where they are handy for the cook – you will not have to trek down to the bottom of the garden in a blizzard for your favourite herb. Herbs, due to their smell, can be used to deter pests that attack other plants near them. A herb garden can look very well as part of the vegetable garden.

A beautiful effect can be created by planting the herbs in a draughtboard style. The herbs are planted in the black squares and crazy paving laid on the white squares to form steps to pick the different herbs. The size of the squares will depend upon the amount of space you have available. Herbs are also planted in a cartwheel pattern – different herbs are planted in each segment of the wheel. Grow the taller herbs, such as fennel, rosemary and sage, at the back with the smaller ones, such as chives, mint and thyme, towards the front. If space is limited, herbs can be grown in pouchs hung on a wall – each pouch can grow four different herbs. The seeds of most herbs are sown in March in a warm place, such as the greenhouse or kitchen window-sill. When the seeds have grown they are hardened off and planted out 6 inches (15 centimetres) apart. Most herbs can be bought from your local garden centre in pots, ready for planting out when the weather and soil conditions are suitable.

Herbs can be classified as annuals (grow for one year only), such as basil, coriander, marjoram and parsley; perennials, such as mint, fennel and thyme; woody perennials, such as rosemary, lavender, bay and sage; and bulbs, such as chives. Some perennials, such as mint, are a bit too vigorous for their own good. To keep them under control try planting them in a large pot and sinking the pot into the ground.

Basil
323

There are a number of varieties of basil such as bush basil (*Ocimum minimum*), sweet basil (*Ocimum basilicum*), lemon basil, sweet basil and purple-leaf basil. Basil is generally grown in a warm place, such as a greenhouse or kitchen window. As the seedlings grow cut the tops of the stems to create a compact plant. Basil is a delicious herb, especially with tomatoes. It also adds great flavour to chicken, vegetable dishes and salad. It is a major ingredient in pesto.

Bay tree (*Laurus nobilis*)
324

The bay tree is a large evergreen tree that can grow to 40 feet (12 metres) tall. The leaves are dark green, tough and very aromatic. Mature plants produce small greenish-white flowers in spring and are followed by small black berries. It likes a well-drained soil in full sun, though it will grow in semi-shade. The plant can tolerate drought, wind and even salt spray.

Bay trees are often grown in pots and they are often trained into topiary specimens, such as spirals or cones. Bay leaves are used to flavour many meat and fish dishes. In ancient Rome a wreath of bay leaves was used as a high honour for heroes and scholars, hence the terms 'resting on your laurels' and 'poet laureate'.

Chervil (*Anthriscus cerefolium*)
325

This is a biennial herb that is generally treated as an annual. It has fine fern-like foliage that resembles parsley but has a subtle aniseed flavour. Sow the seeds where the plant is to grow and carefully thin out later. The plant will not thrive in full sun so a semi-shaded location is needed. The soil needs to be rich with organic humus and kept moist. Chervil can also be grown in a pot. The plant produces flowers in the summer and dies after flowering, so to prolong the life of the plant remove the flowers as soon as they appear.

Chervil can be used to flavour soups and egg and vegetable dishes. It should be used fresh and added in the last minutes of cooking to preserve the flavour.

Chives (*Allium schoenoprasum*)
326

Chives grow as a grassy clump. The round, hollow foliage has a mild onion flavour and the plants make a nice edging plant in the garden, especially if allowed to flower. The flowers are a very attractive pompon shape and mauve in colour. Chives grow from seeds sown in

spring. Clumps of bulbs can be divided in winter and this should be done every few years to prevent clumps becoming congested. Do not allow plants used for the kitchen to flower – cut off all the flowering stems. Pick chives stems from the base and use fresh in egg, chicken and vegetable dishes and in soups and sauces.

Coriander is an annual herb with fine foliage and a fresh spicy flavour. It is sometimes called Chinese Parsley. It likes a position where there is morning sun and dapple shade in the afternoon. Sow seeds in the spring and stake the plant to prevent it falling over in the wind. Water well and fertilise with a liquid feed during the growing season. The plant will quickly produce flowers and seeds if grown in full sun. Coriander is used extensively in Thai cooking and is an essential ingredient in curry powders and mixed spices. It is particularly delicious in chicken, fish and vegetable dishes.

Coriander (*Coriandrum sativum*)

Cress is an annual herb with a sharp peppery taste. Cress is probably the quickest and easiest herb to grow and is often grown indoors in a pot on a brightly lit window-sill. The seed will germinate in a few days and the cress can be used once it has developed a few leaves – the leaves are cut with a scissors. It is a great plant to get children interested in growing seeds. Cress seeds are often mixed with mustard seeds and both leaves used together. The leaves are very nutritious and can be used in salads, soups and egg sandwiches.

Cress (*Lepidium sativum*)

Dill is a feathery-leafed annual that grows to 3 feet (90 centimetres) in height. The plant produces yellow flowers in summer. Sow seed in a sunny position, sheltered from strong winds, in a soil enriched with humus. Keep plants well watered. The plant may self-seed. Dill leaves can be used in most dishes but are particularly used in fish and potato recipes.

Dill (*Anethum graveolens*)
327

The elderberry is a deciduous tree or shrub that grows up to 12 feet (3.6 metres) tall with attractive serrated leaves. The plant produces white flowers in summer followed by shiny purple-black

Elderberry (*Sambucus nigra*)

berries in the autumn. Plant in a sunny or semi-shaded position in moist, rich soil. The berries are used in jams and jellies and to make elderberry wine.

French Sorrel (*Rumex scutatus*)

This is a perennial herb that grows into a clump. The leaves are similar to those of the common dock weed. It grows about 2 feet (60 centimetres) tall, producing terminal small flowers in summer. Flower spikes should be removed as soon as they appear to keep the plant growing vigorously and the leaves fresh and tender. It likes a well-drained soil in a sunny position. The plant is high in vitamin C, has a sharp taste and is used in salads, soup and sauces.

Garlic (*Allium sativum*)
328

Garlic is a perennial bulb. It forms a compound bulb made up of many individual cloves or small bulbs. Each of these cloves is capable of growing into a new plant and producing another compound bulb. The flat grass-like leaves are tasty but removing the leaves will result in smaller clusters of bulbs. Garlic cloves are planted in early spring in free-draining soil enriched with compost. Good drainage is important so plant in raised beds if the soil is heavy clay. Plant the individual cloves just below the surface of the soil. When the leaves turn brown in late summer or autumn the bulbs are dug up with a fork and dried off in an airy shed. Garlic is a favourite flavouring in many dishes. Apart from its wonderful flavour, many people believe that garlic is a useful preventative of disease. Garlic can be grown among roses to reduce attacks of aphids.

Lavender (*Lavandula augustifolia*)

English lavender is generally regarded as having the best perfume of all lavenders. There are hundreds of cultivars available and most of them are grown as ornamental plants. English lavender will grow to about 2 feet (60 centimetres) tall, has silvery-grey leaves and produces mauve-coloured flower spikes on tall, slender stems. Varieties are available that produce white, pink and deep-purple flowers. Lavenders like a well-drained soil in full sun. The plant is available from garden centres in pots. After several years the plant tends to become woody and should be replaced with new plants. A light pruning of the foliage after flowering is recommended. The

plant does not like being pruned back into old wood. Many English gardens use lavender as an edging plant for borders – brushing against the plant as you walk by releases the beautiful perfume of the plant. English lavender is used for a wide range of scented products, such as cosmetics, soaps, lavender pillows and pot pourri. Lavender flowers have been used to keep drawers and clothes smelling fresh and to repel moths. In the garden lavender is highly ornamental and is a good companion plant for vegetables and fruit trees because it will repel insects.

Lemon balm (*Melissa officinalis*)
330

This soft-leafed perennial has leaves with a pleasant lemon aroma. Lemon balm likes a rich, moist soil in semi-shade. It is a spreading plant that can become invasive so it is best to plant it in a pot in the ground. The leaves can be used to add a lemon tang to salads, drinks and desserts.

Lemongrass (*Cymbopogon citratus*)

Lemongrass is a perennial grass that grows into a clump about 4 feet (1.2 metres) tall. The plant needs a sunny, sheltered location with protection from the mid-day sun. It likes a well-drained soil enriched with humus. This is a tropical plant and it will not survive frost so it is best to grow in a container and move to the greenhouse in winter. Lemongrass is a must for Thai cooking – it adds a tangy flavour to curries and stir-fries.

Mint (*Mentha*)
330

There are many species of mint, such as applemint, peppermint, spearmint and gingermint. They all have a creeping habit and produce a highly aromatic fresh-tasting foliage. Mint generally likes semi-shade in moist but not waterlogged soil. It can become invasive so grow in a pot buried in the ground. Spearmint (*Menta spicata*) is a popular flavouring for sauces and dressings. Mint is a traditional flavouring for lamb.

Mustard (*Brassica nigra*)

Black mustard is an annual herb that can grow up to 5 feet (1.5 metres) tall. The plant produces four-petalled bright-yellow flowers in summer, which are followed by pods that contain the black mustard seeds. The plant can become a weed so remove the seed pods before the plant self-seeds itself around the garden. The pods are placed in a paper bag until they dry out and split. The seeds are then crushed and used to flavour meat and vegetable dishes. Black mustard is the favoured ingredient of French mustard.

**Oregano
(*Origanum vulgare*)**
331

This perennial herb forms a low, creeping mound. The soft lime-green leaves are highly aromatic and the plant can also be used in the ornamental garden, where it makes attractive ground cover. It produces small white flowers. It can be grown from seed planted in spring – sow seed in pots and transplant later. Oregano likes a poor, free-draining soil in a sunny location. It can survive drought so is ideal for a rock garden. Cut back the old foliage in spring to promote a fresh flush of foliage. The herb can be used in pizzas, lasagne, pesto and pasta.

**Parsley
(*Petroselinum crispum*)**
332

Parsley is the mainstay of the vegetable garden. Parsley is a biennial herb with curled green leaves. There are two main types of parsley: curled and flat leaf. The curled is good for garnishing while the flat leaf looks elegant on a plate and has a better flavour. Parsley likes a well-drained, rich soil in a sunny location. If grown in a container it needs a tall pot because it has a long tap root. Parsley seed can be slow to germinate – soaking the seeds before sowing can assist germination. It is used to flavour vegetable dishes and soups and is a traditional garnish. The herb is very nutritious, with high iron and vitamin levels.

**Rosemary
(*Rosmarinus officinalis*)**
333

Rosemary is an erect shrub with dark-green, spiky, narrow leaves and produces blue flowers. It likes a sunny, well-drained sandy soil and once established is very hardy and long lived. It can be used to create a dense hedge. Rosemary has a very pungent flavour and should be used with discretion. It is the traditional flavouring for lamb dishes and in the stuffing of the Christmas turkey.

Sage (*Salvia officinalis*)334

Sage is a perennial herb with large grey-green leaves that grows about 2 feet (60 centimetres) tall. It produces purple flowers in

the autumn. It thrives in light, sandy soils in full sun. Sage has a strong flavour and should be used sparingly. It is traditionally used in stuffings for meats, especially pork and poultry.

Summer savoy (*Satureja hortensis*)

Summer savoy is an annual with slender reddish stems and soft leaves. It can be grown from seeds sown in spring and germinates easily. It will grow in a pot or well-drained soil in a sunny location. It is recommended for all types of bean dishes because it tends to reduce flatulence!

Sweet Cicely (*Myrrhis odorata*)
335

This is a large, long-lived herbaceous perennial that can grow up to 4 feet (1.2 metres) in height and width. It has delicate, soft fern-like leaves that have a sweet aniseed flavour. It grows best in a deep, moist soil. The plant produces white flowers, which are best cut off unless you want to collect the seeds. It can be used to reduce the bitter taste of stewed rhubarb or gooseberries so you will need less sugar.

Tansy (*Tanacetum vulgare*)

Tansy is a robust perennial with pretty fern-like leaves and yellow flowers in late summer. It grows to about 3 feet (1.2 metres) tall and has a spreading root system, which can become invasive. It dies down in winter and produces new shoots in spring. Cut the stalks back to ground level in winter. This plant is not fussy about soil type. Tansy is not a culinary herb, as it has a very better taste. It is best used as an insect repellent. Tansy dried in bags is used to repel moths in clothes cupboards. Bunches of tansy leaves on the barbecue table will repel flies.

Tarragon (*Artemesia dracunculus*)
336

This perennial herb has slender stems and long, narrow leaves. The leaves have a spicy aniseed flavour. Tarragon likes a well-drained, sunny location. The herb is delicious in seafood dishes and is also suitable for chicken, turkey and egg recipes. Tarragon vinegar is easily made by steeping the sprigs in white wine vinegar.

**Thyme
(*Thymus
vulgaris*)**
337

Thyme is a low-growing perennial that produces small aromatic leaves. Small lilac flowers are produced in summer, which are quite attractive. Thyme likes a well-drained soil in a sunny location. It will grow well in a stony soil and requires little watering once it is established, which makes it ideal for a rock garden. Plant seeds in pots in spring and transplant out later. Thyme can be used as an attractive ground-cover plant in dry areas. The plant should be clipped lightly after flowering to encourage bushy growth. Thyme is an old favourite for stews and stuffings and gives an excellent flavour to all kinds of meat dishes.

Garden Basics

Garden design

Amateur gardeners find it difficult to design a garden that is pleasing, practical and gives satisfaction throughout the year. If you have moved into a new house you can see nothing except mud. Take a look around your site and see what views you have and which ones you want blocked off. Can you borrow some outside landscape? Are there trees growing nearby or a hill or water that you would like to see from your garden? Look at the type of soil, prevailing winds, amount of sun and shade – all these will determine the type of garden you can have. Consider what skills you have. How much time do you have for gardening? Do you have dogs? Do you like mowing lawns? Do you want a patio area near the house that will catch the morning or evening sun?[341] Some of the best gardens that I have seen were designed by amateurs over several years by adding different features each year and moving plants around to find their ideal location. Garden designers can produce great gardens but unless you have the time and interest to maintain the garden, it will quickly grow into a wilderness.

**Planning
your garden**

Measure your site and draw a map of it, showing all the permanent features, such as the house, the driveway, the direction of the prevailing winds and where north is. Make a list of the things you want in your garden – clothesline, compost heap, fuel shed, lawn, barbecue area, deck, patio, garden pool, pergola, greenhouse – and try to place these on your drawing. This will give you an idea of the amount of space available for planting. Then make a list of the types of plants you would like: trees, shrubs, herbaceous plants, roses, vegetable garden, climbers and roses. Choose plants that are suitable to your particular climate, bearing in mind how tall they will grow and how the colours will complement each other. Take a look at the plants growing well in neighbouring gardens. If there are gardens open to the public in your area visit them to see what plants they grow. The owners of these open gardens will be only too glad to help you select plants suitable for your own garden. Consider how much time is involved in the maintenance of these plants. Then consider what shapes and colours you like – do you want rectangular, circular, oval or curved shapes?[343]

If you want a professional job done, consider getting a garden designer. Garden design has undergone huge changes in recent years – people have more disposable income so the Irish garden is getting as much attention as the rest of the house.

**Choosing
your
plants**

Choose plants that suit the nature of your site rather than trying to change your site to suit the plants you picked. There is no point in trying to grow acid-loving plants in a limy soil. Choose plants that will survive the winter frosts and wind that your garden is exposed to. The amount of sun or shade and type of soil will determine what plants will grow.

If the garden is small the choice of trees is probably the most important landscaping decision you will have to make. Trees determine the amount of shade and therefore what other plants can be grown. They also affect the views around the garden and the local landscape and the amount of light inside the house. Some trees can affect the foundations of the house if they have very aggressive roots, as poplars do. If you want summer shade but winter sun then a deciduous tree is the best choice. The amount of shade will determine the type of plants that will grow underneath the tree: grass will not

grow in deep shade but shade-loving plants, such as ferns, will thrive if the soil is covered with a mulch. An umbrella-shaped tree will give more shade than an erect columnar tree, such as a yew. If you want a tree to produce a screen then an evergreen is more suitable than a deciduous tree. Deciduous trees drop their leaves all at once and these must be collected. Eucalyptus trees are always dropping leaves and bark so do not plant them near a garden pool. Choose trees for their leaf colour, flowers and colour of bark. For the beginner, choose plants that grow well in your area. Look at the plants that are flourishing in your neighbourhood. The experienced gardener will try to grow more exotic plants.

Before planting your newly bought plants, place them in their pots where they are to go. Take a look at them from different parts of the garden and the house and then decide if they are in the right place. Avoid planting in straight lines. Grouping herbaceous plants in groups of threes or fives generally looks better than planting in even numbers. Try to have an interesting mix of colours and textures in the foliage of plants and break up swathes of leafy plants with the occasional spiky or grassy clumping plant for interest.

What's your soil type?

To check your soil type, dig a number of holes around the garden to a depth of 12 inches (30 centimetres). Examine the layers in the soil – the top few inches contain the topsoil, where all the nutrients and earthworms are located; below this is the subsoil, where there is little organic matter. Soils are roughly divided into four types. Chalk soils are alkaline, which acid-loving plants such as rhododendrons and most heathers hate. These soils loose water and minerals quickly so they need regular applications of organic matter and fertilisers. Clay soils are heavy and sticky with poor drainage. They are difficult soils to work with: in winter they are very wet and in summer they dry out and crack. The soil can be improved by working lots of grit and well-rotted manure or compost into it. Sandy soils are easy to work with. They warm up quickly but they are very free draining so they lose nutrients easily. They need lots of organic matter and fertiliser worked into the soil. Loam is the ideal soil: it has a good balance of clay and sand particles. It is a humus-rich soil that holds water and nutrients well.

Soil is divided into two layers: topsoil and subsoil. The topsoil contains organic matter and beneficial bacteria. The layer of topsoil can range from 2 inches (5 centimetres) to 12 inches (30 centimetres) deep – the deeper the better. Subsoil is lighter in colour and has little or no organic matter and bacteria. The texture of soils can be improved by adding organic material such as compost or well-rotted manure. The organic matter will help to hold moisture in soils that are too free draining. Humus is an essential ingredient for good plant growth. It is made from decayed plant and animal material, earthworms and bacteria feed on decayed plants to produce humus. These bacteria and earthworms need an adequate supply of air and moisture to survive.

Test the pH of your soil with a soil testing kit, available at garden centres. The kit is easy to use and full instructions are given on the packet. You can also use a pH meter, which gives you a reading of the soil's pH. A reading of 7 means the soil is neutral, lower than 7 means the soil is acid and above 7 indicates alkaline soil. A reading between 6.5 and 7 suits the widest range of plants. An acid soil can be made more alkaline by adding lime. It is difficult the lower the pH of alkaline soils – adding aluminium sulphate to the soil can slowly change the colour of red hydrangeas to blue, which is the colour in acid soils.

Do you want a lawn?

In a new garden the lawn is one of the first things to do. Lawns are one of the most popular garden features, linking borders, beds and focal points together. An established, well-tended lawn provides a year-round green background, offering contrast to colourful flowers; in winter a lawn may be the only source of green in the garden. Lawns do have their drawbacks. Unlike trees and shrubs, which more or less look after themselves once established, lawns need careful mowing and feeding to keep them looking good. A poorly kept lawn is an eyesore. If you garden is small and you do not have time to maintain it you might consider covering the area with paving and stone chips. Grasses do not like deep shade or waterlogged soils, which should be drained before sowing the grass seeds.

If you are putting in a new lawn, autumn is the best time to grow grass seeds. The new grass has the whole winter to grow and natural rain keeps the grass watered. Weed seedlings are less of a problem in autumn than in spring. I have seen grass sown at different times

of the year develop into good lawns. It takes a few months before you have a useable lawn. The quality of the lawn depends on the soil preparation before sowing the seeds.

Dig the ground to produce a fine seedbed. Rake the ground to level it, removing stones and roots of weeds. Let it stand for a few weeks – any weeds that germinate can be killed with a weedkiller, especially weeds like dock and couch grass. Sprinkle a general fertiliser evenly over the ground and rake it lightly to produce a fine silt. Tread over the whole area, sinking your weight down onto your heels to consolidate the soil. Rake again to cover the footprints and level the ground. The aim is to have a level, firm seedbed, which will give you a level lawn.

Your local garden centre will advise you on the various grass-seed mixtures available for different lawns. You will need about 1 ounce per square yard (35 grams per square metre). If the soil is dry, water well and allow the top inch to dry out before sowing the seeds. Divide the total amount of grass seeds into two halves. On a calm day sprinkle one half as you walk back and forth across the seedbed. Spread the second half at right angles to the first lot. Lightly rake the surface of the soil just enough to cover the seeds. You will not cover all the seeds – expect to see about half of them when you are finished. Go over the area with a light roller to firm the seed and ensure good contact between the seeds and soil. Keep the soil moist until the seeds start to grow, which takes two to three weeks.

It is quite exciting to see grass seeds coming up, to see bare soil covered with a green haze of grass. Do not worry about lots of weeds appearing – this is quite normal and they won't stand a chance once you start to cut the grass. When the lawn thickens up and the longest blades of grass are 2 to 3 inches (5 to 8 centimetres) long, cut the grass with the mower set to cut the tips of the grass. Make sure the blades of the mower are sharp and the grass is dry to prevent the young plants being pulled out of the ground.

If you want an instant lawn you can buy turf. It is more expensive than sowing grass seeds but it can be put down any time of the year. Turf is pre-grown grass cut from the ground and rolled out to produce an instant lawn. The preparation for the turf is the same as for growing grass seeds. The turf is sold in strips about 3 feet (90 centimetres) long by 12 inches (30 centimetres) wide, rolled up for easy handling. When you receive the rolls of turf, roll them out immediately to cover your prepared area and water them well in dry weather.

Maintaining your lawn

In addition to routine tasks, such as mowing and watering, lawns require regular maintenance to keep grass healthy. A cylinder or rotary mower is suitable for grass cutting. A cylinder mower with a roller provides the best finish for a lawn, giving it a classic striped finish. Grass needs to be cut more often with a cylinder mower. Most gardeners will use the rotary mower. Try to cut the grass in different directions to prevent the grass bending in one direction.

If the lawn contains brown patches, where the grass has died, the most likely cause is that the ground is too wet: the grass roots are water logged and unable to get sufficient air. One solution is to drain the area. Another solution is to spike the area with a garden fork and sweep sand into the holes to improve drainage. If you have moss in your garden, you are not alone. Moss thrives in our wet and damp winters. Moss grows on shady parts of the lawn that do not receive sun over the winter months. It can be treated with a moss killer or lawn sand. Lawn sand can be made up by mixing together six parts of sand, three parts of sulphate of ammonia and one part sulphate of iron. For small lawns it is easier to buy a bag of lawn feed, weed and mosskiller. This contains ferrous sulphate (sulphate of iron), which kills the moss and gives a dark-green colour to the grass. It also contains a fertiliser for the lawn and will kill broad-leaved weeds. Apply in spring, at the rate of 2 ounces per square yard (70 grams per square metre), three days after cutting the grass. Do not cut the grass again until at least four days after application. When the moss is dead scarify the lawn by vigorously raking the lawn with a wire rake. This is hard work – if your lawn is large hire out a mechanically powered scarifier from a plant hire firm. This removes all the dead moss and brown thatch so that air can enter the surface of the lawn to produce a dense, healthy sward of grass. Apply an autumn fertiliser in the autumn. This is low in nitrogen. Apply fertiliser when the grass is dry and there is no wind. Fertilisers can be applied by hand but it is easier and more accurate to use a machine. Any weeds that survive can be killed using a liquid weedkiller mixed with water and sprayed onto the weeds – this treatment may need to be repeated to kill all weeds.

The planting of hedges is one of the first jobs done in a new garden after the lawn has been sown. Although we live in a more open and transparent society, and work in open-plan offices, we all have a desire to provide our property with privacy by planting a hedge around it. You may wonder from time to time how to block the view of a neighbour's window or stop children jumping over the low hedge in front of your house to take a short-cut home – what most gardeners want is a hedge that grows rapidly to 6 feet tall, then stops abruptly and needs no maintenance. This is something that nature cannot provide. If you want a plant that grows rapidly you can choose from poplars, willows or an evergreen like leylandii. These plants are not suitable if you live in an urban area because they will not stop growing. They will grow, as nature intended, fast and furious, becoming totally invasive and possibly causing friction with neighbours who are deprived of daylight and direct sun when it shines.

Hedges are a living feature, more attractive than concrete walls – they allow wind to filter through them and support many forms of wild life. They can be used to define boundaries, give privacy, subdivide the garden into regions and provide a backdrop to other plants. When planning your hedge put in a combination of different plants to provide a contrast of dark-green foliage with golden or flowering shrubs. This provides a more interesting hedge than a continuous green line. To brighten up the hedge in spring plant some spring-flowering bulbs near the hedge.

To get your hedge off to a good start dig a trench 2 to 3 feet wide and add in well-rotted manure or compost. Place your plants about 18 to 24 inches (45–60 centimetres) apart, water well and trim lightly the first year.

What kind of hedge do you need?

There are many plants you can choose for a hedge and each one has different strengths and weakness. *Berberis darwinii* is evergreen with a prickly leaf and yellow or orange flowers in spring. Trim immediately after flowering. *Berberis thunbergii* 'atropurpurea Nana' is deciduous with red-purple leaves, ideal as a dwarf hedge. *Buxus sempervirens*, commonly called box hedge, is a slow-growing evergreen hedge that will grow to 2 feet (60 centimetres) tall, so it is ideal as a low hedge for edging around a bed.

Plants to use as hedging

Escallonia is evergreen with dark-green leaves and a pink flower. It is fast growing and needs regular trimming. *Escallonia laevis* 'Gold Brian' is evergreen with a yellow leaf and can be mixed with the green-leaf escallonia. Euonymus is evergreen with green, yellow or variegated leaves and is very hardy against salt winds. *Fagus* (beech) is deciduous with a green leaf that turns brown in the autumn and remains on the plant over winter to give a beautiful winter effect.[347] It is slow to grow and only needs to be trimmed once in summer. It is a hedge that should be planted much more. Forsythia is deciduous with yellow flowers in spring; trim after it has flowered. Fuchsia is a deciduous hedge for the mild garden; trim after the flowers in late summer. This hedge is often seen growing in the hedgerows of west Kerry.

Griselinia is a plant widely used for hedging, available with green or variegated leaves, but it can be killed by severe frost.[345] *Ilex* (holly) is evergreen with green, prickly leaves or variegated yellow leaves. Berries are produced on the female plant if a male plant is present. Trim in late summer. *Lavandula* (lavander) has lovely silvery-grey leaves and fragrant mauve-coloured flowers in summer. It makes a low-growing hedge, ideal along the edge of a path. Trim in spring and after flowering – do not cut into the deadwood. *Ligustrum* (privet) is evergreen with dark-green leaves. It is quick growing so it needs to be trimmed two to three times a year. *Lonicera nitida* forms a dense hedge with small dark-green leaves and needs regular trimming. *Lonicera* 'Baggesen's Gold' has bright-yellow leaves.[346] If allowed to grow over 4 feet (1.2 metres) tall it needs support, such as a chain-link fence in the middle, to prevent it breaking open in the wind.

Olearia is a plant used for hedges in exposed coastal gardens. It has a greyish-green waxy leaf and will tolerate salt but not severe frost. *Taxus baccata* (yew) is evergreen with green leaves and slow growing; trim in summer and autumn.

Creating shape in your garden with borders

Once you have sown the lawn and planted a hedge, the next step is to design some borders for growing shrubs, trees, annuals and herbaceous plants. Most gardens are rectangular in shape, which does not look very attractive. Design your borders to eliminate straight edges and square corners and have a lawn or gravel area in the centre. Create your borders so that you cannot see all the garden

at once. Most borders will contain a mixture of woody shrubs and herbaceous plants, with a high proportion of evergreens for winter interest. Choose a combination of plants that will provide an eye-catching display all year round. Once the plants are in place, create a focal point, such as a statue, that can be seen from the house.

The addition of water to a garden brings an ever-changing pattern of sound, movement and reflections. A water feature, however big or small, is ideal for creating a cool, relaxing atmosphere in the garden on a warm day. It allows you to grow plants that will not thrive in any other part of the garden. There are various ways to introduce water to the garden: you can use a pond that is raised or sunken; a bubble fountain, where water bubbles over stones into a reservoir; or a water spout fixed to a wall, where water spouts out through a lion's head, ideal for the small garden or conservatory.

Are you adding a water feature?

A garden pond may be a regular geometric shape or irregular – the size will depend upon the available space you have.[350] To construct a pond, first mark out the shape and then excavate the hole to a depth of 2 feet (60 centimetres). If you plan to grow marginal plants cut out a shelf about 9 inches (23 centimetres) deep and wide around the edge. Check that the pool is level using a straight plank and spirit level across the length and width of the hole. Remove any sharp stones that may puncture the liner. Measure the size of the liner required – the length of the liner will be the length of the pool plus twice the depth of the pool. The width is the width of the pool plus twice the depth. Add about 6 inches (15 centimetres) to the length and width to allow for a flap at the edges. A number of liners are available. Butyl rubber is the most widely used material; it is also the most expensive. PVC liners are cheaper but do not last as long. Polythene is the cheapest material but cracks where exposed to the sun. It can be used where the bottom and sides of the pool are lined with concrete and stones. Cover the bottom and sides of the pool with a layer of fibreglass before putting in the liner. Position the liner so that there is a flap on all sides. Slowly fill the pool with water. When the pool is full cut off excess liner, leaving a flap 6 inches (15 centimetres) all round. Cover this flap with paving slabs or stones set on mortar. The stones should protrude slightly over the edge to hide the liner.

Preformed moulds made of plastic or fibreglass are available in a range of sizes and shapes. They are more expensive than ponds made with liners but are easier to install. Dig a hole to match the size and shape of the mould, place the mould in the hole and backfill with soil.

Algae in ponds can be a problem, turning the water into a pea-soup colour with scum floating on top. The problem can be reduced by adding a few gallons of water from a clean pond – this water contains a balance of aquatic micro-organisms that reduce the algae. Once you get the balance right do not change the water in the pond: top up in very dry weather with fresh water.

Using a pump in your water feature

A water fountain gives height, sound and movement to a pool. A fountain is very effective if lit at night.[351] A water spout can be attached to a wall and fitted with a pump and pipe.[352] The pump circulates the water through the spout into a small pool or reservoir underneath the spout. There are various shapes of spouts to choose from. There are two types of pumps available for garden use: surface-mounted and submersible. The submersible pump is the most commonly used for fountains and water spouts. They come in different sizes, producing different flow rates. The pump is placed at the bottom of the pool and raised on bricks to prevent debris being sucked into the inlet pipe. The pump contains a filter, which should be cleaned a few times a year. Different heads are available to give different sprays of water. The pump is connected to the mains using waterproof connectors and a residual current device. Seek the advice of a qualified electrician if you have any doubts. A surface-mounted pump is used in very large ponds with a cascade; the pump is located in a near-by house.

Plants for water features

Water plants are planted in baskets with a very close mesh, filled with good garden soil and covered with a layer of stones. Planting should be done between late spring and midsummer, when the plants are in active growth. Water plants can be fertilised using special tablets that are pushed into the basket. Oxygenating plants are one of the first plants added to the pool. They produce oxygen, which is necessary for bacteria and plants in the pool.

When we think of water plants we think of water lilies (*Nymphaea* 'Escarboucle').[353] These are grown as much for their foliage as their flowers. The leaves can vary in size from large dinner plates to just a few inches. The leaves can often be mottled with maroon or streaked with pink. The flower colours range from white to yellow, orange, pink and deep reds.[354] Remove flowers from water lilies in their first year to allow the plant to establish itself and settle into its new environment. Planting depths vary from 6 inches (15 centimetres) to 4 feet (1.2 metres), depending on the variety. Introduce plants to the correct depth gradually over a period of a few years. Do this by placing the potted basket on some bricks in the pool. Take care if your pool has a liner – a layer of gravel will act as a safe foundation for the bricks and prevent damage to the lining. Once established, the plant will need little maintenance other than the removal of old leaves in the autumn. The flowers last from three to five days and only open when the sun is shining. They like still water so plant them away from a fountain. If they become overcrowded the flowers get fewer and smaller and the leaves lift out of the water, in which case they need lifting and dividing. Other plants that can be grown in the pool include irises, *Caltha palustris* (marsh marigold), *Juncus effusus* 'Spiralis' (corkscrew rush), *Lysichiton americanus* (skunk cabbage), *Scirpus tabernaemontani* 'Zebrinus' (zebra rush) and *Glyceria maxima* 'Variegata' (reed grass). Do not over-plant the pond: a pond should have two-thirds water to one-third plant cover to give lots of reflections.

Are you including a rock garden?

A rock garden can look very well in the garden and give you the opportunity to grow alpine and rock plants that have very attractive flowers.[355] Alpine plants grow naturally on the sides of mountains between crevices in the rocks. They are hardy plants, able to survive in extreme conditions. Although they can survive extremes of temperatures, most of them will not survive extreme wet around their roots in winter. In their native habitats they grow in poor, free-draining soil; they develop spreading roots that grow under rocks.

Place your rock garden in an open position facing south. Avoid shaded areas, such as under trees, which cast shade and drop leaves. Pick an area that is easy to get at, as you will have to move large stones. The size will depend upon the amount of space you have. A 30 square foot (3 square metres) area will give you enough space for two to three tiers of rock. Rocks can be expensive to buy and transport so try to get them locally. Buy from a large garden centre or from a local quarry. Try to pick local stone, which will look more natural. Try to select stones that have slightly different shapes and sizes so that your rock garden looks more natural. Ensure that the stones are not too large to handle and move when they are delivered. Buy some gravel, stone chippings or grit to go around the stones and cover the top of the bed.

How to construct a rock garden

Start with a layer of coarse rubble to form a mound, as high as possible, facing south. Cover this with a layer of well-drained, weed-free soil. Position the first row of stones around the base, with the grain running in the same direction.[356] Bury each stone so that about one-third of it is in the ground and tilted slightly backwards, so rainwater will flow backwards towards the plants. Back-fill behind the layer of rocks with rubble and soil. Position the second row of stones behind the first layer and again back-fill with rubble and soil. Ensure there is enough space between the rows for plants. Continue to add further rows of stones until the top of the bed is reached. When all the stones are in place, fill in around them with further soil. Cover the surface of the rock garden with a layer of garden soil, compost or leaf-mould and sharp sand or grit mixed together. Finally add a layer, 1 inch (2.5 centimetres) deep, of stone chippings, gravel or grit to the surface of the rock garden to improve drainage and create a natural finish. Allow the rock garden to settle for a few weeks before planting.

How to plant a rock garden

Most alpine plants are bought as pot plants and may be planted at any time of the year, except when the soil is very wet or frozen. Place the pot plants around the rock garden and move them around until you are satisfied with the arrangement. Some plants grow vigorously so give these space to develop. Make a planting hole with a trowel and make sure the hole is big enough to accommodate the roots. Place the plant in the hole so that the collar is slightly above the surface of the ground to leave room for a layer of gravel or chippings. To place plants between the crevices of large rocks, removing some soil from the crevice. Place the roots of the plant into

the crevice, cover them with soil and fit a stone on top of the soil to keep the plant in place.

Alpine and rock-garden plants need to be trimmed periodically to restrict plants to their allotted space. Remove all dead flowers and leaves with a secateurs or scissors. There is a wide variety of plants to choose from: saxifraga, oxalis, phlox, sisyrinchium, penstemon, sempervivum (houseleek), dianthus, rhodohyposis, achillea, alyssum, aquilegia, arabis, asters, aubrieta, campanula, gentiana, helianthemum (rock rose), primula, pulsatilla, sedum, thymus (thyme) and viola.[357] Check the size and spread of these plants before you buy them to make sure that they will fit into your available space. A number of bulbs produce dwarf plants, such as daffodils, tulips and irises. There are dwarf varieties of shrubs and trees that give height to the rock garden, such as chamaecyparis, cryptomeria, daphne and juniper.

Rock features for smaller gardens

Small gardens that do not have room for a rock garden can grow alpine and rock plants in a stone or concrete trough. Place the trough in an open, sunny position – it can look very well on a patio. Raising the trough about 18 inches (45 centimetres) above the ground allows you to see the plants more comfortably. As with the rock garden, fill the trough with free-draining soil and place a few stones on top. Choose slow-growing plants for the trough and do not over plant it.

Does your garden need a path?

Paths are practical components of every garden, designed to link the house with different parts of the garden. Paths should be comfortable to walk on and have a non-slip surface. A well-designed path can lead the eye into the depths of the garden and entice you to explore more of it. Paths make it easier to maintain the garden, especially in winter. A path is a permanent feature so consider carefully where to place it and what materials you will use.[345] A plant in the wrong place can be moved, not so a path.

The width of the path will depend on its use – it should be wide enough to take a wheelbarrow or maybe a lawnmower. If the path is laid next to a lawn the paving surface should be half an inch (12 millimetres) below the surface of the lawn. The path should have a slight slope so that water will run off it.

A wide range of materials are available to construct a path. Concrete paving slabs are very popular, easy to lay and come in a variety of shapes and sizes. Bricks make a good-looking path and can be laid in various patterns. They are laid on a bed of sand with sand brushed into the joints between the bricks. Crazy paving makes a very attractive path, using pieces of stone of different sizes.[349] The stones are laid on a bed of mortar and the gaps between the stones are filled with mortar. Pavers are special paving bricks, made of clay or concrete, available in different sizes.

Cobblestones are nice to look at but are uncomfortable to walk on and can be slippery when wet. They can be difficult to get and very slow to lay. Gravel or stone chippings are cheap, easy to lay but require a hard edge of stone or bricks to prevent them moving into adjacent beds or lawns. Place a weed-block membrane underneath to stop weeds growing up through it. An old concrete path can be given a new lease of life by covering it with a layer of gravel or stone chippings. The path may need a fresh layer from time to time.

Bark makes an attractive surface and is soft to walk on. It needs edging at the sides and topping up each year. A grass path is beautiful but only suitable for light use. It requires high maintenance, as the edges of the path need regular trimming.

What are garden focal points?

A number of objects can be used to create focal points, drawing the eye towards certain parts of the garden.[340] A stone or terracotta statue can look very well placed at the end of the garden under a canopy of overhanging trees or shrubs.[338] They can be moved around until the most suitable place is found. A birdbath, situated where it can be seen from the house, can be used to admire birds that visit the garden. A tree or shrub such as bay, box, holly or yew can be trained into a topiary shape to attract the eye to where it is grown. Small topiary-shaped plants are now widely available and often used to decorate a patio area.

The garden gate

A garden gate marks the entrance to the garden in the same way that a front door marks the entrance to a house. An open gate between the vegetable and flower garden invites you in to see what is behind the gate. A wide variety of styles and sizes are available.

A gate should not look higher than the surrounding walls or fence, while a low gate set in a high boundary looks well.[364]

How big should a pergola be?

A pergola can be used to make a pleasant walkway between two parts of the garden or to create a shady place to sit in. The overall size of the pergola should be in keeping with the garden: a large pergola will spoil the proportions of a small garden, while a small one will look lost in a large garden. It should be at least 4 feet (1.2 metres) wide and up to 7 feet (2.1 metres) tall. The pergola can be constructed with planed timber but this will rot over a period of time and will have to be replaced. Pillars constructed with brick will give you a permanent structure. Place the pillars at 6-foot (1.8-metre) intervals along the sides. For the crossbeams and rafters, use timber that is 4 by 2 inches (100 by 50 millimetres) and set it on its edge. Treat the timber with a wood preservative. The main purpose of a pergola is to support flowering climbers.[365]

Creating levels in your garden using walls and steps

Retaining walls and steps can be used in a garden with a steep slope. You can divide the garden into terraces by building retaining walls; back-filling behind the wall will give you a level lawn or patio. The wall needs to be strong enough to support the earth behind it and should not exceed 3 feet (90 centimetres) in height. A wall built of bricks or natural stone looks very well.

To gain access to the different levels you will need to build steps or a ramp. Steps create a visual break between the different levels. The steps can be constructed with brick or natural stone.[366] The vertical part (riser) should be less than 7 inches (18 centimetres) high and the part you walk on (the tread) should be at least 12 inches (30 centimetres) long. Start by building the first riser and then fill behind it with hardcore. Next lay the first tread – the tread should overlap the front of the riser by about 1 inch (25 millimetres) and should slope gently towards the front so rainwater will run off. Then start with the second riser, which is built the same as the first. The sides of the steps can be planted with shrubs or a retaining wall can be built.

How do I put in an arch?

Arches are a quick and easy way to provide height and character in a flat garden. Arches can be bought flat-packed and assembled in a short time. They are made of wood or metal. Most garden centres offer a selection of styles. A rustic arch made from forest thinnings can look very natural. A wide and deep arch with a trellis backing and side panels can make a nice hideaway for a garden seat. It can be a focal point and a viewing point from which to enjoy the garden. An arch constructed with brick or stone can create an interesting architectural effect. The arch may be part of a garden wall or extended from the wall of the house.

Use lighting to change the mood of your garden

Outdoor garden lights can transform a garden into a stunning night-time feature or light up a patio. Mains-voltage lights give bright colour but are expensive and need to be installed by a qualified electrician. Low-voltage lights are cheaper, safer and easier to install. They operate on 12 or 24 volts and are not as bright as mains-operated lights. The lights come with cable and spikes, which are pushed into the ground. Lights can make a stunning focal point in a garden pond – they float on the surface of the water and are available in different colours.

Plant diseases and pests

Plants, like most members of the plant and animal kingdom, suffer from disease and pests. Most healthy plants can survive a minor attack of pests and diseases. Some plants, such as fruit, vegetables and plants in a greenhouse, are more prone to damage from pests and disease. Plants that are not growing in the right conditions are more likely to attack from pests and diseases. Growing plants in the ideal conditions with sufficient light, nutrients and moisture will produce healthy plants that are less susceptible to disease. Newly planted plants and young seedlings are very vulnerable until they develop a good root system.

Diseases

Most plant diseases are caused by fungi, bacteria and viruses. Fungi and bacteria can kill plants while viruses will not. Fungi and bacteria thrive in wet, damp conditions. Fungi are classified as parasites: they do not produce their own food and instead live off their host plants. Fungi produce spores that are spread by wind and rain. They need moisture to germinate, which is why fungal diseases such as mildews and moulds are much worse in wet weather. A huge range of bacteria are to be found in the garden. Most of them are beneficial, such as the bacteria that break down garden waste into compost. Some of them cause bacterial infections, such as canker in apple trees and fireblight, which affects apples, pyracantha and cotoneaster. The bacteria are carried by insects from one flower to another or spread by the wind. Viruses are carried by insects from plant to plant; greenfly are common carriers. The effect of viruses on plants is not very noticeable.

Blackspot
379

Blackspot is a common fungal disease of roses whereby the leaves are covered with black spots. The disease will spread until the leaf falls off. The disease is very common in wet, windy weather. Spraying with a rose fungicide when leaf buds open and repeating this through the growing season will reduce the problem. In the autumn pick up and burn all affected leaves. Spraying the ground in winter will kill the spores in the ground and reduce the problem. Some roses are more resistant than others to the disease but no rose is completely immune to blackspot.

Canker
369

Canker is a fungal disease of apples and pears. Brown sunken patches are formed on the stem, which spread to encircle the stem and kill the shoot. There is no chemical cure: cut off the diseased wood and dispose of it. Clean secateurs after use to avoid spreading the disease.

Clematis wilt

Clematis wilt is a fungal disease of clematis and has discouraged many gardeners from growing it. The terminal shoots, especially

the new shoots, wilt and die back. Remove any affected stems by cutting them down to a healthy stem, below ground level if necessary. Spray all the new foliage produced later in the year and the following spring with a fungicide such as Bordeaux mixture. When planting new plants, plant them deeper than they were growing in the pot.

Club root

Club root is a fungal disease of the cabbage family. The roots become swollen and eventually die. When the roots rot, spores are released into the soil where they can remain for years. There is no cure for it. It is a huge problem in the vegetable garden because cabbage cannot be grown in the affected ground for a number of years. Remove and burn infected roots. Adding lime to the soil can reduce the problem.

Coral spot
370

Coral spot is a fungus that attacks dead or dying wood. It produces pink or red raised spots on the bark of dead wood or branches that died back. It can spread quickly so prune the affected branches back to a healthy bud to avoid the disease spreading to the rest of the tree. Burn the affected branches.

Damping off

Damping off is a common fungal disease of seedlings. The young seedlings rot and collapse at soil level. This may affect a few seedlings or spread rapidly through the entire tray of seedlings. The disease is caused by fungi in the potting compost or water used for watering the seedlings. The disease can be controlled by using sterilised compost and watering the seedlings with a weak solution of a copper-based fungicide, such as Cheshunt Compound. Remove any affected seedlings as soon as you see them to prevent spread of the fungus.

Fireblight

Fireblight is a bacterial disease that mostly affects cotoneasters and pyracanthas. The shoots die back, especially the flowering ones, the leaves turn brown and wither and cankers develop at the base of the dead shoots.

Cut out the diseased wood 2 feet (60 centimetres) below the

infection. If the infection is bad remove the whole shrub and burn it to avoid the disease spreading to other plants.

Grey mould
371

Grey mould (botrytis) is a fungal disease that covers dead or dying leaves and flowers with a grey mould. It thrives in damp weather and dull lighting conditions. It is a common problem in greenhouses in winter where there is poor air circulation and low levels of light. The problem is reduced by removing dead leaves and flowers. Ventilate the greenhouse by opening windows to circulate air around the plants.

Griselinia die-off

Griselinia die-off is a fungus that affects griselinia hedging. The disease is caused by a fungus called *Sclerotium cepivorum*, which can survive in the soil for up to seven years Single plants in an established hedge die off and the bark will start to peel. Remove roots and stems of infected plants. Drench the affected soil and protect surrounding plants with Armillatox disinfectant. Repeat the treatment every year. Replant with a different species of plant, such as escallonia.

Honey fungus

Honey fungus is a fungal disease that affects the roots and bark of plants. An early symptom is the growth of toadstools around the base of a plant. Remove soil from around the roots: dark strands of fungus there are an indication that the disease is present. There is no cure: dig up the plant and remove all traces of the roots. Drench the affected soil and protect surrounding plants with Armillatox disinfectant. Water liberally around them. Repeat the treatment every year. New planting in that area will be a risk for a number of years.

Mildew

Mildew is a fungus that covers the leaves, shoots and buds of a plant with a white powdery mould. It affects all types of outdoor and greenhouse plants. It thrives on plants suffering from lack of water and nutrients and poor air circulation. Mildew can be reduced by mulching and feeding the plant in spring and watering thoroughly

in dry weather. Pruning the plant to improve air circulation can also reduce the problem. Cut out infected parts of the plant and spray with a fungicide at the first signs of the disease; spray again a week later.

Rust, like rust on iron, is a fungal disease that produces reddish-brown spots on leaves. Rust on some plants, such as phormiums, will not kill the plant but takes from the appearance of the plant. Some plants, such as hollyhocks, are very prone to the disease so try to grow varieties that are resistant to it. To reduce the disease, feed plants regularly and spray with a rose fungicide.

Rust
372

Tomato blight is a fungal disease of tomatoes grown outdoors and in cool greenhouses. Black blotches develop on the leaves, which can spread to the whole plant and fruit. Treat it the same as blight on potatoes – use a fungicide such as Bordeaux mixture that contains copper sulphate (bluestone).

Tomato blight

Pests

Pests are creatures that like to eat our favourite garden plants. Most of them can be identified by the damage they do. Some of them work underground, such as the vine weevil grubs, where they eat the roots of plants and are not noticed until the plant dies. Some of them eat away leaves. Others suck sap from the leaves to produce distorted leaves. They can vary in size from tiny insects to rabbits or deer in some areas. Not all insects in the garden are pests – some insects, such as ladybirds, will consume large amounts of aphids.

Aphids

Aphids or greenfly are common pests that affect a large number of plants. They form colonies of green or black insects on the bottom of new leaves and suck the sap from the leaves. Their secretions produce a sticky mould on leaves. This mould is not harmful but does not look well and can reduce the amount of light getting at the leaf. Another problem with greenfly is that they can spread viruses from one plant to another. If there are only a few greenfly on a plant they can be removed by hand. For large infestations, spray with an insecticide.

In the greenhouse greenfly can be a problem all year round and can spread very quickly. They can be controlled by spraying or fumigating the house with a smoke cone or using a biological control such as lacewings. Lacewing larvae can be purchased and sprinkled onto the infected leaves. The larvae will produce adult lacewings, who will produce more larvae to keep the process going. Ladybirds will also eat lots of greenfly. Tubs of ladybirds can be purchased to increase their population in the greenhouse.

Caterpillars
373

Caterpillars produce holes on leaves similarly to slugs and snails. They are easily seen on the leaves of plants such as cabbage and some flowering plants. Caterpillars are the larvae of various species of butterfly, in particular the white butterfly. Picking off the caterpillars by hand is one effective way of treating the problem. When white butterflies are seen flying around, cover cabbage plants with fleece to prevent the butterflies laying their eggs on the leaves. Spraying

with an insecticide such as Picket will kill them but is not to be recommended on leaves that you eat, such as cabbage. I would prefer to see a few holes on the leaves of my cabbage – then I would know that the plant was not sprayed with a chemical.

Cuckoo spit is a white froth that appears on plants in summer. The good news is that it will not harm the plant. If you do not like the appearance of it just wash it off with a spray of water.

Cuckoo spit

Red spider mite is mainly a problem in greenhouses. They are so small that you cannot see them with the naked eye. They look like specks of dust on the leaves and take on a red colour in the winter. The leaves will eventually turn yellow and fall off. The mites produce a fine web on the tips of the leaves. They are very difficult to eradicate. They thrive in dry conditions so increasing the humidity of the greenhouse or spraying the leaves with a fine mist of water will reduce them. Spraying with Liquid Derris will help to control them. Removing affected leaves and moving the plant outside for the summer will help to avoid attacks from red spider mite. A biological control called *Phytoseiulus persimilis* is a mite that kills red spider mites. It can be purchased as a powder. Sprinkle the powder onto the leaves of the infected plant. The only problem is that the mite does not work until the temperature in the greenhouse reaches 16°C at night.

Red spider mite

Slugs and snails will eat almost everything except trees and shrubs. They really love hostas and will quickly reduce a leaf to something like Limerick lace. Snails have a shell that they climb inside during the day to give them protection from the sun. They are great climbers and you find them at the top of climbing plants or trees. Slugs have no protection from the sun and are usually found under leaves that touch the ground. Since slugs stay near the ground they can easily be found by natural predators such as frogs and hedgehogs. Slugs can be successfully killed using biological controls such as nematodes. Nematodes occur naturally in the soil but their numbers are too small to deal with the slugs. Nemaslug contains millions of nematodes

Slugs and snails
374–75

and are suitable for organic growers. They are available from Mr Middleton's garden shop in Dublin and some large garden centres. A packet costs about €20. Mix the contents with water and apply to the soil. Use it in spring when the soil temperature has increased. The effects last for up to six weeks. If you can wipe out the slugs in your soil there will be no eggs to start up a new generation of slugs next year. The treatment does not work on snails because they do not spend enough time on the ground.

Most gardeners have their own favourite way of killing snails, such as using beer traps, but none of them really works. Picking them by hand is one effective way of reducing the problem or spraying the leaves with Sluggit, a liquid that is diluted with water and sprayed onto the leaves. Cleaning up decayed leaves in the autumn will reduce cover for them to survive over the winter. Try to encourage more birds into the garden by growing shrubs with berries – birds will eat slugs and snails. Try to reduce the use of slug pellets, as they kill many birds. If using slug pellets use the mini-pellets, which are more difficult for birds to find. If you remove snails by throwing them into a neighbour's garden, remember they are said to have a homing instinct and can travel a long distance back to their original home.

Vine weevil

376–78

Vine weevil attacks a wide range of plants, especially plants grown in pots. It has become the number one insect pest of gardeners in recent years. One of the reasons for this is our tendency to grow more plants in pots and containers. A pot plant is an ideal incubator for the adult vine weevil to hatch its eggs. The adult vine weevil has a blackish-brown colour and a pronounced snout; it cannot fly but can crawl and walk from plant to plant. The adult will attack the leaves of plants to produce notches around the outer edges of the leaves. The damage done to leaves is not bad, however it is an indication that vine weevil is present in the garden. These adults move about from spring to autumn, usually at night, laying hundreds of eggs. The eggs, too small to be seen by the naked eye, hatch out into grubs, which munch away at the roots of the plant. The grubs do most damage in summer and autumn. The grub is white in colour and is curled into a characteristic C-shape. This grub will feed away on roots for up to six months. Plants grown in pots and containers are most at risk and may die in the autumn and winter if the attack is severe. If plants are

not doing well examine the compost for the white C-shaped grub. If present, replace the compost and kill the grubs. In most cases, it is usually too late to do anything – just get rid of the plant and compost. The grub will spend winter in the soil and emerge in spring, when temperatures increase, as an adult vine weevil.

To control the vine weevil, collect the adults at night when they are active. Until recently no control was available to gardeners to protect plants. A new product called Bio Provado Vine Weevil is now available and one application will protect plants for up to six months. Dissolve in water and apply to the compost. If you have problems with vine weevil repot plants grown in containers each spring and examine for the presence of grubs. Commercial growers use a compost with a special insecticide mixed in to kill the grubs. A biological control called Nemasys will destroy the eggs and grubs of vine weevil. It is diluted with water and applied to the compost when the temperatures are above 5°C.

Whitefly

Whitefly are sap-sucking flies that affect many plants, especially tomatoes, fuchsias and pelargoniums. When the leaves are disturbed clouds of white flies take off. They collect under the leaf. They may be controlled by spraying with an insecticide or using biological controls such as sticky tapes. Hang the tape in the greenhouse, shake the infected plants and the whiteflies will fly off and stick to the tape. Another biological control is the parasitic wasp called *Encarsis formosa*. The wasp is sold on cards. Hang a card on the infected plant and the wasp will hatch from the card and lay its eggs on the whitefly scales. These eggs hatch out to produce another wasp instead of the whiteflies. Temperatures in the greenhouse must be above 10°C for the parasitic wasp to work.

Controls against Diseases and Pests

Biological controls

Biological controls are being used more widely to control pests in greenhouses and conservatories. Each biological control attacks one particular pest and the results are as good as using chemicals and will last longer. They are not cheap. Their big advantage is that they will not kill useful insects in the garden. Since biological controls are living organisms, they are not available in most garden centres. They can be purchased from mail-order firms – you will find these listed in gardening magazines.

There are lots of beneficial insects in the garden, such as ground beetles, spiders, ladybirds and centipedes. Encourage these insects to stay in your garden over winter by providing lots of places for them to hibernate. Do not clean away all of your herbaceous plants until spring: the hollow stalks of these plants will give protection to insects in winter. If you have problems trying to identify harmful insects from useful ones, a general rule is that harmful insects move slowly whereas useful insects move fast to catch other insects.

Do not forget birds: they will help to remove many pests from the garden. Attract birds into your garden by growing shrubs that produce berries or feed them in winter with seeds and nuts – also provide a supply of clean water. Robins and blackbirds will eat any grubs in the soil when it is freshly dug. The thrush will eat snails, while the bluetit eats greenflies.

Glasshouse hygiene

Glasshouse hygiene is important in preventing attacks from pests and diseases. A glasshouse provides warmth and humidity, which many pests and diseases thrive on. At the end of the year clean away all debris, such as rotting leaves, and wash all pots and seed trays. If pests have been a problem in the greenhouse it is worth removing all plants and washing all parts of the house with a disinfectant such as Jeyes Fluid or Armillatox. Close all doors and windows and fumigate the house with a smoke cone – this will kill all remaining pests or diseases.

These products are used to kill fungal spores or pests that cause damage to plants. These products are chemicals and should be treated with care. Read and follow the instructions given by the manufactures. Read the small print to see if the plants you want to treat are suitable for the spray – a spray may kill a pest or disease on the leaf of a plant but may destroy the flowers or fruit buds forming on the plant. **Fungicides and pesticides (insecticides)**

Always wear gloves and a mask when applying chemicals. The chemicals are supplied in concentrated form and are diluted with water – use the correct dilution rates. Once the chemicals are diluted with water they do not last, so only make up as much as you need. If spraying edible crops check how many days must elapse between spraying and eating the crop. Do not spray in windy conditions or when rain is expected. Do not spray during the hottest part of the day, to avoid scorching the plants. Keep chemicals locked up, well away from children, and make sure all bottles are clearly labelled. If you want to get rid of a product ask your local council for advice – do not pour it down the drain. The sprays are divided into different categories.

Contact products only work on the parts of the plant that they touch. They will kill insects directly hit by the spray. Contact fungicides will kill germinating fungus spores to prevent further infection but will have little effect on established fungus.

Systemic products are taken into the sap and move around the inside the plant. They are used for killing sap-sucking insects and will give protection for two weeks or more.

Combined products, such as Rose Clear, contain a mixture of ingredients to kill different fungi and pests.

When spraying a plant give it a thorough spraying, especially the underside of the leaves. These chemicals are toxic and can damage plants such as young seedlings, cuttings and flower petals. Plants that are suffering from stress and not growing well should not be sprayed with a chemical. Spraying the plant with a foliage feed may do more good.

Herbicides should only be used in the garden to remove difficult weeds such as dock, dandelion, thistles, couch grass, ground elder and bindweed. Weedkillers are divided into two main divisions. **Herbicides (weedkillers)**

Non-selective weedkillers will kill all green plants that they come in contact with. Glyphosphate is the active ingredient in weedkillers such as Roundup or Tumbleweed. It is absorbed by the leaves and works its way down to the roots, killing the plant and roots. It is slow acting and it may take a few weeks to see its full effect. Wait for a few weeks and if new growth occurs spray again so that the weeds do not get a chance to recover. Use it on a mild day to avoid drift onto nearby shrubs. Use a sprayer fitted with a hood to reduce spray drift. Choose a day when no rain is predicted for twenty-four hours. The spray works best when weeds are in active growth in late spring. It does not persist in the soil so it is safe to cultivate as soon as the weeds are dead.

Selective weedkillers such as Verdone will kill broadleaf weeds like clover and dandelion without killing the grass growing around them. Some lawn weeds, such as daisies, are killed by one or two applications of weedkiller; other weeds, such as veronica (speedwell), may need three or more applications at four- to six-week intervals. If a weed shows no response to various weedkillers the only solution is to remove it by hand. It is a good idea to feed lawns with a fertiliser before you kill the weeds. Use lawn weedkillers in late spring when weeds are growing actively and before they start flowering.

Propagation and plant care

Seeds

Seeds are one of nature's great inventions. Plants have survived on this earth due to their ability to grow from seeds. Each seed is different, like the plant that produced it. Raising plants from seeds is not difficult for many plants – after all they do it naturally themselves in the open. Sowing seeds signals the start of another growing season. It offers you the opportunity to grow a large selection of different plants economically. Sowing seeds can be fun. Watching a tiny seed germinate, grow and produce a flower or fruit is one of the most rewarding things about gardening.

Buying and collecting seeds

A wide variety of seeds are available for sale from the main seed distributors. The seeds are sold in foil sachets that preserve them until opened. Always read and follow the instructions on the packet – the instructions contain details on time of sowing, temperature needed and planting distances of the young seedlings. It is worth collecting seeds from your favourite plants in the garden. Do not collect seeds from F1 hybrids because these plants are specially bred and do not produce viable plants from their seeds. Collect seeds, on a dry day, from healthy plants when the seeds are mature but before they are too ripe and blown away. Place the seedheads in a paper bag until fully ripe, shake the bag and collect the seeds. Place the dry seeds in an envelope and label it with the name. Store the seeds in a dark, dry, well-ventilated place. Some seeds, such as myosotidium, dierama and lychnis, can be sown fresh after collection. These seeds are sown in the autumn and will germinate the following spring.

What is germination?

This is the growth of a seed into a plant. To germinate, most seeds require moisture, oxygen (air) and a suitable temperature. Some seeds, especially very small ones, require light. Seeds that come from the forest-fire regions of South Africa and Australia require smoke to germinate. It is possible to buy special chemicals from the botanic gardens in South Africa to simulate this smoke. The heat required for germination can be provided by a propagator, a sunny window-sill or an airing cupboard. A consistent temperature of about 16°C is essential for most seeds to germinate. Seeds of most tropical plants will not germinate below 20°C. Seeds with a hard seed coat that are slow to absorb moisture can be nicked with a knife or rubbed with sandpaper or soaked in warm water overnight. This is called scarification. Some seeds need to be placed in a refrigerator for a period of chilling to simulate winter conditions. This technique is called stratification and it tricks the seeds into thinking that it is time to start growing.

Trays, propagators and compost

Most seeds are sown in plastic trays – make sure these trays are clean to avoid disease killing the young seedlings. Some trays have a number of internal divisions or modules.[381] A few seeds are sown in each module and when they germinate one seedling is

allowed to grow in each module – the weaker seedlings are removed. The seedlings can be left in the modules until they are planted on into larger pots or planted outside. Some trays, called root trainers, have deep modules to allow roots of plants such as sweet pea and beans to grow down straight.

The simplest propagator consists of a tray with a plastic lid that fits over it.[380] This will prevent the seedlings from drying out and increase the temperature. To grow exotic plants a heated propagator is required. These heated propagators can be purchased or home made. A heating cable with a thermostat is bought and placed in a wooden box. The cable is covered with sand and the thermostat is set to give the required temperature. The box is covered with a sheet of transparent plastic. A cold frame constructed with wooden sides and a glass top, situated in a warm place, can be used to raise many seeds.

Choose a potting compost as a planting medium for your seeds because its fine texture will give better seed-to-compost contact. Mixing some vermiculite or perlite with the seed compost will increase the water and air content of it. After mixing your potting compost, moisten it with a dilute solution of a copper-based fungicide, such as Cheshunt Compound, to prevent damping off.

Sowing the seeds

Fill the seed tray with the potting-compost mixture and rub your fingers through the compost to break up any large lumps and make sure it fills every corner. Tap the tray on a table to settle the compost and then level it. Firm the surface using a flat piece of wood – do not pack it down too tightly because the seeds need air within the compost. Sprinkle the seeds over the surface of the compost so they seeds fall in ones or twos onto the compost. If using modular trays place three seeds in each module. Large seeds can be inserted into the compost using your fingers. Read the instructions on the seed packet. Cover the seeds with a thin layer of sieved, moist compost or perlite. Sowing seeds too deeply is one of the reasons for poor germination. Some seeds, such as very small seeds, do not need any compost over them – light helps them to germinate. Stand the tray in warm water until moisture has soaked up to the surface of the compost. Cover the tray with clingfilm and place it in a warm place. Most seeds need a temperature of 16°C to germinate. The length of time it takes seeds to germinate varies from a few days to a few weeks and some seeds, such as trees, can take twelve months or more.

Caring for seedlings

When the seed germinates the first thing it does is produce a root (radicle); this is followed by a shoot (plumula). The first pair of leaves produced are called 'seed leaves' and they look similar on all plants.[384]

These seedlings need good light, not direct sunlight, to produce sturdy, healthy plants. If they do not have enough light the seedlings will grow tall and thin and topple over, because the thin stems cannot support the weight of the leaves. A fluorescent tube can be used to increase the amount of light available for the seedlings. Do not allow the seedlings to touch the fluorescent tube. Seedlings thrive on about sixteen hours of light each day so do not leave the light on all the time – seedlings need their sleep too. Brushing your hand lightly across the tops of the plants daily will increase the size and strength of the stems.

Damping off is a fungal disease that kills many young seedlings – the seedlings topple over and die. This can be avoided by using sterile compost, good drainage and good air circulation. When watering seedlings use lukewarm tap water and water from the bottom up. Water from a tank or barrel contains bacteria that can kill seedlings.

How to 'prick out' seedlings

As the seedlings grow and develop true leaves they become root bound and stunted in their confined space. If grown in modules remove the weaker seedlings in each module to leave only one seedling. It is easier to cut the weak seedlings than to pull them out, which can disturb the compost. Use an old fork to gently lever the seedlings and their roots out of the tray and replant them in a small pot. Handle the leaves by their 'seed leaves' rather than the stem. If a leaf breaks it is no big deal; if the stem breaks the seedling is lost. Give the potted-up seedlings a liquid feed every two weeks.

What is 'hardening off'?

Seedlings that were raised in the greenhouse or that you bought in must be hardened off before planting out. This process gradually weans plants away from warm indoor conditions and acclimatises

them to the variable weather outside. Pots and trays of bedding plants can be placed outside during the day and moved back under cover at night. Alternatively, place them in a cold frame, open the lid each morning and close it at night. Do this each day for a week or so and the plants will have hardened off enough to plant them in their permanent position outdoors.

Planting out the young plants

Plant out the hardened-off young plants when the weather is suitable and the threat of frost is over. Add some well-rotted compost into the planting hole and firm the soil around the plants with your fingers. Water the plants well and protect from slugs and snails. Place plastic bottles, with the bottom cut off, around each plant. This will protect it from slugs and snails. It will also warm up the soil and get the young plant off to a good start. Pinching out the growing tip of flowering plants will produce a bushier plant with more side shoots and many more blooms.

Propagation

As seed is produced by cross-pollination between flowers from different plants, new plants produced from seeds may not be identical to the parent plant. Plants propagated by division or from cuttings will produce new plants identical to the parent plant.

Propagation by division

This is the easiest way to produce new plants. Most herbaceous plants can be propagated by division. This is best done from autumn to spring when the plant is dormant.

Using a fork, dig around the clump and lift it out of the ground. Pull the clump apart by hand or using a garden fork. Separate out the sections with healthy roots from the outside of the clump. Cut away any roots that are dead or damaged. The centre of the clump normally contains many dead roots and this section can be discarded. Mature clumps can have a thick mat of roots, which can be difficult to divide. To divide these clumps use two garden forks back to back: pushing the fork handles together will separate the clump. Replant the divided pieces in soil that has been enriched with compost and water well. Very small sections can be placed in pots and over-wintered in the greenhouse.

Plants that grow from rhizomes, such as irises, monarda, physalis, polygonatum and cannas, are best divided in early spring when the new growth buds are starting to emerge. Lift them with a garden fork and shake off any soil. Cut the younger rhizomes from the outside of the clump, making sure each rhizome has a few growth buds and healthy roots. If the plant has leaves cut them back to about 6 inches (15 centimetres) – this will reduce rocking by the wind. Replant in well-prepared soil. Plant iris rhizomes so that the top of the rhizome is just exposed.

Most spring-flowering bulbs increase to form a congested clump with poor quality flowers. These clumps can be lifted and divided after the foliage has died down. Separate the bulbs with your fingers, discard any diseased bulbs and put aside the small bulbs. Replant the bulbs immediately. Bulbs of daffodils, tulips and crocus can be allowed to dry off and replanted in the autumn. Snowdrops are best divided and replanted while the foliage is still green. Most herbaceous plants need to be divided every three years to produce quality flowers.

Layering is a simple way to produce new plants – strawberries do it naturally. This method can be used with plants that have flexible stems growing near the ground. Select a flexible stem that has grown in the current year and that can be bent down to ground level. Remove the leaves where the stem touches the ground. Using a knife, remove a strip of bark from the bottom of the stem. Dig a small hole and gently bend the stem into the hole and peg it down with a piece of wire. Fill the hole with potting compost and place a stone on top. Water the area and make sure it does not dry out.

Most shrubs take six to twelve months to form roots, while rhododendrons and magnolias can take up to two years. When the roots are well developed sever the new plant from the parent plant. Climbing plants such as clematis, honeysuckle and jasmine can be propagated by layering.

Air layering is used to propagate branches that are too stiff or too high up to be layered at ground level. This method is best done between late spring and midsummer. Select a branch from the current year's growth, remove a strip of bark and put rooting powder on the cut. Wrap a piece of black plastic around the stem below the cut and tie with a piece of string. Fill the area around the cut with a mixture of damp compost and sand. Cover this with the plastic sheet and tie it at the top. Once the plastic is sealed there is no need to water any more. When the roots are developed, cut off the stem below the roots and pot up the new plant in a pot filled with potting compost. You may need the help of a colleague to successfully hold the plastic in place. The Comet is a patented device that makes air layering easy. The comet is placed around the cut stem, filled with compost and tied in place. It is available from some garden centres.[382]

Propagation by layering

Air layering

Taking cuttings is one of the most popular ways of producing new plants.[383]

Softwood cuttings of plants such as dahlia, fuchsia, penstemon and argranthemum are taken from spring to summer. Cut a section, about 4 inches (10 centimetres) long, from the top of a non-flowering stem. Cut the stem just below a leaf joint and remove the lower leaves so that two or three leaves are left on the stem. Dip the stem into hormone rooting powder and tap to remove excess. Using a pencil, insert the cutting into a suitable compost, firm it and water. Enclose

Propagation using cuttings

the cutting in a plastic bag or propagator. Make a suitable compost by mixing equal parts of potting compost and sharp sand.

Semi-ripe cuttings of climbers, conifers and evergreens are taken from midsummer to mid-autumn. Take a cutting from the current year's growth that is moderately firm and woody towards the base. Cut the stem just below a leaf and remove the leaves from the lower part of the stem. Remove the soft growth at the top of the stem so that the cutting is about 4 inches (10 centimetres) long and insert it into compost as for a softwood cutting. Cuttings root better if they are placed in a heated propagator.

Hardwood cuttings of deciduous trees and shrubs and roses are taken from late autumn on, when the leaves have fallen off the plant. Stems about 9 inches (23 centimetres) long are cut just below a bud. The cuttings are inserted in a trench in the open that is sheltered from north and east winds. Place a layer of sand in the bottom of the trench to improve drainage. The cuttings are placed about 4 inches (10 centimetres) deep in the trench. The cuttings may take a year to produce sufficient roots to transplant the cuttings.

Root cuttings can be used to propagate many herbaceous plants in winter, while the plant is dormant. Expose a section of the plant's root system and cut off a thick root close to the main stem. Cut the root into sections about 2 to 3 inches (5 to 7 centimetres) long, cutting straight across at the top and using an angled cut at the bottom. Place the cuttings into a mixture of potting compost and sand so that the section with the straight cut is flush with the top of the soil. Cover with a thin layer of sand and spray with water. Place the cuttings in a cold greenhouse or cold frame. In spring leaves will appear but wait until you see roots at the bottom of the pot or tray before transplanting into individual pots. To get cuttings to root you need clean pots or trays to avoid fungal diseases. Disinfect pots, trays and secateurs before you start. Cuttings must not be allowed to dry out so place them in a plastic bag. Do not expose them to full sun – light shade is best. Most cuttings root more easily if the propagating medium is kept warm until the roots begin to emerge. Then remove the heat to prevent too much root growth at the expense of shoot growth.

Pruning

Many gardeners get into a tizzy when it comes to pruning. Many plants need little or no pruning if you have a large garden where you can allow plants to go naturally. Unfortunately gardens are getting smaller and we need to prune more to restrict the size of trees and shrubs. Most gardeners will know how to prune roses but are afraid to prune anything else. Timing is vital – if you prune a flowering shrub at the incorrect time you may lose a whole year's flowers but the shrub will flower the following year. Plants that flower on the current year's growth can be pruned from autumn to early spring. If a plant flowers on the previous year's growth it is pruned immediately after flowering.

This pruning is carried to remove branches that are dead, diseased or damaged by wind to prevent the disease spreading. This type of pruning can be carried out at any time of the year. The damaged branch is cut back to a healthy shoot or bud. Removing weak branches or branches that are crossing each other will help to maintain the shape and vigour of a plant. These weak branches are produced at the centre of the plant, where they are starved of light. Removing these will open up the centre of the shrub to more light and allow more air to circulate freely around the branches.

Maintenance pruning

Spring is the traditional time to prune trees, before the sap starts to rise. Removing the lower branches of trees and shrubs will produce more space underneath them to grow smaller shrubs and bulbs. When removing large branches use a pruning saw. First cut halfway through the branch from underneath. Then cut from above to remove the branch – this prevents the branch from breaking off and tearing the bark on the main stem. When removing a large branch paint the cut surface with a sealing paint to prevent infection. On trees that have developed two leading branches, remove one to produce a straight tree-like structure. Variegated trees and shrubs often produce shoots with green foliage. These should be removed as soon as they appear because the green foliage is more vigorous than the variegated foliage and would eventually take over. Plants that are grafted onto a rootstock, such as corkscrew hazel, produce suckers that grow straight up. These must be removed when they appear to avoid them taking over and reducing the vigour of the grafted plant.

Pruning Roses

Roses such as hybrid teas and floribundas are pruned back hard in winter to encourage new growth. In general floribundas are not pruned as hard as hybrid teas. Hybrid tea roses are pruned back to within 8 inches (20 centimetres) of the ground. St Patrick's Day was the traditional last day for pruning hybrid tea roses. Our winters are getting milder so these roses should now be pruned before spring.

After pruning spray the ground with a dilute solution of Jeyes Fluid to kill the spores of blackspot. Then give the base of the roses a mulch of well-rotted compost.

Cut back the main shoots of floribunda roses to about one-third of their length. Cut out all dead wood and weak, thin stems. Cut all roses just above a bud or young shoot that is facing outwards. This will open up the centre of the rose bush to more light and air. Roses need continuous pruning. Cut stems that have produced flowers in summer back to a strong outward-facing bud.

Rambling and climbing roses are best pruned in late summer. Ramblers flower on stems produced the previous year near the ground. Cut the old stems that have produced flowers down to ground level in the autumn and retain the new young stems. Climbing roses produce a main stem with lots of side shoots. Prune back the side shoots to about one-third in the autumn.

Pruning early-flowering shrubs

Plants that flower in spring and early summer on stems produced the previous year should be pruned after flowering – for example, forsythia, philadelphus, deutzia, spiraea and chaenomeles. These shrubs can be pruned each year immediately after flowering. Pruning will control the size of the shrub and produce larger flowers the following year. Cut each shoot that has produced flowers back to two or three buds from the main stem.

Pruning mop-head hydrangeas

Mop-head hydrangeas flower in late summer on stems produced the previous year. Leave the old flower heads on until spring

when the danger of frost is over. Prune the plant lightly, removing old stems by about 12 inches (30 centimetres) down to a pair of healthy buds. Do not cut away last year's growth.

On established hydrangeas remove about one-third of the oldest growth down to the ground. This should be done every year, so after three years you will have a completely new plant. This will open up the centre of the plant and encourage new growth from the base.

Hydrangea paniculata flowers on stems produced in the current year's growth; these are pruned in spring.

Pruning shrubs that flower on new shoots

Plants such as abutilion, *Buddleja davidii*, cotinus, fuchsia, indigofera and perovskia produce flowers on stems grown in the current year. These plants are pruned in spring, just as the new growth is starting to show. Cut all last year's shoots back to two or three buds from the older wood. Do not cut back into the older darker-coloured wood because this wood may not produce new shoots. After pruning mulch around the plant with a layer of compost or well-rotted manure.

Pruning to produce good foliage and stem colour

Eucalyptus can be pruned hard in spring to produce new stems with foliage that is more attractive than the old foliage.

Plants such as cornus (dogwood) and salix (willow) that are grown for their colourful stems in winter are pruned down to the ground in early spring.

Pruning sambucus (elder) hard in spring, before growth starts, will produce stems up to 3 feet (90 centimetres) long with beautiful variegated or golden leaves, depending on the variety.

Pruning clematis

The late-flowering clematis that flower from midsummer on are pruned to the ground in spring and given a mulch of compost. All the other clematis need little or no pruning but they may be tidied up after flowering.

If a clematis gets too big it can be pruned back hard in early spring and let grow all over again. Depending on the variety, you may get little or no flowers the first year; after that it will flower each year.

Pruning trees

Most trees grow naturally to form a tall spreading plant. Prune trees in the winter when the leaves have fallen – it is easier to see the shape and the layout of the branches. Remove branches that are crossing each other and branches that are growing too close to the ground. If the tree has two or more leaders at the top, remove all leaders except one; leave the most upright, vigorous stem as the new leader.

Coppicing and pollarding

This method of hard pruning is used to produce large, beautiful foliage with no flowers. Pollarding is a special pruning technique used to control the size of a mature tree. Cut back all branches to leave short stumps in early spring before growth starts. These stumps will produce lots of new shoots from the cuts. Trees grown along the streets of towns are often pollarded to make space for traffic underneath. This technique can be used on eucalyptus and paulownia. Coppicing involves cutting back all stems to ground level in spring and is often used with plants such as cornus and elders.

Fertilisers

Every garden needs fertilisers from time to time to provide plants with sufficient nutrients. Fertilisers can be divided into two types: organic or artificial.

Organic fertilisers

Organic fertilisers such as compost and well-rotted farmyard manure do not provide many nutrients but they are very effective for soil improvement. They open up heavy clay soil, making it easier to work with. In very dry soil they hold moisture for plants in summer. Organic fertilisers can be dug into the soil at the time of planting or placed as a mulch on the ground.

Artificial fertilisers

Artificial fertilisers are chemicals that contain nutrients only. The contents are clearly labelled on the bag. Artificial fertilisers are quick and easy to use. Plants are like small factories: they take in water from the soil, carbon dioxide from the air, chlorophyll (green colour) from the leaves and sunlight to make starch. In addition to the above, plants need other chemicals from the soil to carry out their chemical reactions. The most important nutrients or chemicals required by plants are nitrogen (N), phosphorus (P) and potassium (K).

Compound fertilisers contain a mixture of the above three elements with the NPK ratio, the relative amounts of these chemicals, printed on the bag, for example 10:10:20. Nitrogen stimulates the growth of green leaves and is used to make protein. It is washed out of the soil by rain so it needs to be applied each year. Phosphorus is required for root formation and the ripening of fruit and seeds. It remains in the ground for two or three years. Phosphorus is supplied in phosphate fertilisers such as Superphosphate. Potassium is required for flowers and fruit formation. It also protects against disease and remains in the soil for two or three years. Potassium is supplied in the form of potash in fertilisers such as sulphate of potash.

Plants require different proportions of the nutrients at different stages of their lifecycle: more nitrogen at the seedling stage; a higher proportion of phosphorus and potassium at the flowering and fruiting stage.

When applying fertilisers read the instructions carefully. Do not over fertilise: more plants have been killed from too much fertiliser than from a lack of it. Remember artificial fertilisers are chemicals that can burn roots, especially in dry weather, so always water the fertiliser into the ground. When applying fertiliser, sprinkle it around the base of the plant, making sure none touches the leaves or stem.

Liquid fertilisers are mixed with water before application and are easier to apply. Plants grown in pots benefit from a weekly feed of liquid fertiliser.

Slow-release fertiliser granules are mixed with potting compost when planting in pots or containers. These work by releasing the nutrients slowly into the compost during the growing season.

Liquid foliage feeds are applied to the leaves using a pressure sprayer. This gives a rapid boost to plants and is ideal for supplying trace elements. Foliage feeds should be regarded as a supplement to the manures and nutrients in the soil rather than as the sole means of feeding plants. They are very useful in very dry weather when plants have difficulty drawing nutrients up from the soil. To avoid scorching the leaves, do not apply them in hot sun.

Mulches

Mulches are materials that are added to the surface of the soil. Nature has been using mulches for centuries with great success. Mulch protects the ground with a natural cover that provides excellent protection against bad weather such as cold winds, frost and excessive sunshine in the summer. It also stops the soil drying out and helps to keep soil temperatures at a constant level. Mulches help to suppress weeds. Spring is the ideal time to apply a mulch, while the soil is still moist and beginning to warm up. Remove all weeds before applying the mulch. If you have a lot of weeds and do not like weeding, cover the ground with a weedblock membrane and then cover it with mulch. A number of organic mulches, such as compost, leaf-mould and wood bark, and inorganic ones, such as gravel and stone chips, are available.

Organic mulches

Organic mulches such as compost will break down slowly, producing nutrients for the soil. Leaf-mould is ideal for woodland gardens or for bulbs. Wood bark is available in various grades from fine to course and will last for a number of years before it needs to be topped up. Organic mulches should be applied to a depth of 4 inches (10 centimetres) to control weeds and retain moisture. These mulches are alive with bacteria and other soil life that convert the mulch over a period of time into very valuable humus.

Inorganic mulches

Inorganic mulches have become very popular in recent years. They are ideal in the rock garden and around plants that need good drainage. Gravel and stone chips are available in different colours and can make very attractive mulches in modern small gardens, where they often replace lawns. They last a long time and do not need to be topped up every year. Coarse stone chips can help to deter slugs and snails around plants such as hostas. These mulches are applied to a depth of 2 inches (5 centimetres). Nice patterns can be created using paving stones or slate with stone chips.

Compost

The increased cost of waste collection should make all of us think about converting our waste into compost. Composting is the decomposition of organic material – anything that has lived can be composted. Over one-third of household waste is suitable for compost. This reduces waste and saves you money. All plants, especially food crops, benefit from regular applications of compost to promote strong growth. It breaks down in the soil to form humus, which binds the soil particles into small groups, leaving space for water and air to circulate. Compost should not be confused with potting compost, which is used for growing seeds and pot plants. The largest compost heap in Europe is at Kew Gardens: it covers one acre and is 12 feet (3.6 metres) high. The benefit of this compost can be seen everywhere in the garden. Compost is like dinner for plants.

Constructing a compost heap

The size of the compost heap will depend upon the amount of material you have available for composting. The minimum size of the compost heap should be 3 feet square (1 square metre). For the small garden, buy a compost cone – these are available from garden centres. You add the waste at the top and remove the compost at the bottom. If you are worried about attracting rodents place a layer of fine mesh wire at the bottom of the cone and turn it up around the edges. Place the cone directly on the soil so that useful earthworms can move in and out.

For the larger garden, construct a compost bin using planks of timber or wooden pallets or build one using concrete blocks or bricks – make sure to leave plenty of air gaps between the blocks. The advantage of concrete blocks is that they will last a long time and you can grow climbers up the sides to conceal the compost bin. A bin measuring 5 feet (1.5 metres) long by 5 feet (1.5 metres) wide by 4 feet (1.2 metres) high will suit the average garden. The bin should be constructed directly on the soil. Ideally you need two compost bins: while the material in one is breaking down, fresh material can be added to the second bin. Place a removable front on the bin so that you can access the organic-rich compost when you need it.

Making compost right is a bit like baking a cake: the right mixture of ingredients will produce the best result. The ingredients for your compost bin can be divided into two types: green and brown material.

The green material is full of nitrogen and includes grass cuttings, vegetable peelings, flowers and leafy hedge trimmings.[385] Do not use cooked food. The brown material contains a high percentage of carbon and is slow to break down. The brown material is made up of bark or wood chips, autumn leaves, straw, contents from vacuum cleaner, shredded newspaper, cardboard and eggshells. Materials like fish, dairy products, coal ashes or magazines should not be added to the compost bin. Most people find it difficult to collect enough brown material for composting, try to collect a few bags of autumn leaves to add to your compost throughout the year. Newspapers, cardboard, woollen and cotton clothes will break down if they are cut into small pieces and soaked in water. Branches and strong stems, collected after pruning, can be shredded using an electric garden shredder. Do not use diseased plant material to avoid spreading the disease with the compost. Avoid the roots of perennial weeds like couch grass, bindweed and dandelions. Also avoid annual weeds that have seed-heads on them. As a rule of thumb, roughly equal amounts of green and brown material should be mix together.

Begin your compost heap by placing a layer of brown material at the bottom and then adding alternate layers of green and brown material. The more varied the ingredients are, the better the process will work. The material in the heap is broken down by bacteria and other micro-organisms, which will thrive if given sufficient air, water and heat. Keep heat in and rain out by covering the heap with a sheet of plastic or carpet. If you are adding dry material to the heap wet it first with water. If your heap is warm this is a sign that the bacteria are working. Supplying enough air to all parts of the heap is the key to successful composting. Turning the contents of the heap will help to speed the decomposition of the material but it is not essential. Poking holes in the heap with a garden fork or crowbar will help to improve air circulation. The length of time it takes to produce good quality compost will depend upon the mixture and the amount of air and moisture in the heap. In general it will take twelve months to produce nice compost. The advantage of having two compost bins is that while one is being filled, the second one is breaking down.

Using leaf-mould as a soil improver

Leaf-mould, made from fallen leaves in the autumn, is one of the best soil improvers available. Collect the leaves of deciduous trees using a wire rake or garden vacuum. The advantage of the vacuum is that it shreds the leaves and speeds up the decaying process. Place the leaves in a black plastic refuse bag with some holes punched in the sides of it. Pack the leaves down and leave the top open for rain to enter. The leaves are broken down by fungi, which work better in cooler conditions. The leaves will take a year to break down to leaf-mould, which can be mixed with potting compost for pot plants. If you have pine needles keep them in a separate bag because they can take up to two years to break down and you can use them around lime-hating plants to reduce the pH of the soil.

Wormery
386–87

A wormery can be used to break down household waste such as cooked food. It has never been easier to start a wormery. You can buy a flat-packed unit from a number of suppliers who will post the kit to you. It costs about €170 plus postage. The kit comes with a collecting tray, three working trays, a lid and the worms. The kit is easy to assemble. The collecting tray has a tap and is placed on legs. The first working tray is placed on top of the collecting tray. Soak the bedding block supplied in warm water and spread it over a layer of cardboard in the first working tray. Empty the bag of worms on top of the bedding and spread a thin layer of household waste on top. Cover this with a moisture mat, which is supplied. Slowly over the next few weeks add small amounts of waste until the first tray is full. Then place the middle working tray on top of the first working tray and add waste until that is full. Then add the top tray and add waste to it. When the top tray is full remove the bottom working tray and empty out the contents to produce your first nutrient-rich compost. Place this empty tray on top and continue to add waste to it. The worms work their way up from the bottom tray. It can take up to nine months to harvest your first compost.

The worms take time to breed – the more worms you have the more waste they will consume. Worms can eat their own weight in food every day and can double their population every few months. The worms like a mixture of about 25 per cent fibre and 75 per cent food waste, such as cooked or uncooked vegetables, tea bags, pasta, rice, crushed egg shells, bread and vacuum-cleaner dust. Use shredded

newspaper to provide the fibre. The kit is designed for household waste so it is not suitable for grass-cuttings. Do not add citrus fruits or glossy printed paper and add very little meat, which should be cut into very small pieces as worms do not have teeth. The liquid fertiliser produced is collected from the tap in the collecting tray at the bottom. This fertiliser is diluted ten parts to one with water to produce a valuable liquid feed for plants. The worms, like humans, work best at temperatures between 8 and 27°C so place the kit in a shaded part of the garden in summer and in a garden shed in winter, or place a layer of bubble-wrap around the kit outside in winter. If the temperatures drop too low the worms will stop feeding.

Garden jobs for the months of the year

This chapter lists some of the garden jobs to be carried out during the year. They should be taken only as a guide: if you live in a cold area you may have to delay some jobs; gardeners in warm areas may start these jobs earlier and finish later. Every garden is unique – its location and soil type will determine when plants grow and therefore the time when various jobs are best undertaken.

January

With Christmas over, most people are glad to get back to some level of normality. In cold parts of the country, such as the midlands, there is little to do in the garden. In warmer gardens, around the coast, plants are starting to grow and camellias will start to flower.

❋   Take time to browse through seed catalogues: they are a cheap way of getting lots of colour in the summer. The earlier you order you seeds, the sooner you will have them.

❋   Prune roses if there is no frost.

- ❀ Prune trees, especially fruit trees.
- ❀ Dig over bare ground in the vegetable garden, if not already done, and add in lots of compost or well-rotted manure.
- ❀ Examine bulbs such as dahlias and begonias that are in storage.
- ❀ Feed the birds and provide them with fresh water.
- ❀ Bare-rooted fruit trees and bushes can be planted when the ground conditions are suitable. Bare-rooted trees are much cheaper than pot-grown ones.
- ❀ This is a good time of the year to move trees or shrubs that are growing in the wrong place or have outgrown their position.
- ❀ Do not walk on the lawn when there is frost because you will break the frozen blades of grass.

February

- ❀ Sow seeds of half-hardy annuals and bedding plants under glass.
- ❀ Sow vegetable seeds like lettuce and cabbage under glass.
- ❀ Sow tomatoes in a heated propagator.
- ❀ This is a good time to clean the greenhouse. Clean out any pots or trays that can provide shelter for pests such as slugs and vine weevil. Wash pots and trays with a dilute solution of Jeyes Fluid or Armillatox to kill any disease or pests present. Clean the glass with water and some bleach to remove algae but be careful that plants are not damaged.
- ❀ Plant anemone bulbs in pots in the greenhouse to provide an early display of colour.
- ❀ Tidy up the rock garden, removing debris after the winter.
- ❀ Prune late-flowering clematis down to 6 inches (15 centimetres) from the ground and give them a mulch of compost.
- ❀ Firm the soil around the base of newly planted plants. Check the ties on trees after the winter storms.
- ❀ Tidy up clumps of pampas grass, removing all dead material using a sharp knife and wearing gloves.
- ❀ Place a mulch of compost around hostas before the new leaves emerge, to give you wonderful, lush leaves.
- ❀ Have your lawnmower and other power tools serviced for the coming season.

* Plant deciduous hedges when conditions are suitable.
* Sow sweet peas in the open.

March

This is a busy time in the garden: the days are getting longer and soil temperatures rise to a level where most plants will start to grow. Now is the time to get those jobs done that you missed out on over the last two months. The weather in March can be cold, wet and windy, with some good spells of sunshine that dry out the soil.

* Apply a mulch of bark on flower and herbaceous beds to reduce weeds.
* Cut the lawn as early in the month as possible when it is dry. Towards the end of the month feed the lawn with a spring lawn fertiliser and apply moss killer if moss is present.
* Make an early sowing of salad vegetables such as lettuce and spring onions when the soil has dried out. Covering the soil with a sheet of plastic a week or two before sowing will warm up the soil and improve germination. If the soil is not too wet sow seeds of parsnips and Brussels sprouts. Onion sets, garlic and early potatoes should be planted as soon as soil conditions allow – the sooner they are planted the sooner you will be able to harvest them.
* The end of March is the last time for planting bare-rooted plants.
* Snowdrops that have finished flowering can be divided and replanted.
* Plant hedges to provide shelter in the garden.
* The middle of March is the last time for pruning hybrid teas and floribunda roses.
* Houseplants will need more water and a feed.
* Feed fruit trees and bushes with a high-potash fertiliser. After removing all weeds, mulch around the base of fruit trees with compost.
* Plants growing in pots and containers will need a feed. Remove the top few inches of compost and replace with fresh compost and a slow-release fertiliser.
* Prune forsythia and chaenomeles when they have finished flowering.

- ✳ Prune eucalyptus and sambucus hard to produce new, more attractive foliage.
- ✳ Prune shrubs, such as *Buddleja davidii*, cotinus and fuchsia, that flower on stems grown in the current year, cutting them back to within 6 inches (15 centimetres) of old wood.
- ✳ Shrubs grown for their colourful bark in winter, such as cornus and willows, should be pruned back to within a few inches of the ground.
- ✳ Prune hydrangeas and remove all dead flower heads. Remove about one-third of old stems, cutting them down close to the ground.
- ✳ Clip winter-flowering heathers with hedge clippers, removing most of the old flower stems to keep the plant compact.
- ✳ Plant begonia tubers in moist compost, just covering the top. Keep in a warm place and only water when the compost dries out.
- ✳ Plant or transplant conifers and other evergreen shrubs.
- ✳ Harden off seedlings of lettuce and other vegetables.
- ✳ Tidy up the herbaceous bed by cutting back all the old dead stalks to ground level. If you have a shredder shred the old stalks and spread them on the bed. Remove any weeds grown and apply a mulch of compost. Do not prune penstemons until much later, when all dangers of frost are over. Divide clumps of herbaceous plants that have been grown in the same spot for three years or more and replant the healthy parts in soil enriched with compost.
- ✳ Sow seeds of cucumbers, chillies, peppers, aubergines and celery in the greenhouse.
- ✳ Pollinate flowers on peach and apricot trees with a light brush and cover at night with fleece if frost is forecast.
- ✳ This is the last chance to prune wisteria before it starts to grow. Trim shoots back to two or three buds from the main stem to produce short stumps that will bear the flowers. Prune only in mild weather.
- ✳ Cover rhubarb with old buckets or forcing jars to exclude light and encourage long, tender stalks.

April

This is a very busy month for the gardener: the days are getting longer and with summer time in you have an extra hour of daylight to do all those jobs you were putting off since Christmas. Check over the list of jobs for March and get these done as soon as possible.

* Weeds are growing fast at this time of the year so control them by hoeing, by hand or by weedkiller if you have a lot of them. Use Roundup on weeds such as bindweed, thistles and dandelions.

* Plant dahlias and gladiolus in the garden where they are to flower. The danger of frost will be over by the time they appear.

* Lawns will need to be cut regularly and a spring fertiliser applied if this has not already been done. The edges of the lawn will need to be remade.

* Remove any grass or weeds growing around the base of trees or hedges. The growth rate of trees is reduced from competition with the grass.

* Plant new shrubs: the soil is starting to warm up so roots will develop quickly.

* Check that trees and shrubs planted last autumn and winter have not been rocked by winter gales. Check the ties on the trees to see if they are too loose or too tight and adjust if necessary.

* Dead-head spring-flowering bulbs that have finished flowering but allow the leaves to grow on and die back naturally. Feed them with a general fertiliser to build up the bulbs for the following year.

* Check climbers growing on walls and tie in any loose stems to the support wires.

* In the vegetable garden sow seeds of beetroot, broad beans, peas, carrots, parsnips, turnips and spinach. Covering them with a fleece will speed up germination and will keep cats off the new soil.

* Vegetable seeds sown last month can be pricked out and replanted in pots. If grown in modular trays, thin out so that there is only one seedling in each module.

* Take cuttings of argyranthemums, fuchsia, Virginia creeper, honeysuckle, jasmine, passion flower and clematis and place them in the greenhouse.

- Canna rhizomes can be divided and potted up in the greenhouse for planting out in summer.
- This is a good month to sow a new lawn: the soil is warm enough for grass seeds to germinate.
- Spray roses every fortnight with a fungicide to reduce blackspot.
- Sow hardy annuals outside in the garden. Rake the soil well and sow the seeds in shallow trenches – do not plant them in straight lines.
- If roots are appearing through the pots of household plants, repot them.
- Keep an eye out for slugs and snails – they love to eat the new emerging shoots of many plants, such as hostas and delphiniums.

May

- There is an old saying that a 'wet and windy May fills the barn with hay'. If the month is dry, water trees and shrubs that were planted in the autumn or spring.
- *Cordyline australis* looks untidy with dead leaves hanging down and falling onto the lawn. Pull them off, one at a time, starting at the bottom. They will clog up the lawnmower if they get onto the lawn.
- Garden pools can become covered with algae because of the increased sunshine. Use a brush to remove it.
- This is the time of the year to move and divide grasses and bamboos as they come into active growth. Remove pieces from the outside and replant them somewhere else.
- Ferns can be replanted as the new fronds appear.
- Start to plant up hanging baskets and patio containers for summer colour. If vine weevil has been a problem in recent years treat the pots with Bio Provado. Pots that remain in the greenhouse can be treated with nematodes to kill the vine weevil.
- Plant and divide aquatic plants growing in the garden pool.
- Plant out sweet peas that were grown in the greenhouse but harden them off first.
- Place stakes or supports around tall-growing herbaceous

plants such as delphiniums and alstromeria. If using canes put eye guards such as corks on top to protect eyes.

❋ Remove green shoots from variegated plants.

❋ Continue to take softwood cuttings of shrubs.

❋ Trim evergreen hedges.

❋ Sow seeds of herbs such as coriander, dill and parsley in the open ground. Sow basil in the greenhouse.

❋ Prune the dead flower stems of hellebores, cutting them back to the base to make room for new shoots.

❋ Plant gladiolus corms any time during the month in good size groups. Tuberous begonias and dahlias can be planted out in the garden towards the end of the month, when the danger of frost is over.

❋ In the vegetable weeds are growing fast among many vegetable seeds so remove the weeds while they are small to avoid damaging the young vegetable seedlings.

❋ Lawns will need to be cut about three times every fortnight. Spray weeds growing in the lawn with a lawn weedkiller.

❋ Trim the dead flower heads on alpine plants such as phlox and saxifrage once they have faded. Trim the plants to restrict their size and keep them tidy.

❋ In the greenhouse prune the vine to two leaves beyond a fruit bud.

❋ Now is a good time to kill weeds on driveways and paths using any of the available weedkillers. Weedkillers work best when weeds are in active growth.

June

June is often the best growing month of the year: the days are at their longest and there is lots of sunshine.

❋ In the vegetable garden thin out seedlings of carrots, parsnips and turnip and then water to settle the soil around the remaining seedlings. Place fleece over carrots to prevent carrot fly. Plant out celery seedlings sown in the greenhouse – plant the self-blanching varieties in blocks 9 inches (23 centimetres) apart so that the plants shade each other. Seedlings of leeks grown in the greenhouse can be planted out now in rows. Continue to sow seeds of lettuce to provide a continuous

supply of tender, fresh leaves. If the weather is dry water the vegetable garden in the evening.

❀ Feed roses with a rose fertiliser and water in if the weather is dry.

❀ Before moving them outside, harden off hanging baskets and containers that were planted up last month in the greenhouse. Feed these plants with a liquid feed every week to produce strong growth and plenty of flowers.

❀ Cover the greenhouse with a blind or netting on very warm days to provide shade for the plants growing in it. Water the floor of the house daily to increase humidity. Remove side shoots from tomatoes and feed weekly with a liquid tomato feed. Keep an eye out for greenfly and other pests in the greenhouse.

❀ Many flowering shrubs, such as buddleja, potentilla, deutzia, lavender and philadelphus, root easily from softwood cuttings taken at this time of the year. Take cuttings early in the morning from stems that grew this year.

❀ If the compost heap gets dry wet it with water and cover with a sheet of plastic.

❀ Sow seeds of biennials such as wallflowers and sweet william to flower next year.

❀ Move houseplants out on a mild, rainy day.

❀ As the weather warms up keep a look out for pests attacking flowers, fruit and vegetables. If you get them in time you can pick them off with your fingers.

❀ Cut the old flower heads off lupins and you may get a second crop of flowers later in the year.

July

❀ All the hard work in the vegetable garden in spring will now be paying off, with fresh vegetables available daily. If the weather is dry, water plants thoroughly once or twice a week. Onions need lots of water to produce a good yield.

❀ Trim hedges – most will be at the peak of their growth. Some fast-growing hedges, such as escallonia and *Lonicera nitida*, will have been clipped already and will soon need another clip.

* Trees and shrubs planted in the last eighteen months may be suffering from lack of water. Water these plants well but do not feed them with a fertiliser. Remove weeds from around the base and mulch with compost or bark to conserve moisture.
* In the greenhouse, watering and looking out for pests is a continuous job. Plants growing in grow bags can dry out very quickly. Open doors and windows in the morning to improve ventillation.
* Keep up the battle with weeds by pulling them before they go to seed.
* Some trees that are grafted, such as apple, pear and corkscrew hazel, produce suckers from the base. Remove these down to ground level.
* Remove faded flowers on lupins, delphiniums and other perennials. Cut them down to just above a new shoot and feed them with a liquid fertiliser. They may produce a second crop of flowers later in the year.
* Cut down the stems of bearded irises when the flowers have faded.
* Remove the sharp tips of yucca to avoid damage to eyes.[294] Always wear gloves and eye protection when working around these plants.

August

* Many vegetables will be reaching maturity at this time of the year: these can be used as soon as they are mature. Some of the vegetables that you cannot use can be frozen for use later in the year. Plant strawberry runners and spring cabbage.
* In the greenhouse continue to pinch out side shoots in tomatoes and when the plant reaches the roof pinch out the growing tip and continue to feed. Protect pot plants against vine weevil by watering the compost with Provado.
* Trim evergreen hedges to give them time to recover before the winter.
* Continue to take cuttings of shrubs and tender perennials – they root quickly at this time of the year to produce strong young plants that will survive the winter.
* Prune wisteria, cutting the long, thin stems back to three or

four leaves from the main stems. If the plant did not flower well this year give it a feed of high-potash fertiliser.

* Buy spring-flowering bulbs: the quality and variety of bulbs will be much better at this time of the year than later, when the best bulbs will be gone.
* If the weather is dry water your camelias and rhododendrons to encourage flower buds for next year. If the soil is too dry these plants have a tendency to drop their flower buds.

September

* In the greenhouse, plants like tomatoes, peppers, chillies and cucumbers will continue to produce a plentiful supply of fruit. Removing the ripe fruit will encourage the green fruit to ripen. Stop feeding pot plants, except winter-flowering plants such as cyclamen and chrysanthemums. Pot up hyacinths for Christmas.
* Apply an autumn lawn fertiliser to give the lawn a boost before winter starts. It is a good time to sow a new lawn.
* In the vegetable garden lift onions and garlic, allow the foliage to die back and dry them off in a shed.
* Prune rambling roses, cutting all stems that have produced flowers this year down to ground level.
* Houseplants that were placed outside for the summer should be brought indoors or into the greenhouse before the weather gets too cold and wet.
* Lift gladioli plants towards the end of the month in cold gardens and store the corms in a dry, frost-free shed.
* Lift tuberous begonias at the end of the month and dry them off before storage.
* In the herbaceous bed many plants will have finished flowering: leave the old stems until next spring to provide shelter and a friendly habitat for useful insects to hibernate. This is a good month to plant a new herbaceous bed.
* Plant spring-flowering bulbs, such as daffodils, crocuses, fritillarias, erythroniums and irises, towards the end of the month in large drifts.

October

❋ In the vegetable garden lift carrots, beetroot and potatoes before the garden becomes too wet and store them for the winter. Remove all weeds and dig the soil, leaving it in rough heaps to expose it to winter frosts.

❋ Lift dahlias once the leaves have been burned by the first frost, dry them off and store for the winter.

❋ Collect seeds of your favourite perennials and store them in a dry place. The seeds of some plants, such as myosotidium, dierama and lychnis, can be sown fresh after collection to germinate the following spring.

❋ Remove cannas growing in pots to the greenhouse and keep the compost moist but not wet over the winter months.

❋ Move tender plants such as *Heliotropium arborescens*, *Salvia patens* and *Cosmos atrosanguineus* to the greenhouse. Lift the entire plant using a fork, cut down all stems to about 3 to 4 inches (7 to 10 centimetres) from the base, tidy up the root ball and replant in a pot filled with free-draining compost. Keep the compost just moist during the winter

❋ Move tender plants growing in pots to the greenhouse or to a warm, sheltered part of the garden.

❋ Protect tender plants growing in the ground, such as tree ferns and palms, with a layer of fibreglass. Large multi-stemmed plants can be protected with horticultural fleece when frost is expected.

❋ Continue to plant spring-flowering bulbs – a few hours' work now will provide lots of colour next spring.

❋ Collect leaves that have fallen, using a wire rake, and place then in plastic bags with holes in the sides. These leaves will break down over the next twelve months to produce very valuable leaf-mould.

❋ We normally associate hanging baskets and pots with summer but a winter hanging basket or pot can be planted up with spring-flowering bulbs, winter pansies, ornamental cabbage and with variegated trailing ivy around the edges to provide colour through winter into spring.

❊ The clocks have gone back, the length of the day is decreasing and the first winter gales and frost appear in most gardens. Growth has slowed down considerably due to falling soil temperatures.

❊ Continue to rake up the last of the autumn leaves and place them in plastic bags to make leaf-mould. Sweep up all leaves from paths: leaves left on paths and other secluded places will provide shelter for slugs and snails to survive the winter.

❊ Insulate the greenhouse with a layer of bubble wrap to protect against frost.

❊ Plant deciduous trees and shrubs during this dormant period, when soil conditions are suitable. Plant trees and shrubs that have colourful barks or berries, which look very well at this time of the year.

❊ Prune roses and rake up all diseased leaves; apply a layer of compost to the soil.

❊ Move Japanese maples growing in pots to a sheltered part of the garden, away from cold winds.

❊ Plant fruit trees such as apple, pear, raspberries and gooseberries in a sunny position, sheltered from cold winds and hard frost. Check the varieties of apple trees: are they self- pollinating.

❊ Remove fallen leaves from the garden pool – these leaves will reduce oxygen levels in the pool as the leaves decay and starve fish of oxygen. Place water pumps at the bottom of the pool to protect against frost.

❊ In the vegetable garden continue to harvest parsnips, Brussels sprouts and leeks as you need them. Tidy up the garden, remove weeds and dig it, adding compost if you have not done it yet.

❊ The growth of grass will have slowed down; cut the lawns when the grass is dry.

❊ Houseplants will need less water as temperatures drop.

❊ Check that tree ties and stakes are secure for the winter gales.

❊ Place a mulch of compost around tender plants to protect them against frost.

December

❋ This is the month when most gardens can look very bare but it does not have to be like that. If you plant evergreen variegated shrubs and shrubs with berries they will provide colour and food for the birds over the winter months. This is the month when most gardeners will retreat indoors and content themselves with browsing over seed catalogues. It is an ideal time to look around your garden and see where it can be improved. It is a time to reflect and take note of the things that went wrong in the previous year and try to rectify them for the coming year.

❋ Check bulbs and tubers that are in storage over the winter. Remove any bulbs that are damaged or rotting.

❋ Take hardwood cuttings of plants such as deutzia, roses, cornus and Virginia creeper.

❋ Large evergreens and shrubs that have grown too big for their position can be lifted and replanted. Try to lift as large a rootball as possible and plant in their new location with lots of compost added.

❋ This is the time of the year when many gardeners will buy pot plants such as poinsettias, jasmine, azaleas, Christmas cactus and cyclamens for Christmas. Try to buy Irish-grown plants – they are hardier and will survive in our climate much better. Watering these plants will often determine how long they will last. Water the plants to thoroughly soak the soil and do not water again until the soil is almost dry. Give the plants as much natural light as possible.

❋ Use home-grown foliage to make Christmas decorations – they will look better than anything you buy and you will be able to enjoy foliage plants from your garden in the comfort of your home.

Glossary

Acid soil: soil with a pH less than 7.

Alkaline soil: soil with a pH greater than 7, often referred to as a soil with lime.

Annual: a plant that grows for one year.

Anther: the part of the stamen that produces pollen, which contains the male sex cell of plants.

Aquatic: any plant that grows in water.

Bare root: plants that are sold with no soil around their roots.

Biennial: a plant that takes two years to flower and then dies.

Bloom: a flower head.

Bolt: vegetables that produce flowers and seeds prematurely.

Bract: a colourful leaf, like the petal of a flower.

Brassica: a member of the cabbage family.

Calyx: a layer of leaves or sepals that protects the flower before it opens.

Chlorophyll: the green colouration found in plants that combines with sunlight, carbon dioxide and water to make food (starch).

Cloche: a plastic or glass dome used to protect seedlings from the cold.

Conifer: an evergreen tree or shrub with needle-shaped leaves.

Cross-pollination: the transfer of pollen from the flower of one plant to another.

Crown: where the stems of a plant join the root system.

Cultivar: a variety of a plant that has evolved in cultivation and which is sufficiently different from all others to receive a unique cultivar name. The names of cultivars are written with initial capital letters within single quotation marks.

Cutting: the part of a stem or root that roots to form a new plant

Damping off: a fungal disease that rots the stems and roots of young seedlings.

Dead-heading: removing the dead flowers from plants to stop them producing seed; it also helps the plant to produce more flowers.

Deciduous: a tree or shrub that loses its leaves in the autumn.

Dioecious: plants that produce either male or female flowers so plants of both sexes are required to produce fruit or berries.

Disbudding: removing surplus buds from a flowering stem to produce bigger flowers or removing buds from fruit trees to get bigger fruit.

Dormant: plants that stop growing when the temperatures drop down to low levels.

Double flower: a flower that has very few stamens but much more petals than a similar plant growing in the wild.

Drill: a narrow, hollow furrow created with a stick in the soil in which seeds are placed.

Espalier: used to train fruit trees so that there are pairs of horizontal branches on each side of the main stem.

F1 hybrid: first-generation hybrid plants that produce larger flowers or fruit; seeds collected from these plants do not breed true.

Fastigata: a plant with branches that grow almost vertical, parallel to the main stem.

Fertile soil: soil that has a high concentration of nutrients necessary for plant growth.

Frost hardy: plants that can withstand temperatures down to -5°C.

Frost tender: plants that can withstand temperatures down to 5°C.

Fully hardy: plants that can withstand temperatures down to -15°C.

Genus: like the surname of plants – it contains plants that share a wide range of characteristics. The genus name is printed in italic type.

Germination: the growth of a seed into a plant.

Glaucous: stems and leaves with a bluish colour.

Graft: a plant produced by joining together part of a plant (scion) to the rootstock of another plant – for example, roses.

Ground cover: low-growing plants that spread out to cover the ground, often used to suppress weeds.

Half hardy: plants that can withstand temperatures down to 0°C.

Hardening off: gradually acclimatising plants that were grown indoors to colder conditions outdoors.

Hardwood cuttings: cuttings taken from mature wood in late autumn when the leaves have fallen off.

Herbaceous: plants with non-woody stems that die back in the autumn and shoot again the following spring.

Herbicide: a chemical used to kill weeds.

Humidity: a measure of the amount of moisture in the air.

Humus: material found in the soil produced by the decay of organic matter.

Insecticide: a chemical used to kill or control insect pests.

Leader: the main central stem of a plant.

Leaf-mould: leaves that have rotted down over a period of time, usually one year.

Liquid feed: a dilute solution of fertilisers in water used to feed plants.

Oxygenator: an aquatic plant that releases oxygen into the water.

Palmate: with all leaves originating from a central point. The leaves look like the fingers on a hand.

Parasite: an organism that does not produce its own food but lives off another plant. It takes food and moisture from its host plant – for example, misletoe.

Perennial: a plant that lives for more than one year.

Perlite: a lightweight inorganic compound that aerates compost and improves drainage.

Pesticide: a chemical used to kill or control pests and diseases.

PH: a scale from one to fourteen that measures the acidity or alkalinity of soil.

Photosynthesis: the process that plants use to make food or starch.

Pinching out: removing the soft growing tips of stems to produce a bushy plant.

Pinnate: a series of leaflets arranged on either side of a central stem.

Pollination: transfer of pollen from one plant to another by wind or insects.

Pompon: a flower that is spherical in shape.

Pot on: to transfer a plant or seedling into a larger pot with new compost.

Pricking out: transferring seedlings from a seed tray to pots filled with potting compost.

Propagate: to increase plants from seeds, division or cuttings.

Prostrate: a low-growing plant with spreading stems that grow flat on the ground.

Repot: to transfer a pot plant from a smaller container into a larger one.

Rhizome: a modified stem that grows horizontally underground.

Root ball: a mass of roots and soil attached together.

Root: the part of the plant that grows underground – its function is to anchor the plant and absorb water and minerals from the soil.

Sap: the juice of a tree or shrub.

Saprophyte: an organism that lives on dead or decaying organic matter. Most of the bacteria in a compost heap are saprophytes.

Semi-evergreen: a plant that holds most of its leaves through the year.

Side shoot: a shoot that grows from the main stem.

Specimen plant: a tree or shrub that looks well planted on its own.

Sport: a shoot that is different in leaf or flower colour from the rest of the plant. A sport can be propagated by cuttings to form a new cultivar.

Spray: a cluster of flower heads on a single stem.

Stamen: the male part of the flower containing the anther where the pollen is produced.

Standard: a tree or shrub trained to grow on a single stem.

Stigma: the female part of the flower on which the pollen is deposited.

Sucker: a shoot that grows from underground, usually from the roots. Grafted plants often produce suckers from the rootstock.

Terminal bud: the bud at the end or top of a stem or branch.

Thatch: a layer of dead material that collects on the surface of lawns.

Topiary: clipping trees or shrubs to grow in a geometric shape.

Umbels: round or flat-topped flower heads.

Variegated: leaves that have patches or margins with two or more colours.

Vermiculite: a heat-treated natural mineral called mica that retains water and improves the drainage of potting compost when mixed with it.

Index